MOTORCYCLE JOURNEYS THROUGH THE
APPALACHIANS

by Dale Coyner

A Whirlaway Book
Whitehorse Press
North Conway, New Hampshire

A Whirlaway Book. Published November 1995 by
    Whitehorse Press
    3424 North Main Street - P.O. Box 60
    North Conway, New Hampshire 03860 U.S.A.
    Phone: 603-356-6556 or 800-531-1133
    FAX: 603-356-6590

Whirlaway and Whitehorse Press are trademarks of
Kennedy Associates.

ISBN 1-884313-02-7

5 4 3 2

Printed in the United States of America

For Mom and Dad, Sandy and Carl, family and friends.

Acknowledgments

· ·

If you're like me, you probably skim through the first ten pages of any book, looking for the introduction or Chapter One, paying scant attention to the acknowledgments. After experiencing the book writing process first-hand, I hereby vow to read every word written, especially the acknowledgments.

Thanks to Dan Kennedy and the staff at Whitehorse Press for this opportunity and for being patient with a novice author. Thanks to my wife for being patient, period. I also appreciate the suggestions made by my extended motorcycling family, including Marty Berke, Doc Smith, and friends on the cyberslab. Susie LeBlanc, trusted friend, your opinions and efforts are appreciated as well.

Finally, thanks to all those who have hounded and cajoled me into finishing this work; your enthusiasm sustained me in the tough times. I can at last say to you, "It has arrived."

Contents

Motorcycle Journeys Through the Appalachians

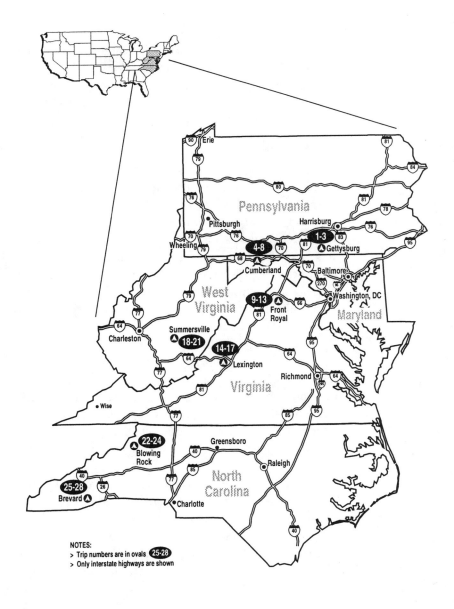

Erie

90

79

81

84

Pennsylvania

76

80

81

78

Pittsburgh

Harrisburg

76

70

76

Wheeling

79

4-8

70

1-3

83

81

Gettysburg

95

68

Cumberland

70

Baltimore

270

79

West Virginia

9-13

66

Washington, DC

81

Front Royal

Maryland

64

Charleston

Summersville

18-21

95

77

14-17

64

Lexington

Richmond

64

81

Virginia

Wise

77

85

95

22-24

Greensboro

40

Blowing Rock

85

Raleigh

25-28

77

North Carolina

Brevard

26

40

Charlotte

40

NOTES:
> Trip numbers are in ovals **25-28**
> Only interstate highways are shown

Introduction

So, you want to go on a ride, eh?

To my mind, there's nothing that can restore the spirit and refresh the mind like a good long ride on two wheels. As you and the bike settle into a comfortable rhythm, the warm sunshine, fresh air, twisty pavement, and rolling countryside work a magic on a person that's better than any $2 tonic.

As I peck out the words that fill this book, I can still vividly recall many of the experiences I've had over the years exploring the hills and valleys of the Appalachians, my family's home for generations on end. I can still feel the cool, crisp Canadian air blowing over the Blue Ridge, signaling the arrival of autumn and carrying with it the strains of bluegrass music from a small town square. I can taste the sweetness of freshly-squeezed apple cider and hand-turned ice cream purchased from a roadside stand. I recall the memorable people I've met, and there have been many, all of whom would strike up a conversation as easily as blinking an eye. On the next breeze, the blast of cannons in the great War Between the States echoes through the hollows. Or could that be the fury of a late afternoon thunderstorm pounding the hills with relentless energy? Closing my eyes, images of mile upon mile of empty highway play out in my mind like an arcade game, and as the sun sinks low beyond the Alleghenies, the distilled fragrance of the forest intoxicates me in a way no perfume ever could. No doubt about it, I would be content to ride here forever.

As these memories come flooding back, I cast a longing glance out the window at the grove of trees behind my comfortable and secure suburban home, as though the greenery might offer some solace to my wandering mind. The responsibilities of life keep me from fulfilling the dream of becoming a gypsy (for now), as I suspect they do for many of you. To that end, I write this book.

Bring 'em on . . .

The fact is that most of us pursue motorcycling as a pleasurable hobby, and we have to get the most out of the time and money we have allotted to it. If you're lucky enough to string together a few consecutive days when you can leave work and home behind, you've got to make them count. You want to spend your time cruising open, free-wheeling highways making the best of your American experience, not paddle-walking through bumper-to-bumper traffic to get into an overcrowded tourist trap. Therefore, I present for your approval *Motorcycle Journeys Through the Appalachians.*

Why the Appalachians?

It's the dead of winter. Cabin fever has nearly set in and the promise of springtime and motorcycling is the lone remaining sparkle in your eye. With maps and travel guides (this one among them, I should hope!) laid out across the table, chairs, and floor, you realize that this is an awfully big country.

I'll spare you the big sales pitch and put it to you this way: few regions of the country are as culturally diverse and rich in history as the Appalachians. A tour of this region is a living history lesson. You can't count ten paces without crossing the path of a pioneer, patriot, or Native American. And don't forget to add the splendor of sprawling green valley pastures, scenic vistas from a dozen or more mountain chains, and the quiet, bucolic byways that lead you through towns where Elvis is still The King and the front porch light is on just for you. If you really want to discover the roots of America, I daresay they grow deeper in the Appalachians than anywhere else.

Remember, too, that this is not a comprehensive guide to the region. It's a starting point to aid you in avoiding the overcrowded, urbanized areas of the East, and finding those better suited to two-wheeled wanderers such as yourself. Popular attractions and destinations are often treated lightly, while the not-so-obvious towns and points of interest are given much more coverage. Buy yourself a good map, cultivate some ideas, and grow your own personal journeys. Consider these suggestions only the seeds.

A Few Notes From The Road

I've compiled a few notes from the miles I've covered over the years and I thought it might be useful to share them with you.

- It is not safe to assume that you can do 20 mph over the posted "maximum safe speed" signs in West Virginia. In fact, don't assume anything about West Virginia.
- There is no louder sound than that of a twig snapping outside your tent in the middle of the night.
- Turkeys in the wild are not as tame as domestic ones.
- Not every place named "Mom's" serves good food. Some of these "mothers" have no place in the kitchen. A gaggle of touring sofas in a restaurant parking lot is a much more reliable indicator of good food (not to mention unlimited trips to the all-you-can-eat buffet).
- If you wear your rain gear on a ride, the sun will come out.
- If you leave your rain gear at camp, it will rain on your ride that day.
- If anyone tells you that mountain oysters are a delicacy cultivated in the freshwater streams of the Shenandoah Mountains, don't buy it. Ask any hog farmer why.

How This Book Is Organized

Motorcycle Journeys Through the Appalachians is a collection of tours ranging from the patchwork farmlands of Amish country to the deep recesses of western North Carolina. As a matter of convenience, comfort, and peace of mind, the tours have been arranged around a series of base camps, with four or five rides plotted from the same spot. Unless you're traveling across a region, it's unnecessary to break camp every day, pack the bike, and haul everything with you everywhere you go.

The range of most tours makes them a comfortable day's ride at a leisurely pace with plenty of opportunity to visit, explore, hike, and eat. Some of the longer trips can be broken into two days or more if you prefer. You could easily spend a week in each region, riding in a different direction each day without retracing a single path.

I tend to camp out when I tour, and as a result, most of the base camps are at state or national campgrounds. However, all of them are near towns that afford a good range of accommodations and travel services, so you aren't likely to be stranded if you need assistance.

One of the goals of this book is that it should pay for itself—that is, it should suggest ways to increase your travel experiences without lightening your wallet. If I didn't feel like I got my money's worth out of an attraction or restaurant, I didn't list it here. The same is true of lodging. And while these are not exhaustive lists of travel services, I did try to include a range that would suit a variety of budgets. Heck, you can always find ways to spend more money for something if you want to, right?

Maps

Throughout the book, we've placed map segments to help you find your way. The Map Legend shows the conventions we used when making the maps:

Map Legend

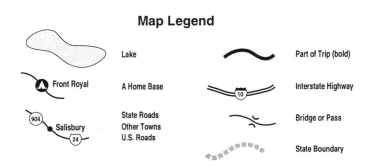

Additional Travel Resources

If you really want to get off the beaten path and explore for a lifetime without the fear of getting lost, invest in a set of DeLorme maps. Most of the good roads I found weren't shown on the complimentary state maps offered by departments of tourism, but rather in the DeLorme Atlas and Gazetteer series. DeLorme's topographical maps of each state include all the back roads. Detailed maps are available for Pennsylvania, Virginia, North Carolina, Maryland/Delaware and Tennessee as of this writing. I was disappointed to find no such map for West Virginia, but DeLorme now sells a product called the *Street Atlas* CD-ROM which remedies that problem. It contains every road in every state.

The Mid-Atlantic area is fortunate to have an excellent bi-monthly publication for motorcyclists, *Motorcycle Times Magazine,* 2550 Albert Rill Rd., Westminster, MD 21157; Phone 410-374-6282. Each issue contains an exhaustive listing of events for the area, including poker runs, open houses, dirt track races, and anything else related to motorcycling. It's a great way to find out about things happening in the area that aren't nationally promoted.

Weather Notes

The Appalachians experience all four seasons in equal measure and though you can travel the region most any time of the year, some are preferable to others. My favorite months for long tours are March through June and September through November. In the early spring months, the higher elevations are chilly, but the cold air brings expansive views. The spring thaw has begun in earnest by the end of March. Early spring flowers are beginning to poke through the damp soil and tree buds are nearly ready to burst. At the higher elevations, winter still lingers but roads are easily passable. Spring arrives on the mountain tops some time in May while the valleys below are vibrant shades of green. Temperature ranges are usually in the 70s and 80s, perfect for a leisurely tour.

Some time in June, the weather patterns change and the valleys are shrouded with the haze of moisture-laden air from the Gulf. It's humid and hot. Feels like Florida, except in the mountains. If you come in late June, July, or August, camp at higher elevations. Temperature differences of ten degrees or more are common between the valleys and summits. What is a miserable day below is a pleasant one on yonder ridge. If you plan to change altitudes, take along layers of clothing so you can add or subtract as the change in temperatures dictates.

By September, most of the Florida snowbirds who came in June to escape the heat of the lowlands are packing up and heading south for the winter. The days become cool and the nights downright chilly. This sets off a domino effect in the hardwoods which begin to tinge with color. The change begins at the top of the mountains and descends to the bottom, quite the opposite of the arrival of spring. By early to mid-October, most of the foliage in the region is blazing with color and there isn't enough Kodachrome in the world to capture all the beauty.

Let's see . . . a few other tips. Bring a rain suit and keep it handy. There's a reason why "Allegheny" rhymes with "always rainy." Zip up your tent before you leave camp for the day, even if it dawns bright and sunny. It's uncanny how those stray thunderstorms will make a beeline for your bag if you leave the tent open to air out. If you are camping out, move between regions on any day other than Saturday and you'll usually find your destination campgrounds nearly empty. Ride Skyline Drive or the Blue Ridge Parkway during the week and the road will be yours alone, even during the peak of fall foliage.

Average temperatures are roughly the same throughout the region, though my personal experience has been that the Cumberland area is cooler than the other regions.

Average Temperature	Jan.	April	July	Oct.
Summersville,W.Va.	33	55	74	56
Brevard, N.C.	37	56	73	56
Cumberland, Md.	27	50	72	53
Front Royal, Va.	34	53	74	53

Last Words

I'd love to hear about your experiences touring the Appalachians—what you found interesting, the good roads and fun places you found that I haven't yet, or the places you wouldn't recommend. Your suggestions and comments will be incorporated to make future editions of this book even more useful. Write to me in care of the publisher, or contact me directly via Internet e-mail at dale@his.com.

I hope you enjoy riding in my home country as much as I do. Have a safe, enjoyable journey, and don't forget to write!

Dale Coyner

The Northern Front

Gettysburg, Pa.

· ·

Before the War Between the States, Gettysburg was a sleepy little town in the rolling piedmont of southern Pennsylvania. Three days in early July of 1863 ensured that it would never sleep again. The worst battle since the war's inception two years earlier left Gettysburg littered with the devastating legacy of bloodshed.

In the end, the Battle of Gettysburg claimed 51,000 casualties. Five thousand horses, broken cannons, shelled and burned homes, trees felled by heavy fire, and soldiers, some still barely alive, were scattered across the fields. The wise and considered words of Abraham Lincoln's Gettysburg Address some months later helped people understand what had happened there.

Little by little, as the nation pieced itself together after the end of the war, monuments were erected to commemorate the dead. Together with cannon placements, they total over 1,000. The battlefield has been preserved in its original state. But most of all, the shadows and spirits of those who were here still roam the fields and woods, at times so tangible you can feel them walk through you as you look across the battlefield. Place your hand on a cannon and it still feels warm. If you don't believe in ghosts or spirits when you come here, you will when you leave.

Today the town rests a bit easier, though it still does not sleep. People from around the world are drawn to this town, some for the glory, some to learn, others to remember. Fortunately for the motorcyclist, there is ample opportunity to do all three from the seat of your motorcycle. There are 40 miles of scenic tours marked in the immediate area, and the tours in this section venture well beyond those limits. If you aren't tied to a particular schedule, the best time of year to visit Gettysburg is either end of the summer vacation season.

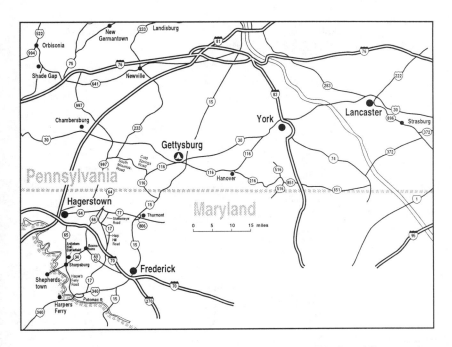

April, May, September, and October offer fine riding weather with less competition for travel resources from the masses.

In town, you'll want to visit several places associated with **Gettysburg National Military Park.** The first is the visitor center, which houses the museum and electric map room. The free museum features a collection of artifacts displayed and interpreted in typically excellent National Park form. Get your National Parks Passport stamped here. Behind the center is an electric map room with a 30-minute program that helps you understand what happened more clearly when you go out to the battlefield and see things firsthand. Just across the road from the visitor center is the Gettysburg National Cemetery where Lincoln made his Gettysburg Address on November 19, 1863. At certain times of the day, a park ranger will guide you on a walk through the cemetery and offer some commentary on the things that happened in this area.

After the walk, you might want to follow the marked tour route of the battlefield. The observation tower on Culp's Hill gives you a good view of the town below and Little Round Top to the south. These two points held the greatest concentration of Union strength and saw the most action in the first two days of the battle.

Almost overshadowed by the military park is the farm and home of Dwight D. Eisenhower at the **Eisenhower National Historic Site.** Ike purchased the farm in 1950 and retired there with his wife Mamie after serving as commander of NATO forces in Europe and 34th President of the United States. They intended to remodel and live in the farmhouse already on the property, but found that it was nearly ready to collapse. Instead, the Eisenhowers built a new home on the site, salvaging as much of the original structure as possible.

Gettysburg is also home to a plethora of private museums, gift shops, and diversions to entertain you during your evenings. One must-see is **Michael Garman's Magic Town.** Garman is an artist who resides in Colorado and creates what he calls accessible art, meaning that it is both affordable and of artistic value. His specialty is creating figures of people and places which capture American moments. The front part of the store features the figures from his collection which you can buy. The rear part of the store is Magic Town. For a couple of bucks you can walk through this miniature city brought alive with mixes of street sounds and the clever use of holograms and mirrored images. Look in the windows of the buildings and the scenes change before your eyes. Glance down the alleyway between two buildings and you'll see a poet-mechanic who tells you how his '57 Chevy taught him the meaning of life. In the richly-detailed movie theater at the end of town, a woman behind the counter fills you in on what's been happening there lately.

Down the street from Magic Town, the **Farnsworth House Inn** features an attraction perfectly suited to the Gettysburg area—ghost stories. After descending a narrow set of stairs into the basement, guests are seated on benches. It takes a few minutes for your eyes to adjust to the candlelight, but you can feel the cool damp walls and sense the low overhead beams before you can see them. In the front of the room, a black mound of cloth rises to reveal a seated woman. She puts on a spine-tingling performance, telling grisly stories about the things that took place around the time of the Battle of

The guns are silent at Gettysburg, but the memories linger . . .

Gettysburg. The show will have you seeing more than shadows on your way back home.

Lodging and food in every price range are easy to find. On the south end of town, right on the battlefield, you will pay an average of $50 per night for a room. I hung out at the **Colton Motel.** It was within walking distance of the major National Park facilities, and it was clean and comfortable. If you prefer the added luxury of a bed-and-breakfast, the **Old Appleford Inn** on the north end of town has a dozen nicely decorated rooms.

Many local restaurants are in the immediate vicinity of the battlefield. My favorite is the **Avenue Restaurant,** located at the corner of Baltimore and Steinwehr Avenues. Inside, the fifties-era Formica and chrome decor is sparkling. Slightly more upscale yet reasonably priced is the **Gingerbread Man.** This is a small franchise operation offering Greek and Mexican specialties. If you're in the mood for pizza, **Tommy's Pizza** is the answer. And on the other end of town, the **Lincoln Diner** offers standard American diner fare. If you want to really do it up in style, the **Farnsworth House Inn** offers fine dining, featuring dishes from the Civil War era, including game pie, peanut soup, spoon bread, and pumpkin fritters. Reservations are a must.

Trip 1 Pennsylvania Heartland

··

Distance	*180 miles*
Terrain	*Narrow, twisty back roads through orchards and farms, several passes over mountain ridges, short stretches of gravel on bridge detours*
Highlights	*Scenic overlooks, covered bridge hunt, East Broadtop railroad, fall foliage, Appalachian Trail, Penn State Arboretum*

The Route from Gettysburg

→ PA 116 west to Cold Springs Road
→ Cold Springs Road becomes South Mountain Road
→ South Mountain Road to PA 233
→ PA 233 north to PA 850
→ PA 850 west to PA 274
→ PA 274 west to PA 75
→ PA 75 south to PA 641
→ PA 641 west to US 522
→ US 522 north to PA 994
→ PA 994 west to East Broadtop Railroad
→ PA 994 east to US 522
→ US 522 south to PA 641
→ PA 641 east to PA 997
→ PA 997 south to PA 233
→ PA 233 east to South Mountain Road
→ South Mountain Road becomes Cold Springs Road
→ Cold Springs Road to PA 116
→ PA 116 east to Gettysburg

If time is short and you have the chance to try just one route through Pennsylvania, make it this one. This route features more varied terrain, sights, smells, and sounds than any other I've found yet. Go in early October when the trees are heavy with apples and the leaves are at their peak. It will be chilly when you begin, but you'll soon forget about that, I assure you. The route begins by following Route 116 west out of Gettysburg , the Confederate Army's trail of retreat from the

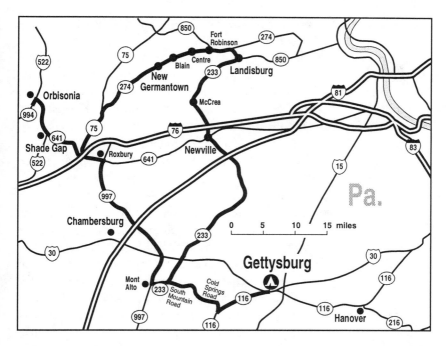

Battle of Gettysburg. The retreating train stretched out 17 miles along this road. At the time it was so bumpy that many of the wounded who were able walked the route rather than endure the hardship of riding in wagons without springs. About five miles outside town, look for Cold Springs Road on your right.

Cold Springs Road is a direct route to nowhere, but runs through some beautiful orchard country. When the trees are loaded with fruit, the air is fragrant with the smell of ripening apples. It isn't the smoothest road; an easy pace will be comfortable. You're not in a hurry anyway, right? Just keep plugging away until you reach Route 233 north.

A good portion of time spent on Route 233 will be through state forest land, first **Michaux State Forest** and then **Tuscarora.** Along the way, our path crosses that of the **Appalachian Trail** for the first of many times throughout our travels. The trail, which stretches 2,144 miles along Appalachian ridges from northern Maine to Georgia, is managed and maintained by a coalition of public and private interests and has often been called "a gift of nature Americans give themselves."

By early October, the foliage in central Pennsylvania has turned and your route is lined with a fantastic assortment of fall colors. Your encounters with several major thoroughfares that cross your path are blessedly uneventful. As you ride under Interstate 81 and hear the traffic thunder overhead, you can't help but wonder where all those people are going. They seem to be in such a hurry to get there, and it makes your 40 mph pace feel even more comfortable.

As Route 233 passes through McCrea, the front of Blue Mountain looms in front of you. It doesn't look like there is much place for a road to go unless it tunnels under the mountain, but it craftily follows a narrow valley through Doubling Gap and into another small valley. Just ahead at Landisburg, you can take a brief detour to a long covered bridge still in use over Sherman Creek. At the intersection with Route 850, make a right. Turn right on Kennedy Valley Road and follow it for a few tenths of a mile.

There are more covered bridges in the United States than anywhere else in the world, and more in Pennsylvania than any other state. At one time, there were more than 1,500, but that number has now dropped to 221. (Next in line is Ohio, 140; Vermont, 99; and Indiana, 93. Iowa, the setting for the best-seller *The Bridges of Madison County,* has 12.)

Wooden bridges became popular in the mid-1800s with the development of a support system called the triangular truss. This allowed bridges of substantial length to be built at a lower cost than ones using stone or iron. They were covered to shelter them from the elements and preserve their longevity. Many of the spans in Pennsylvania were built in the nineteenth century, with those built near the end of the era still in use today, like the bridge here at Landisburg.

If you are interested in finding more bridges, they are near the main route and easy to find. Follow Route 850 west out of Landisburg until it joins Route 274 near Fort Robinson, then follow Route 274 to the left when it splits from Route 850. All of these roads are wide open with gentle sweeping curves and made for power road sofas like my Honda Gold Wing. However, any bike will enjoy tracing a smooth line through the curves, taking in rural Pennsylvania framed on either side by gentle ridges of the Alleghenies.

Pennsylvania is home to 221 covered bridges—more than any other state.

Just past Centre, make a left turn on Couchtown Road, SR 3008. The bridge along this route is to your left off the main traffic route. Make a right on SR 3005 and follow it over the covered bridge, then turn left on Red Rock Road, and make a left on Adams Road to the Enslow Bridge. This is a particularly pretty bridge, framed by trees. To the right of the bridge down the creek is a bench perfect for a brief stop to soak in the atmosphere of the countryside. Follow SR 3005 until it ends on SR 3006. Turn right on SR 3006 and follow it through Blain, returning to Route 274 where you resume your westward trek. Two other bridges are close to the road along your way, though neither was open to traffic when I passed by. Along 274, look for bridges down Mount Pleasant Road and New Germantown Road, both on your left.

There isn't much in the way of food service along the route, so your best bet might be to bring along a picnic lunch for your stop at Enslow Bridge. If you can hold out until you reach New Germantown, stop by **Ginger's Country Kitchen** for a diet-busting lunch. It appears out of nowhere along Route 274 and you have to wonder how they stay in business. One taste will tell you though—the food is good. This is a friendly little place and except for the occasional passersby, the clientele is all local. Sitting at the back of the restaurant, you can look across a broad field and see the northern ridge of Blue Mountain while eavesdropping on conversations nearby. If you really want to be bad, finish off your lunch with a piece of Ginger's toll house pie. Prepare for a sugar buzz!

After New Germantown, the route enters the **Tuscarora State Forest** again and **Big Spring State Park.** There are some quick switchbacks in this section, so don't let the relatively easy ascent fool you. Descending rapidly, you'll meet wide-open Route 75. Turn left and follow it south, then turn right on Route 641. This is a fun road that jumps over Tuscarora Mountain with pretty vistas along the upper ridges. To the west, you can see the Shade Mountain Gap. That's where we're headed. Route 641 meets US Route 522 at Shade Gap. Follow Route 522 north to Orbisonia and the **East Broad Top Railroad** (EBT).

The EBT began operating in 1872 to connect the isolated southwestern coal and iron fields of the state with iron furnaces and the Pennsylvania Railroad. In the fall, the railroad hosts a weekend special when they draw out nearly their whole line of rolling stock. If you're anywhere near the railroad, you'll hear another tradition: the annual whistle salute. Not only does each train have a distinctive whistle, each conductor has his own unique way of using it. This is perhaps the one safe time you can pass through town and rev your straight pipes for all they're worth without disturbing anyone. The EBT offers rides to passengers from June to October. If you're interested in a ride, call ahead for an exact schedule. (Another attraction located near the EBT is the **Rockhill Trolley Museum.** This working museum has a collection of eighteen trolley cars and operates on a schedule in conjunction with the EBT.)

As I stood in front of the railroad taking pictures, a few folks stopped to take a look at the Gold Wing and comment on its enormous size and array of gadgetry. One older gent and his wife stopped for a look. "Nice bike," he said. "What is that, an Indian?" I guess it had been a while since he was part of the motorcycling scene. A few minutes later, an Amish family strolled by, mother and father and two young children in tow. Mother and the children passed by with a polite nod, but the father paused just a moment and glanced at the bike. "Nice Wing," he said and shot me a grin. Now do you suppose he is a closet . . . ? Naah.

The return route passes by another covered bridge near Saint Mary's Catholic Church near Shade Gap and then enters open farmland, much of which is maintained by Amish farmers. You will often see them working the land with a harnessed mule team, or traversing the highway in their familiar black buggies. This setting, quiet and isolated, seems more suited to the Amish than the much-hyped Pennsylvania Dutch country. In Penn Dutch country, the Amish are like a novelty attraction that you pay to view; here they blend into the countryside. But I'll bet that if one particular Amish farmer had his way, his buggy would have a flat-six, reverse gear, and two wheels.

When you arrive back at Route 75 where you turned off, continue on Route 641, following it over Kittatinny Mountain. This is a nice stretch of road with some good lines for taking curves. When you reach Roxbury, turn right on Route 997. This section of the route passes the Letterkenney Army Depot and skirts just to the east of Chambersburg. As a result, there is more traffic to contend with, but it isn't too bothersome and won't last for long. Once you are past Chambersburg, the scenery becomes rural again. When you approach the intersection of Route 997 and Route 30, note that you must turn right on Route 30 and then a quick left to resume your tour on Route 997.

Upon arriving in Mont Alto, you have come nearly full circle in the tour. If you need to get off the bike for a stretch, the Mont Alto campus of Penn State University offers just the place. The **Mont Alto Arboretum** on the grounds of the campus features more than 300 species of shrubs and trees from the U.S., Europe, and Asia. There are self-guided walking trails you can explore at your leisure.

The return route closes the loop on this tour at South Mountain. Be sure you turn onto South Mountain Road rather than continuing on Route 233, otherwise you'll ride in circles! South Mountain Road becomes Cold Springs Road again, and this in turn leads back to Route 116. Follow Route 116 east to Gettysburg to complete the tour. On second thought, maybe riding in circles through the Pennsylvania heartland isn't such a bad idea after all!

Trip 2 Harley Country

Distance	*165 miles*
Terrain	*Predominantly rolling hills and farm country. All roads are paved but some sections are a little rougher than others. Light traffic except for stretch between York and Lancaster.*
Highlights	*Harley-Davidson manufacturing facility, Pennsylvania Dutch country, Strasburg Railroad, Railroad Museum of Pennsylvania*

The Route from Gettysburg

→ PA 116 east to US 30 east at York
→ After I-83 overpass in York, take a left at the H-D plant sign at the fourth light
→ US 30 east to Lancaster
→ PA 896 south (Eastbrook Rd.) to Strasburg
→ PA 896 south (Georgetown Rd.) to PA 372
→ PA 372 east to PA 74
→ PA 74 south to PA 851
→ PA 851 west to PA 516
→ PA 516 north to PA 216
→ PA 216 west to PA 116
→ PA 116 west to Gettysburg

No self-respecting tourbook of this region would be complete without including the mecca of motorcycling, the **Harley-Davidson Motor Company** assembly plant in York, and the famed Pennsylvania Dutch country. The time of year you visit plays a big part in determining how much time you spend seeing things and how much time you spend standing in line. Unless you are coming to the area for the specific purpose of attending the annual *Rider* magazine rally held in the Lancaster area each spring, my advice is visit another time. Otherwise, you'll be battling hundreds of fellow motorcyclists for the same roads, restaurants, motels, etc. Fall is a good time to visit. Whether you are a Harley rider or not, you are always invited to the open house held at the plant during the last weekend in September.

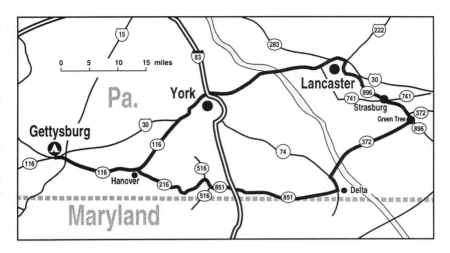

This event usually draws a few thousand Harley fans and is worth visiting just to stroll through the parking area and browse the incredible array of bikes, many of them heavily modified. As added incentive, you can take a free demo ride on a new Harley, an opportunity you won't often have at your local dealer. The open house also features tours of the plant and free food. Who can resist?

Our tour begins by picking up Route 116 on the northern end of Gettysburg and following it through Hanover to Route 30 just outside York. This route is a little less traveled than following Route 30 straight from Gettysburg, but there will be traffic to contend with from here on until you are past Lancaster. Following Route 30 east through York, start counting lights after you pass under the Interstate 83 overpass. The Harley plant is marked by a big sign on your left at the fourth traffic light.

Though the immediate area is disguised with a heavy layer of industrial development, 51 percent of the land in York County is still agricultural, and historical notes abound. York bills itself as the first capital of the United States because it was here, in November 1777, that the Continental Congress adopted the Articles of Confederation, the first document outlining federal powers over the colonies. York's industrial heritage includes the first iron steamboat and first coal locomotive to be built in the U.S., as well as an early cottage industry in horseless carriages.

Following Route 30 east will take you through Lancaster and deposit you into the heart of Pennsylvania Dutch country. It's surprising how much commercial development has sprung up along the Route 30 corridor, but I found you need only slip off onto any side road to return to a gentle pace and find countryside that better represents the true character of the area. After a brief map consultation, I turned off Route 30 onto Route 896 and traced a southeasterly route through the region. This offers a good combination of scenery and passes through some of the out-of-the-way attractions in the area.

As you follow Route 896 through Strasburg, watch for Route 741 on your left. Follow it to the **Strasburg Rail Road** and the **Railroad Museum of Pennsylvania** just a few tenths of a mile down the road. If you are a railroad buff, or just a fan of things mechanical, this is a must stop. Established in 1963 to collect and preserve the elements of Pennsylvania's railroading heritage, the museum has a great variety of loco-motives, from some of the earliest to a few of recent diesel-electric origin. When you first walk in the museum, you suddenly feel as if you have shrunk to two inches tall and are walking amid a huge toy train collection.

Don't miss the trains outside in the rolling stock yard. You may find members of local railroad interest groups on hand conducting tours of the stock yards inside and out, and working to preserve and restore some of the locomotives and cars to their original condition. There are several engines you can climb aboard if you want to feel what it was like to command one of these giant iron monsters. As you look ahead out the side window and take in the length, breadth, and weight, imagine how much easier commuting would be in one of these babies during rush hour . . . no one would make the mistake of turning left in front of you!

After you've explored Strasburg to your satisfaction, return to Route 896 to continue the route. The route now becomes Georgetown Road and gently winds through farm country, eventually intersecting with Route 372 at Green Tree. From this point, turning right will start the return trek to Gettysburg. There is plenty of interesting riding left though. Route 372 is wide open and fast, but lightly traveled and soon ends on Route 74, another wide-open road. Follow

Pennsylvania's railroad heritage is alive and well.

Route 74 to Delta, where you'll want to stop for a bite to eat if you haven't had anything for a while. It will take a couple of hours from here to negotiate the twists and turns before you return home. The **Delta Family Restaurant** is conveniently located at the very intersection where you need to make your right turn onto Route 851. The menu is standard fare, but better than fast food and just a couple of dollars more.

Now you're ready to tackle Route 851. It's a challenge to follow, not because it is particularly twisty—though it has its moments—but because of the extraordinary variety of roads it follows to get from one place to another. It has to be a route designed by committee and drawn by connecting the dots on the map. It must touch every single hamlet, burg, and 'ville along the way. You'll have some scouting to do, but this is a fun route to travel. It follows creeks, fence rows, and railroad beds. It gets narrow and bumpy, then turns wide and smooth. It passes through towns like New Freedom, Constitution, and my personal favorite, Sticks.

Eventually you end up in the general vicinity of nowhere. After a brief stint on Route 516, follow Route 216 west. Just outside of Hanover, you will ride through **Codorus State Park** and over Lake Marburg. The lake doesn't look like much from this view, but this is only a small portion; the rest is hidden away in the forest. From here it is three miles into Hanover and a simple matter to find Route 116 to Gettysburg.

Trip 3   Monument Valley

• •

Distance   *120 miles*

Terrain   *Twisty roads over and around small hills*

Highlights   *Cunningham Falls, The Cozy, Catoctin Mountain Park,*
Washington Monument State Park, Antietam National Battlefield,
Harpers Ferry National Historic Park

The Route from Gettysburg

→ West Confederate Avenue to US 15
→ US 15 south to MD 806
→ MD 806 north to Water Street
→ Left on Water Street to MD 77
→ MD 77 west to MD 64
→ MD 64 east to MD 66
→ MD 66 west to Alternate US 40
→ Alt US 40 east to Washington Monument
→ Return Alt US 40 west to MD 34
→ MD 34 west to Sharpsburg
→ MD 65 north to Antietam
→ MD 65 south to MD 34
→ MD 34 west to Harpers Ferry Road
→ Harpers Ferry Road to Keep Tryst Road
→ Keep Tryst Road west to US 340
→ US 340 north to MD 17
→ MD 17 north to Harp Hill Road
→ Harp Hill Road north to Stottlemeyer Road
→ Stottlemeyer Road east to MD 77
→ MD 77 east to US 15
→ US 15 north to Gettysburg

I call this loop "Monument Valley" in honor of the real
Monument Valley on the Arizona/Utah border. In this case,
the monuments aren't towering rock formations, but rather
the memorials raised to those who served in the Civil War.
This loop is relatively short in mileage because you'll want

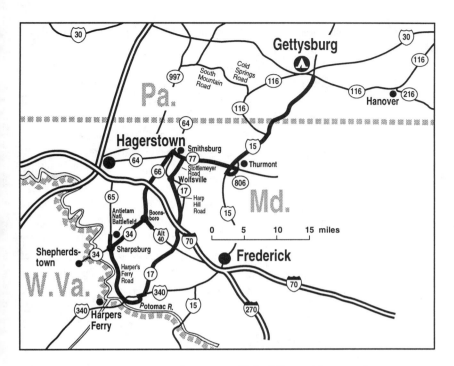

an opportunity to get off the bike and browse the museums, walk the trails, or meander the battlefields at a leisurely pace.

A good way to start is by following West Confederate Avenue out of town. You are behind Confederate lines, looking over the meadow that separated the western ridge from the town of Gettysburg. On the third day of the Battle of Gettysburg, in a last-ditch attempt to take the town and shift the momentum of the war to the South, General Lee hesitantly approved a bold plan—to allow George Pickett, one of his field generals, to lead the army of Northern Virginia across the wide open expanse directly into the strongest point of the Union line.

Pickett's Charge, as it came to be known, was a disaster. As the rebels marched toward the entrenched Union position on the other side of the field, a barrage of Union musket and artillery fire raked the Confederate lines. In a matter of minutes, the Rebel advance was shattered. The Union army held off the strongest offensive the Confederate states could mount. This would be the last significant invasion the Rebel army would make into Union territory, prompting historians in later years to label this battle "the high water mark of the Confederacy."

West Confederate Avenue intersects with Route 15. Take Route 15 south and stop in Thurmont, Maryland for breakfast at the **Cozy Restaurant.** The Cozy is a favorite of local motorcyclists. You'll often find a group of bikes in the parking lot, especially on the weekends. On Sundays the Cozy puts out a tremendous brunch buffet that stretches 20 or 30 feet. Not only is it a huge spread, everything is freshly prepared and tastes great.

After tanking yourself and your bike up, the journey begins straight out of Thurmont into the Catoctin Mountains. Follow Route 806 north into town, make a left on Water Street, then turn left on Main Street, MD 77 west. Close at hand are **Catoctin Mountain Park** on the right side of the road and **Cunningham Falls State Park** on the left. Route 77 threads through the middle, an inviting strip of pavement that will whet your appetite for the curves that follow. The short hiking path to Cunningham Falls is perfectly suited to working off a dozen or so of those 10,000 calories you just ate for breakfast. Don't forget to stop by the visitor center at Catoctin Mountain to get your National Parks Passport stamp.

Once Route 77 reaches the summit of Catoctin Mountain, the pace picks up as the road straightens out. It ends on the outskirts of Smithsburg. Make a left on MD 64 for a couple of miles, then another left on MD 66, then slip under the roar of Interstate 70 and pass into the rolling rural countryside of western Maryland. At Boonsboro, make the left turn onto Alternate 40 and follow the signs for **Washington Monument State Park.** Just outside of town you'll begin climbing again, this time ascending South Mountain.

There are countless monuments to George Washington scattered all over the country, but the large stone tower erected on this site by local patriots in 1827 was probably the first. Enter at the base of the tower and ascend the narrow circular stairs to reach the platform at the top. From here you can see well into West Virginia across the upper Shenandoah Valley, known here as the "Great Valley." Members of local conservation groups are often present, observing the movements of migrating hawks that follow the thermals created by

This stone tower was the first monument to George Washington. There are great views from the top!

the mountains. You can also impress your friends by telling them that while you were at it, you hiked a portion of the Appalachian Trail on your vacation. You don't need to tell them it was only from the parking lot to the monument and back.

Return to Boonsboro on Alt 40 and make the left turn onto MD 34 towards Sharpsburg and the **Antietam National Battlefield.** The Battle of Antietam marked an earlier attempt by General Lee to take the offensive in the Civil War. His goal was to capture the Union capital, Washington, DC, which, if attained, might generate European support for and recogni-

Miss Kitty poses on a bridge near Gettysburg.

tion of the Confederate States. Fighting between the opposing forces was ferocious. A field of corn which stood between the two armies was cut to the ground by the exchange of fire. So many soldiers from both armies fell at Antietam Creek that for a while during and after the battle, the creek ran red with blood. The battlefield is preserved in a state much as it was when the war raged, and a series of drives allows you to tour the battlefield on your bike to see how the engagement was played out. Stop by the visitor center and add another stamp to your passport.

In the town of Sharpsburg, pick up Harpers Ferry Road east out of town. If you've been looking for a little more riding excitement to go with your scenery, this road delivers. It's a favorite route of area riders and you're apt to meet up with a few along the way. The ride gets even more twisty as you near the Potomac River at Harpers Ferry and parallel the C&O Canal Park Towpath for a mile or two. The towpath is great for a leisurely stroll alongside the river. Just ahead, the Potomac and Shenandoah rivers meet before turning southeast toward Washington, D.C. A bridge near the confluence allows you to cross the Potomac and enter **Harpers Ferry National Historic Park.** You can get yet another passport stamp here. (See Mosby's Confederacy, Trip 11, for more information about Harpers Ferry).

Follow Harpers Ferry Road underneath the railroad bridge and make the left turn onto Keep Tryst Road. A short distance will put you northbound on U.S. Route 340 toward Frederick, Md. and Route 15. Rather than get caught in the urban clutter of Frederick, follow MD Route 17 north. Pasture land abounds on either side of your view, and sharp right angle turns that once marked property boundaries will keep you interested. Route 17 is wide and smooth, a great touring road. As it makes its way north, the ride entertains you with several series of tight curves that will have you swaying your bike from side to side to stay with it. A nice diversion is to follow Harp Hill Road north over higher ground. You'll have to drop down a gear or two as some portions of the road rise and fall like the streets of San Francisco. Harp Hill Road rejoins MD 17 at Wolfsville. In Wolfsville, a right turn on Stottlemeyer Road will bring you back to MD 77 just outside Catoctin Mountain Park. Follow MD 77 east to Thurmont, then US 15 north to retrace your path to Gettysburg.

Lodging

••

Colton Motel
232 Steinwehr Avenue
Gettysburg, PA 17325
Phone 717-334-5514. Price varies according to season: from $45
to $79 for a single.

The Old Appleford Inn
Frank and Maribeth Skradski
218 Carlisle Street
Gettysburg, PA 17325
Phone 717-337-1711. Rooms from $88.

Places of Interest

••

Antietam National Battlefield
Sharpsburg, MD 21782
Phone 301-432-5124. Daily, 8:30 a.m. to 5 p.m. $

Big Spring State Park
New Germantown, PA 17071
Phone 717-776-5272.

Catoctin Mountain Park
MD Route 77 West
Thurmont, MD 21788
Phone 301-663-9388. Visitor Center is open 8:30 a.m. to 5 p.m.
Free.

Codorus State Park
Hanover, PA 17332
Phone 717-637-2816.

Cunningham Falls State Park
Thurmont, MD 21788
Phone 301-271-7574. Free.

East Broad Top Railroad
P.O. Box 189
US 522 North at Orbisonia
Cresson, PA 16630
Phone 814-447-3011. Weekends, June to October. Call for exact
times and dates. Tours of shop available. Ten-mile round trip re-
quires about an hour to complete. $7.50 adults, $5 children.

Eisenhower National Historic Site
97 Taneytown Rd.
Gettysburg, PA 17325
Phone 717-334-1124. Shuttle runs to farm daily, every fifteen
minutes from 9 a.m. to 4 p.m. during the summer. Off-season
weekdays, 4 times a day; off-season weekends, hourly. $3.60.

Gettysburg National Military Park
97 Taneytown Rd.
P.O. Box 1080
Gettysburg, PA 17325
Phone 717-334-1124. Open daily, 8 a.m. to 5 p.m. Contact point
for Eisenhower National Historic Site. Museum free; Electric
Map $2; Cyclorama $2; Eisenhower Tour $2.50.

Harley-Davidson Motor Company
US Route 30 East
York, PA 17401
Phone 717-848-1177. Factory tours Mon. through Fri., 10 a.m. to
2 p.m. Call for specific tour times. Open house with demo rides
last Thurs. through Sun. in September. Free.

Harpers Ferry National Historic Park
Harpers Ferry, WV 25410
Phone 304-535-6115. Best time for tours is between Memorial
Day and Labor Day. Frequency depends upon staffing. $5 per ve-
hicle.

Michael Garman's Magic Town
49 Steinwehr Avenue
Gettysburg, PA 17325
Phone 717-337-0442. Sun. through Thurs., 11 a.m. to 7 p.m.; 'til
9 p.m. on Fri. and Sat. $2.75 per person; group rates available.

Michaux State Forest
Fayetteville, PA 17222
Phone 717-352-2211.

Mont Alto Arboretum
Pennsylvania State University
PA Route 233 at Mont Alto
Mont Alto, PA 17237
Phone 717-749-3111. Daylight hours. Self-guiding trails through area with 725 trees and shrubs of 300 species from United States, Europe, and Asia. Free.

Railroad Museum of Pennsylvania
P.O. Box 15
Route 741 East
Strasburg, PA 17579
Phone 717-687-8628. Mon. through Sat., 9 a.m. to 5 p.m.; Sun., noon to 5 p.m. Closed Mondays, November through April, and certain holidays. $5 admission.

Rockhill Trolley Museum
US Route 522 North at Rockhill
Cresson, PA 16630
Phone 814-447-9576 or 814-447-3011. Weekends, Memorial Day through October; rides begin every half-hour, starting at 11 a.m. $3 adult; $1 children.

Strasburg Railroad
P.O. Box 96
PA Route 741 East
Strasburg, PA 17579-0096
Phone 717-687-7522. Trains run daily, Memorial Day through October. Weekends off-season. Call for scheduled times. In the summer trains depart Sun. through Fri. at 12 noon, 1 p.m., 2 p.m., and 3 p.m.; Saturdays, every hour between 11 a.m. and 3 p.m. $7 adults; $4 ages 3 to 11.

Tuscarora State Forest
PA Route 74 West
New Germantown, PA 17071
Phone 717-536-3191.

Washington Monument State Park
21843 National Pike
(At the intersection of Monument and Zittlestown Roads, one-half mile off Alternate US 40)
Boonsboro, MD 21713
Phone 301-432-8065. Open Fri. through Mon., 8 a.m. to sunset.

Restaurants

• •

Avenue Restaurant
21 Steinwehr Avenue
Gettysburg, PA 17325
Phone 717-334-3235. Open 7 a.m. to 9 p.m.; closes 10 p.m. Fri.
and Sat. $

Cozy Restaurant
105 Frederick Rd.
Thurmont, MD 21788
Phone 301-271-7373. Weekdays, 11 a.m. to 3:30 p.m. for lunch;
4 p.m. to 8:45 p.m. for dinner. Open weekends at 8 a.m. for
breakfast. Huge, delicious buffet spread that is popular with rid-
ers. $$

Delta Family Restaurant
Route 2, Box 468
Intersection of PA 851 & PA 74
Delta, PA 17314
Phone 717-456-5233. Daily, 6 a.m. to 9 p.m. (10 p.m. Fri. and
Sat.). Breakfast $2.25; lunch $3.50; dinner $6 to $11.

Farnsworth House Inn
401 Baltimore Street
Gettysburg, PA 17325
Phone 717-334-8838. Daily, 5 p.m. to 9 p.m. Reservations for
dinner strongly suggested. Ghost stories in basement in season;
call for dates and times. $$ - $$$

Ginger's Country Kitchen
PA Route 274 West
New Germantown, PA 17071
Phone 717-536-3410. Sunday, 9 a.m. to 8 p.m.; Mon. through
Thurs., 10 a.m. to 8 p.m. Fri. and Sat., 10 a.m. to 9:30 p.m.
Closed Tuesday. $

Gingerbread Man
217 Steinwehr Avenue
Gettysburg, PA 17325
Phone 717-334-1100. Open 11 a.m. to 11 p.m. $ - $$

Lincoln Diner
32 Carlisle Street
Gettysburg, PA 17325
Phone 717-334-3900. Daily, 24 hours a day. $

Tommy's Pizza
105 Steinwehr Avenue
Gettysburg, PA 17325
Phone 717-334-4721. Sun. through Thurs., 11 a.m. to 11 p.m.;
'til midnight Fri. and Sat. Very limited delivery. $

Travel Information

. . . .

Appalachian Trails Conference
P.O. Box 807
Harpers Ferry, WV 25425
Phone 304-535-6331. Guidebook available from ATC with infor-
mation about hiking the Appalachian Trail. Information only.

Gettysburg Travel Council
35 Carlisle Street
Gettysburg, PA 17325
Phone 717-334-6274.

York County Visitors Bureau
(contact for information on the Pennsylvania Dutch Country)
1 Market Way East
P.O. Box 1229
York, PA 17405
Phone 717-848-4000.

The Trail West

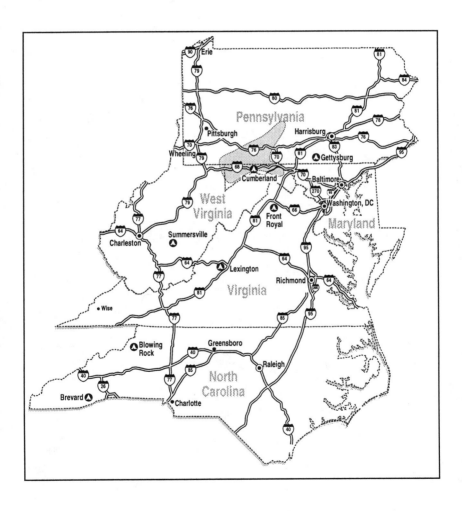

Cumberland, Md.

• •

Cumberland was for many years a destination of travelers heading to points west by road, rail, and canal. The town sprang up around a large gap in the Allegheny Mountains called The Narrows. This corridor, first discovered by Native Americans, marked the route for the National Road, the first federally funded highway.

During the 1800s, thousands of settlers poured through The Narrows on their way to claim homesteads in the territories of the Great Plains. Situated at the end of a day's journey along the route, Cumberland was a popular stopover on railroad and stagecoach routes.

Today, Cumberland can be reached in two hours from metropolitan areas of the mid-Atlantic, making it little more than a convenient rest stop on the way west. For us, however, it remains the perfect strategic position from which to discover the byways that wind through the mountains that surround it.

From Cumberland you can launch a day trip into southern Pennsylvania to discover the hundreds of tiny farming valleys that lie between the ridges. You'll meander through quiet little towns that have successfully resisted the urge to keep pace with modern America. No pay-at-the-pump gas stations, automated teller machines or fast food restaurants in this region. You can also venture west into Maryland's **Deep Creek Lake** area. West Virginia is just over the Potomac River, and some of that state's greatest beauty can be found along its northern border.

Cumberland itself is like a large patchwork quilt spread out over uneven ground. Its streets are a tangled web of intersections, underpasses and access roads. The only way to figure out how to get around town is to navigate by points of the compass rather than by street directions. "I think the

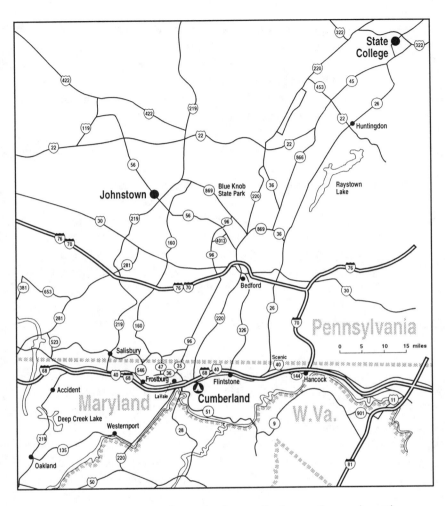

restaurant is south of town. Let's see, the sun is setting over there so that must be west . . . let's go down this street."

While you are in town, there are a few places you will want to check out. The **History House** on Washington Street is a restored 1867 town house that is now a museum of Allegany County history. While you are on Washington Street, check out the other large homes that line the street. These were all built around the same time, during Cumberland's economic peak during the mid-1800s. To get a better idea of the forces that shaped this region, visit the **Transportation and Industrial Museum** at the Western Maryland Station Center. While you are there, you can book a ride on

the **Western Maryland Scenic Railroad.** The 16-mile trip
from Cumberland to Frostburg passes through The Narrows
and through a tunnel. You are conveniently dropped off at the
Old Depot Center and Restaurant in Frostburg for a 90-
minute layover before returning. Gee, what should you do
with that hour and a half? Eat? Shop? The folks in Frostburg
sure hope so.

One of my favorite places to camp is just outside Cumberland at **Rocky Gap State Park.** This is one of the newest
and largest state parks in Maryland, with almost 300 sites.
None of them have hookups, though, so this park isn't popular with the home-away-from-home RV set. Rocky Gap bor-
ders a large lake with three beaches and rowboats and canoes
available for rent. At night, the conversation of nearby campers filters through the heavily wooded site, but the sounds are
dampened by the heavy undergrowth. During the summer
season, make reservations at Rocky Gap early to avoid disap-
pointment. You might do well to avoid the last weekend in
July at Rocky Gap altogether. This is the week normally
reserved for the three-day Rocky Gap Country Music Festival, which draws tens of thousands and swamps the area.
Some people like that kind of mass hysteria, but I come here
to get away from it. If you would like to attend the festival,
plan to make your reservations about a year in advance.

If motelling it is your idea of minimum accommodations, check out the **Maryland Motel** just a few miles from
the campground on Route 220. **Mason's Barn** is convenient
to both town and the campground and is your best bet for a
good meal. There are numerous fast food places and chain
restaurants on the west side of town. Just follow Alternate 40
through the Narrows and into LaVale to get to the travel
services strip.

The view from outside Rocky Gap State Park near Cumberland.

Trip 4   Pioneer Loop

Distance   *140 miles*

Terrain   *Wide, well-paved roads through mountains and valleys. Big sweepers and a few tighter ones.*

Highlights   *Casselman River Bridge, Penn Alps, Deep Creek Lake, Westernport*

The Route from Cumberland

→ I-68 or Alt. US 40 west to US 219

→ US 219 south to MD 135

→ MD 135 east to US 220

→ US 220 north to Cumberland

The Pioneer Loop begins on I-68 west at Cumberland. I-68, also known as the National Road, has had a long history. It began as an Indian trace, then became a pioneer road, and is now a major gateway to the west. It wasn't always as smooth as it is now. Thomas Jefferson signed the enabling legislation

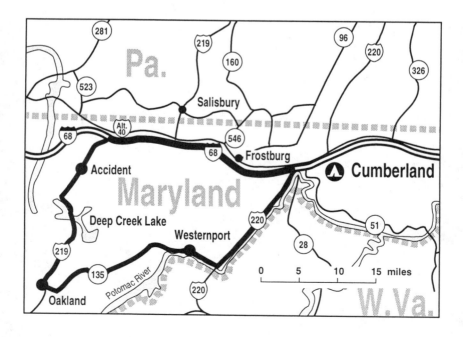

A recreation of the old Compton School at Penn Alps. Sit up straight and mind your manners!

that created the National Road in 1806 and construction began in 1811 near Cumberland. By the time the road reached its terminus in Vandalia, Illinois, nearly 40 years later, it was obsolete—train travel was all the rage. The road fell into a five-decade decline, with some sections becoming virtually impassable. It wasn't until the introduction of the automobile in the early twentieth century that these sections of the National Road were improved and resurfaced. In the early part of this decade, the first American interstate was officially added to the interstate highway system.

Despite the fact that it carries the much-maligned title "interstate," I-68 is a smooth scenic ride and good for making time. It isn't hard to get the feeling that you own I-68; it is rarely crowded. When you feel like taking things at a slower pace, follow Alternate US 40. It hops on and off the interstate, but it is a little more curvy and challenging than auto-piloting down the superslab.

Thirty miles west of Cumberland is a wide spot in the road called Penn Alps. The tug of the highway would ordinarily pull you past Penn Alps without a second thought, but a visit to the **Spruce Forest Artisan Village** there is worth the time. The village is a group of restored log cabins occupied by Appalachian artisans who demonstrate their crafts and sell their wares. These are not weekend woodworkers either. Many of the artists-in-residence have won international recognition for their work.

Other buildings have been restored just to display frontier life. One is a restored log schoolhouse which is authentic right down to the books on the desk and boots arranged neatly in the rear of the building. On the day we visited, a schoolmarm was there to tell us about how school was conducted. From her description, it was clear that she had firm control over her classroom. On the way out the door, she even reminded me to mind my manners and to "say please and thank you!"

Adjacent to the village is the Casselman River Bridge, built in 1813 as part of the National Road project and in use until 1933. The night before it was to be officially dedicated, the builder came to take away the scaffolding to make sure it wouldn't fall down in front of everyone at the ceremony. He was convinced it wouldn't stand on its own! The bridge didn't fall, so the workmen were directed to put the scaffolding back into place for the official dedication ceremony the next day.

The bridge was originally built much larger than was required as a political ploy to attract the C&O Canal project through the area. Local government officials thought that by building a large bridge over the Casselman River, they would provide a route for the engineers that wouldn't require any further bridge construction. Good idea, but the Ohio end of the canal never got past Cumberland. But when you consider the bridge was in use for 120 years, they probably got their money's worth out of it anyway. Today the state has set aside the bridge area as a state park with tables and grills.

Continue west to US 219 south. A scenic overlook to the right gives you a superb view of the valley below as pretty as any you'll ever see. For the most part, the pace is relaxed on 219, there isn't a great deal of traffic, and the view is nice. You might get a little tense, though, as you pass a storefront along the way called "Accident Ambulance Sales." Shortly thereafter 219 winds through the town of Accident, Maryland. Well, that explained things a little, but I didn't stop to find out how the town got its name. Perhaps one day I'll write to find out—from the safety of home.

Outside of Accident, traffic will increase as you approach the **Deep Creek Lake State Park** and resort area.

Despite the builder's concern, the Casselman River Bridge still stands.

Deep Creek is popular both as a summer resort and—because the area receives an average of 82 inches of snow each winter—as a popular skiing destination. The result is an abundance of places to stay if you wish to layover, and a good range of places to eat from casual snacks to fine dining. One place I especially enjoyed was **Doctor Willy's Seafood.** Another fact to file for Really Trivial Pursuit: Deep Creek is 72 feet deep.

Eventually 219 runs into the town of Oakland. From there, hang a left onto Route 135 east. About ten miles out of Oakland, 135 falls off the top of a mountain ridge in one straight, fast four-mile descent. Signs every 50 feet warn trucks to stay in first gear and not to exceed 10 mph. The road didn't seem that steep to me, but at the bottom of the mountain I found a road crew picking up the remains of a shattered guard rail and a log truck—guess the signs were right after all. Route 135 makes an abrupt right face at the end of the downhill run and then hugs the north bank of the Potomac River for the next 20 miles.

Maryland's entire southern border is etched on the map by the course of the Potomac River from the Fairfax Stone at the far southwestern corner to the Eastern Shore. In the 1700s when Lord Thomas Fairfax commanded a massive stretch of land known as the Fairfax Proprietary, he was told that the western boundary of his claim would be defined by the headwaters of the Potomac. It was in Fairfax's best interest to see that the headwaters be as generously defined as possible. At the Fairfax Stone, you can literally step across the Potomac.

The area's primary employer is Westvaco, a large paper mill, which has spawned several towns. On my way through one of them, Westernport, I stopped for a breather at a town park next to the river. There is a bright red caboose on display in the park. I thought that maybe this was just the hull for youngsters to crawl on. Luckily, I was wrong.

Inside, the caboose has been completely refurbished and is crammed full of old photographs, lanterns, and dozens of other mementos of the railroad. I was lucky enough to even get a personal guided tour, front to back, by Ellsworth Kenealy, a 40-year veteran of the rails. Each item or picture he picked up had a story associated with it, and Mr. Kenealy's personalized tour meant a lot more than if I had simply walked through an exhibit in some museum. Thanks, Mr. Kenealy.

From Westernport, continue on 135 to Route 220 north. This runs back into Cumberland to conclude the Pioneer Loop.

*Ellsworth
Kenealy and
grandson Aaron
await your visit
to Westernport.*

Trip 5   Lion Country

Distance	*240 miles*
Terrain	*Mostly well-paved state roads with long sweepers. Back roads are narrow, with some tight curves and occasional gravel hazards.*
Highlights	*Miles of beautiful Pennsylvania farm country and small towns framed by low ridges, Old Bedford Village, Indian Caverns, Pennsylvania State University campus, Boal Mansion and Museum, Raystown Lake*

The Route from Cumberland

→ I-68 east to Pleasant Valley Road
→ Pleasant Valley Road becomes SR 3005 in Pennsylvania
→ SR 3005 north to SR 3007
→ SR 3007 north to PA 326
→ PA 326 north to US 30
→ US 30 west to Bedford
→ Business 220 north to Old Bedford Village
→ Business 220 north becomes SR 4009
→ SR 4009 north to T707
→ T707 north to PA 869
→ PA 869 east to PA 36
→ PA 36 north to PA 866
→ PA 866 north to US 22
→ US 22 east to PA 453
→ PA 453 north to PA 45
→ PA 45 east to Business 322 in Boalsburg
→ Business 322 west into State College to PA 26
→ PA 26 south to US Scenic 40 in Maryland
→ US Scenic 40 west to I-68
→ I-68 west to Cumberland

This is a long route, one of the longest included in this book. It is here because of the important lesson it teaches to the patient rider: by no other means of transportation (save perhaps a bicycle) could you absorb as much of the scenery and atmosphere of a place as by riding a motorcycle. You have probably read often that travel is its own reward and the fun

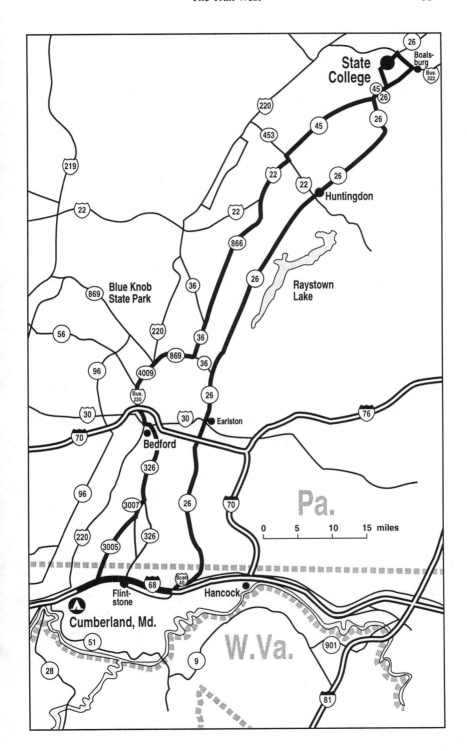

is not where you are going but in getting there. This route proves it.

We begin our journey to the center of the Keystone State from **Rocky Gap State Park,** following Pleasant Valley Road north toward the state line. There is no sign to announce your arrival in Pennsylvania, but you will begin seeing route markers with "SR 3005" on them and know that you have arrived. SR 3005 is a narrow, twisty, bumpy, and delightful back road that inches its way through Buchanan State Forest. It crosses over Tussey Mountain and enters the Martin Hill Wild Area with rewarding snatches of scenic vistas through the thick stand of trees. Even though there are few vehicles to compete with, the road surface will keep your pace down. If your scoot is apt to drop nuts and bolts, be prepared to stop in Bedford and check for missing hardware. Hang a left on SR 3007 and then another left on PA 326. You can now relax; the remainder of the route is largely smooth.

PA 326 joins US 30 at a gap in Evitts Mountain just outside of Bedford. Here you need to exercise a little caution and patience because US 30 is a busy highway. Once you are able to negotiate the left turn, follow US 30 into the town of Bedford. If you took off without breakfast, I can recommend the **Landmark Restaurant.** You'll see it on East Pitt Street as you meander through town. If you're really hungry, try the pancakes. They were almost more than I could eat, but I was somehow able to put them away.

You could spend a couple of hours in Bedford just cruising the streets checking out the variety of historic homes and buildings. Two of the most popular are **Fort Bedford Museum** and **Old Bedford Village.** The fort is built near the site of the original and features exhibits of frontier life. Of the two, I preferred the fort. Old Bedford Village strikes me as too touristy and though the purpose is to recreate the atmosphere of an old village, there's something about it that doesn't ring true. Maybe it's the endless roar of the Pennsylvania Turnpike which runs along the back boundary of the property.

Follow Business 220 out of Bedford along Black Oak Ridge and exit onto Route 869. As you reach the summit of Dunning Mountain, you can see Morrison Cove spread out below you. Slow down and enjoy the countryside as you pass

The Amish horse and buggy is a common sight in rural Pennsylvania.

through. Occasionally you will catch up to an Amish horse and buggy, as I did along the route. Give them a wide berth to prevent spooking the horses.

All the roads through Morrison Cove will lull you into a slow touring rhythm with their gentle sweeping curves and peaceful scenery. I passed through the area just after the harvest and the aroma of sweet rich earth filled the air. Farmers were in their fields tilling under the stubble after the year's harvest to prepare for the next year, returning my wave as I drifted by. Route 869 ends on Route 36 where I turned north. I followed that for a few miles before turning right on Route 866 on a whim. It turned out to be a good one, too. I passed neatly kept farmhouses and small towns so perfect they looked nearly like scale models. Finally winding out of the cove, the route follows US 22 for a short way, left on Route 453 and shortly a right on Route 45. Be sure to follow Route 45 and not the special route for trucks. Somewhere along the route, you will begin to see signs for **Indian Caverns.** I stopped there. You should stop too, but perhaps not for the obvious reasons.

Indian Caverns is one of those tiny little enterprises that manages to eke out an existence by selling the touring public on a notion based partly on fact and largely on imagination. Traveling along Route 45, you can't miss the place. Holding a brochure of the caverns up against the real thing shows that the place could use a little more upkeep, but then you notice that the cars parked outside the cavern in the brochure can now sport antique license plates. At least one of the cars in the picture hasn't moved since.

To me, the gift shop is the real attraction at Indian Caverns; pure all-American kitsch with genuine rubber tomahawks, plastic Indian dolls, and a wide assortment of gimmicks and gadgets with the Indian Caverns logo stenciled on them. There is no lack of authentic souvenirs to choose from.

I stood in the gift shop for ten or fifteen minutes waiting for a guide to return from the caverns, wondering if I was simply being given ample opportunity to browse the merchandise. Eventually a small group of two adults and two children appeared from the cavern and descended upon the gift shop, snatching up plastic bow and arrow sets, cedar boxes of myriad shapes, and an official Indian chief's headdress. The register happily rang up a $75 sale and the proprietor gave them a wide, toothy grin. He could afford to.

The ticket for the cavern tour is $7. Frankly, I suggest you take the tour not to see the cave, but to listen to the tour guide recite her speech. I was an audience of one, but our relationship was strictly tour guide-tourist. This meant I was the entire audience, and when she dutifully executed each pause in her script, I was clearly expected to respond with some exclamation of wonderment. The tour would simply not continue until I made the appropriate comment. I obliged as best I could, but it was awkward. Occasionally she would ask, "Does anyone have any questions?" Anyone??

As you enter Boalsburg on Route 45, hang a right on US Business 322. You will soon find signs pointing to the **Boal Mansion and Museum** and the **Columbus Chapel**. This tour is worth $7 but only costs $1.50. It contains some of the oddest and oldest artifacts of our country's European heritage to be found anywhere on the North American continent. It is the most fascinating museum I have ever visited.

The Boal family was highly placed in colonial social circles, influential in trade, politics, law, the military, and so on. As a result their home is a living history of our ties to the European continent. The home had humble beginnings but was gradually expanded and enlarged until it assumed its present grandeur. Members of the Boal family still live in the home. Only a few rooms are open to the public, but they are stuffed with antiquities and oddities.

In one corner stands a piano which once belonged to Dolley Madison. Could this have been an heirloom Dolley sold from Montpelier to pay her son's gambling debts? (See Home Country, Trip 9, for details.) In a picture hanging on the wall, a stern-faced elderly woman stares at you from ages past. The chair she occupied sits in the corner. Bronze busts and statuettes of famous people are scattered throughout. Dueling pistols are displayed in cabinets in the living room, along with locks of Napoleon's hair, given to one of the members of the family who was highly placed in Napoleon's army. Gazing on Napoleon's hair on American soil is a little amazing, but it gets more amazing still.

Theodore Davis Boal was a fifth-generation family member who married a descendant of Christopher Columbus. Through this connection, a good many artifacts from the Columbus family found their way across the same ocean their ancestor had navigated hundreds of years before. Eventually Theodore Davis erected a chapel on the grounds of the Boal Mansion to the exact specifications of the original chapel building in Spain. He then imported all the contents of the original chapel. Inside is a wealth of treasures from the family, including the wooden Admiral's desk Columbus used in his voyages as well as a few of the wooden crosses he planted on newly discovered lands. Many of the papers and other items housed in the chapel also date back to the 1400s, including the intricately carved door on the front of the building.

The whole area of Boalsburg and State College deserves a full day of your time because the Boal Mansion is just the first point of interest. Just across the street from the mansion is the **Pennsylvania Military Museum.** It displays a range of weaponry and military gear from colonial times to the present day, but its outstanding feature is a full scale World War I battlefield. To complete your tour of Boalsburg, turn right on Church Street and follow it to the downtown area where you will find quite a few quaint (read dangerous to the wallet) shops and boutiques.

Just a few miles west of Boalsburg lies the town of State College, home to Pennsylvania State University. When school's in session the size of this quiet, small town of 35,000 triples. On a warm autumn afternoon, the town is literally buzzing with activity.

Plans for Penn State started in 1850 with the desire of some area residents to begin a farmer's high school. Since those humble beginnings, it has grown into one of the nation's largest universities, complete with a nationally-recognized football dynasty. There are five different museums on the main campus ranging from anthropology to the history of cable television, all of them free to the public. If you don't want to deal with the crowd on your visit to State College (though it's kind of fun, actually), go during the summer months when there is less activity at the university.

Asking around for a good place to eat, I kept getting the same answer—"Baby's"—so I decided to check it out. **Baby's** is a fifties diner on the northern end of town. It's a little hard to find if you don't know where to look, but if you like the fifties era and good burgers, this place is worth the effort to find. When you leave Boalsburg, follow 322 west into downtown until you reach PA 26 northbound. You'll go almost through town, past a number of large residence halls, offices, and campus buildings. On your left, look for a large stand–alone automatic teller. The next street on your left should be Garner Street. Baby's is on your right. If you miss it, drive through to PA 26 southbound, go down a couple of blocks and circle around. You'll eventually find it. If you don't, just about anyone on the street should be able to point you in the right direction.

This is a long tour and you might want to stay over the night in the area and make your return the following day. This is an especially good idea if you want to take advantage of any of the recreational opportunities at Raystown Lake. There should be no problem finding a room in town unless something special is going on. With the large selection, you can find prices under $30. If you are keen on bed-and-breakfasts, contact the **Rest & Repast Bed & Breakfast Service** for a list of more than 60 private homes and small inns in the immediate area.

As I worked my way south on Route 26, I passed through
a dozen more small townships and countless villages of a few
homes backed up to the long Tussey Mountain ridge. It was
early evening and the air, no longer warmed by the sun, was
taking on a real autumn chill. It was television time and the
front windows of many homes had that eerie, faint phospho-
rescent glow. While these gentle people watched the evening
news and Jeopardy, my machine and I glided past silent and
unnoticed like a ghostly shadow.

A large portion of Route 26 parallels the western shore
of Raystown Lake, the largest lake in the state. Want a cabin
with a view of the lake on four sides? At Raystown you can
rent a houseboat! You can motor one of these beauties away
from the dock at **Seven Points Marina** for a three- or four-
day vacation on the water, exploring every cove and island of
the lake, starting at $500. If you're shy of making such
long-term commitments, you can rent an open utility boat for
the day for $65.

The remainder of Route 26 below Earlston finishes in
fine Pennsylvania fashion, becoming narrow and crooked
and full of fun twists and turns. It ends all too soon, crossing
over into Maryland and soon returning to the National Road.
Your best bet for a final dose of riding satisfaction is to follow
the scenic portion of Scenic Route 40 for as long as it lasts
before returning to the wide, sprawling, and blessedly empty
superslab.

We've covered a lot of real estate in this tour, but I think
you will gain an appreciation, as I did, for the tremendous
diversity of things to do, places to go and ways to get there.
With a good map, you could explore the back roads for weeks
along this route and never travel the same road twice. It's a
tough job, but somebody has to do it. It had just as well be
you as anyone, right?

Trip 6 The National Road

....

Distance	*180 miles*
Terrain	*Pennsylvania's "high country"*
Highlights	*Mount Davis, Ohiopyle State Park, Springs Farmers' Market, Springs Museum*

The Route from Cumberland

→ Alternate Route 40 to MD 546
→ MD 546 becomes SR 2010 in PA
→ SR 2010 to T325 in Salisbury
→ T325 (Ord Street) through Salisbury to PA 669
→ PA 669 to Springs (Farmers Market & Museum)
→ Return PA 669 to SR 2002
→ SR 2002 to SR 2004
→ Right on SR 2004 east to Mount Davis
→ Return SR 2004 west to PA 523
→ PA 523 south to US 40
→ US 40 west to PA 381
→ PA 381 north to PA 653
→ PA 653 east to PA 281
→ PA 281 south to PA 523
→ PA 523 south to US 40
→ US 40 east to Cumberland

It isn't often that the weather turns hot in the Alleghenies, but when it does, this ride takes you to a good cooling off spot, namely the Youghiogheny (pronounced YOK-ah-ganey) River.

Follow Alternate Route 40 through The Narrows of Cumberland, and once you work your way past the strip shopping centers, chain restaurants, gas stations and the like, the real tour begins.

You probably won't want to stop now, but make a mental note to revisit the town of Frostburg on your return trip, or one evening for dinner. Frostburg is a college town that features a clean, homey Main Street that invites you to hop

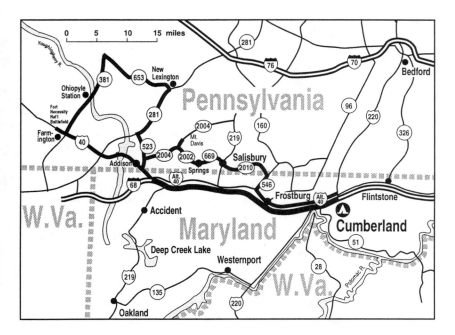

off the bike for a stroll. Continue following Alternate 40 out
of town and into the countryside. The turn onto Route 546 is
a little strange. You'll ride past it, or rather under it, then make
a left turn and drive back to get onto it. Head north for the
state line. Over the state line, the route changes to SR 2010.
This intersects with Route T325 just outside the town of
Salisbury. Stay on T325 through town (fifteen, twenty seconds), and you'll reach Route 669. Make a left here to
proceed south on Route 669.

　　Unless someone told you, you might not notice that this
is Pennsylvania's high country. The mountains look more like
tall hills out here, but in Pennsylvania, that's about as big as
they get. Much of the country is farmland and much of that is
worked by the Amish. If you want to see what real work is
like, stop by the roadside some time and watch an Amish
farmer work the field with a team of horses. I didn't catch any
out on this occasion, but I did see fields filled with precision
rows of hand-gathered bundles of grain, a sure sign that the
autumn harvest was about to approach in earnest.

　　A good place to sample some of the fruits of that harvest
is at the farmers' market in Springs. Out here a farmers'

market is as much a social occasion as it is an opportunity to buy food. You'll find a wide assortment of vehicles at the market with horse and buggy tied up next to a tractor, or sometimes, actually to a tractor. You won't find better picnic lunch supplies anywhere. Also be sure to stop by the **Springs Museum.** For a buck and a half you can wander through a massive collection of household items commonly used by people of the region from a few hundred years ago to the present day. Not only that, you'll learn the origin of the term "stogie" and how the phrase "I'll be there with bells on" came to be. When you're ready to depart the museum, turn back north on Route 669 and make a left turn on SR 2002 just a mile or two up the road. This is the route to Mount Davis.

The ascent to Mount Davis, the highest point in Pennsylvania, can be attempted from a southern approach on SR 2002 as the signs will indicate, or from the north. I suggest you pass the south entrance and go around to the north unless you're on a dual sport machine or prefer several miles of rough gravel washboard. Follow SR 2002 to the intersection with SR 2004 and turn right.

The northern entrance to the summit is just a few miles ahead on the right and is paved. Once you've turned on the road to the summit, you can skip the summit itself and continue for a short distance to a large wooden observation deck. This will give you the best view of the region, known locally as the Laurel Highlands. To continue the tour, retrace your path to SR 2004 and follow it to Route 523.

This section of SR 2004 is my favorite little stretch of road in the Keystone state. It's not particularly winding, though there are a few good sweepers. There's a spot along this road just after you pass a church that ascends a short hill and when you look to the south you see green pastures falling gently off the ridge. Behind that the forested slopes and gentle folds of Winding Ridge stand firm and silent. I just like to get off the bike, turn off the engine, and listen to the silence here. It's good for whatever ails you.

Your ride down Route 40 could be a straight shot to the next turnoff, but you'd miss an interesting site if you let time be your guide. Soon after you turn onto Route 40 there is a turnoff on the left (Route 3002) for the town of Addison.

The toll house at Addison could tell many tales of life on the National Road.

Make the turn and follow it a short distance to the **Old Petersburg-Addison Toll House.**

The National Road hadn't been around more than 20 years or so before Congressional controversies raged over who would pay for its maintenance and upkeep. Congress decided the best way to resolve the issue was to dump it on the states. The states promptly established toll houses and began to charge for the use of the road. This road has seen all kinds of traffic: covered wagons, stage coaches, and even flocks of sheep and cattle. On weekends you can usually find members of the Daughters of the American Revolution giving tours and answering questions about the toll house (they now own the building).

Other remnants of the old road remain besides the name—a marker here, an historic home there, an occasional bridge. As you breeze across the Youghiogheny on a modern steel and concrete bridge, another old link to the past remains, submerged under fifty feet of water. Lurking somewhere below is an original stone arch bridge similar to the one preserved at Casselman Bridge State Park. This one was the longest bridge on the National Road. In the winter, if water levels drop far enough, the old bridge emerges from the water like a monster rising from the depths of a Scottish loch.

If you're a fan of old forts and battlefields, you'll want to drive past the turnoff for Ohiopyle at Farmington and make the short trip (a couple of miles) to the **Fort Necessity National Battlefield.** This was just one of many wooden stockade forts that once marked the western boundary of settled territory. It's pretty amazing to imagine that at one time, venturing far beyond this point was a suicide mission. Today you just breeze by, scarcely recognizing a fort is here. To continue the tour, turn back on US 40 to Farmington and make a left turn on Route 381.

Ohiopyle State Park is situated on the banks of a broad, calm spot in the Youghiogheny River. Tubing, canoeing, and just plain wading are big business here. In Ohiopyle Station, a dozen outfitters will rent you nearly any type of device that floats. But if you prefer to picnic and perhaps just get your feet wet, there is a nice park on the northern end of town with big grassy areas.

North of town the road sweeps along the ridges, flowing with the geography. Route 653 has different ideas though, running directly across the ridges. Here you would expect the potential for big switchbacks, but I'm afraid you won't find them. Instead, the road runs right at a ridge, only to find a seam and duck through it at the last moment. It's still worth a ride for the scenery, and you'll find another of Pennsylvania's covered bridges along the route.

The return home begins with Route 281 in New Lexington. A rarity among Pennsylvania roads, this one has a freshly paved, smooth-as-glass surface, combined with long

My riding buddy Jeff Markham proudly displays the elusive Appalachians.

sweepers—a nice way to cap off the ride. Pick up Route 523 south when the two roads meet and you'll soon find yourself back at Route 40 where you came out at Addison. All that remains is to make your trek home, as so many have, along the National Road.

Trip 7   In Search of Prospect Peak

Distance	*140 miles*
Terrain	*Several mountain passes along the National Highway followed by a course tracing the Potomac River and more mountain passes*
Highlights	*The National Road, Sideling Hill, Park-N-Dine, C&O Canal, Fort Frederick, Berkeley Springs, Prospect Peak, and the Paw Paw Tunnel*

The Route from Cumberland

→ I-68 east to Scenic US 40
→ Scenic US 40 east to I-68
→ I-68 east to MD 144
→ MD 144 east to I-70 at Hancock
→ I-70 east to MD 56
→ MD 56 east to MD 68
→ MD 68 east to US 11
→ US 11 south to WV 901
→ WV 901 west to WV 9
→ WV 9 west to MD 51
→ MD 51 west to Cumberland

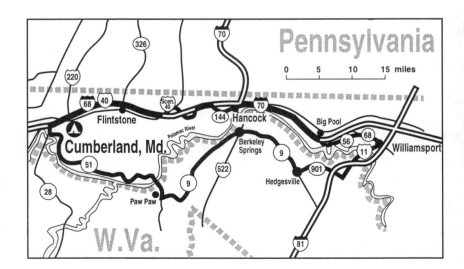

Nature's dramatic architecture is on display at Sideling Hill.

Begin your search for Prospect Peak by following Interstate 68 east out of Cumberland. Along the way you can hop off and follow the older alignments of the National Road, which parallel the entire route between Cumberland and Hancock.

There are some special sections of highway waiting for your personal discovery along Scenic 40, graceful curves that lead you into a turn at a quick pace and set you up perfectly for the next. They beg to be ridden on two wheels. Thank the interstate highway system for taking most of the traffic off this road and opening it up for pleasure riding.

Topping out at Town Hill, you can see Sideling Hill in the distance, identified easily by the big notch carved into the mountain, marking the point where I-68 passes through. The **Town Hill Hotel** is perched atop the ridge, looking neat and trim. This would be a great place to stay on a warm summer evening, enjoying great views and refreshing breezes. A few miles past Town Hill, Scenic 40 intersects with I-68. Jump back on the Interstate to catch the **Sideling Hill** exhibit just ahead.

Sideling Hill is a western Maryland landmark. In order to straighten a challenging section of the roadway, engineers blasted down a few hundred feet through the middle of the mountain to a point where a straight section of road could be made. During construction they found that during the time the Appalachians were being formed the mountain had sagged in the middle like a fallen layer cake. Perhaps it

should have been baked another million years or so. The state
built a pedestrian bridge across the highway to give you the
best opportunity to view this natural wonder without the risk
of parking on the side of the road. A visitor center is accessible from the walkway with more information and displays
explaining how the mountain was formed, plus general travel
information.

The ride into Hancock is short, eight or ten miles. If you
wait on breakfast till you get to Hancock, I promise you will
not go unrewarded. Hancock is home to the **Park-N-Dine,**
one of those places where the cooking is good, the plates are
loaded, and the price is laughably low. When you order a $3
breakfast, you'd better be ready to let out your suspenders
and pop the top button on your trousers. Riders of all brands
flock to the Park-N-Dine, especially on the weekends.

Directly behind the restaurant is the Potomac River and
the **C&O Canal National Park.** In the early 1800s specula-
tors and politicians were all afire about finding new ways to
move goods between the East Coast colonies and the newly
opened Midwest. The ridges of the Appalachians made that
no ordinary task. Some people thought roads were the answer, some gambled on the canal, and others built railroads.
Canal construction began in 1828 in Washington, D.C., and
reached Cumberland 22 years later, but was made obsolete by
speedier railroad service almost as soon as it was opened. The
towpath along the canal is now a trail for hiking and biking

The piper still plays at Fort Frederick. Hasn't aged much, has he?

and is a good place to walk off that third stack of pancakes you polished off. Also in Hancock is the **C&O Canal Museum,** which features a slide show, artifacts, and photos. Maybe after a short hike to the canal and museum you can swing your leg over the bike again. Then again, maybe you'll need a hoist.

The route out of Hancock follows Interstate 70 for a brief period, making an exit at Big Pool. Turn right and follow Route 56 east. **Fort Frederick State Park** is just about one mile down the road. Fort Frederick is the only remaining original fort from the French and Indian War (1756, for those who snoozed in history class). You can tour the fort and visit the barracks, which have been restored to show you what a soldier's life was like. Be glad you live in the twentieth century, friend. You can have equal fun touring the well-appointed museum or just strolling around the large open grounds. The quiet, green lawns would make a great place to spread out a blanket for a picnic lunch.

Resume the tour on Route 56 east and take advantage of the whoop-de-doos—those sections of the road that lift you out of your seat and cause your co-rider to hold on tighter. Route 56 ends on Route 68, turn right. Route 68 starts wide then narrows and remains a straight shot into Williamsport, a small blue-collar city on the West Virginia border that was once considered for the federal capital. Your best bet is to follow Route 68 into town where it intersects with U.S. Route

11 into the Mountain State. Route 11 passes through a small section of suburbia, then Route 901 appears on your right. Follow Route 901 west and get set for some good riding.

It's too bad Route 901 is only a few miles long, because it winds through beautiful countryside. Side roads in this area are bound to reward you with more good riding. It ends all too quickly on Route 9 at Hedgesville. Turn right on Route 9.

Between Hedgesville and Paw Paw, some 42 miles distant, there are far more good riding miles than there are bad. The initial traffic you encounter in Hedgesville quickly fades as you remove yourself further in country. Soon the entire roadway is yours. Entering the town of Berkeley Springs and seeing all the traffic is almost a culture shock. **Berkeley Springs State Park** is the site of a watering hole that has been popular since colonial times. Imagine soaking your tootsies in the same refreshing waters as our founding fathers did! Okay, maybe that image doesn't capture your imagination, but these springs have long been known for their restorative powers. West of Berkeley Springs, the road winds slowly up Cacapon Mountain on a steep incline, testing the bottom end of your bike's power curve.

I remember the first time I toured this area a few years ago, my wife clinging to me on the back of a little 600cc sport bike. We were searching for a spot called Prospect Peak. The peak has been named by National Geographic Society as one of the ten prettiest spots in America. Road trip! As you reach the summit of Cacapon (KAK-upon or CAKE-upon) Mountain you'll find an overlook for the peak on your right. In the valley below, the Potomac looks like a thin silver ribbon draped over the landscape. Sideling Hill starts here and runs from left to right into Maryland. To the far right lies Pennsylvania and to the left, the small village of Great Cacapon slumbers. These are the Appalachians as few people see them.

When you descend the ridge and ride through the country you've seen from above, it's like stepping through the frame and into the painting. Route 9 follows the contours of the Cacapon River in places accounting for some of the curves. Other times it takes a turn seemingly for the fun of it. Forest lines the road on both sides so thick it looks as though you are flying through a long green waterslide.

Your entry into Paw Paw is likely to go unnoticed. The road enters the edge of town and quietly exits on the north side. Just over the line in Maryland, look for the **C&O Canal Paw Paw Tunnel** sign. The tunnel was constructed in the mid-1800s and cut through 3,118 feet of rock to avoid laying six miles of track along the Potomac River—a major engineering feat in its time. You can walk through the tunnel now, but bring a flashlight. There is also a hiking trail that crosses over the top of the tunnel.

When you cross over the river, Route 9 becomes Route 51 in Maryland. In addition to the tunnel, there are a number of spots along the route marked to indicate the remains of locks along the canal. They represent a good chance to hop off the bike for a quick stroll. Dual sport fans will find a plethora of side roads leading over the ridges and into the arms of the mountains. When you're ready to wrap up the loop, just follow MD 51 west to return to Cumberland.

Trip 8   Johnstown Loop

* *

Distance	*180 miles*
Terrain	*Low hills and ridges, farming country, and state parks*
Highlights	*Covered bridges, Blue Knob State Park, Johnstown Flood National Memorial*

The Route from Cumberland

→ Alt 40 west to MD 36

→ MD 36 east to MD 35

→ MD 35 north becomes PA 96

→ PA 96 north to SR 4013

→ SR 4013 north to PA 56

→ PA 56 west to PA 96

→ PA 96 north ends at Blue Knob State Park and becomes PA 869

→ PA 869 north to Johnstown Flood National Memorial

→ PA 869 south to PA 160

→ PA 160 south becomes MD 47

→ MD 47 south to MD 36 east

→ MD 36 east to Alt 40

It was spitting rain the day my wife Sandy and I traced the loop that took us to the **Johnstown Flood National Memorial,** and somehow it seemed appropriate that it should. Johnstown is the site of the 1889 flood that caused the second largest loss of life in US history. In addition to the memorial, there are a couple of detours along the way to discover a few old covered bridges, small towns, and a few suggestions for exploring further north and west.

Pick up the tour at Maryland's Route 36, just east of the point where Alt 40 passes through The Narrows. Route 36 ambles through the clutter of the greater Cumberland area for a few miles. You'll make the right onto Route 35, which becomes a nice two-lane country road as you enter Pennsylvania. You don't need a sign to tell you when you've crossed

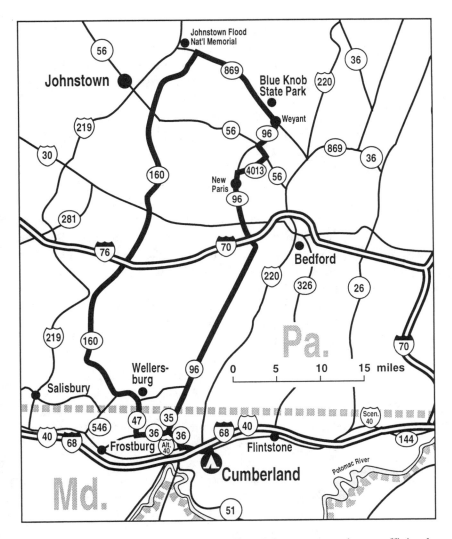

the state line. The quality of the pavement drops sufficiently to tell you.

At this point, you really can't make a wrong turn. Dozens of roads branch off to the right and left of Route 96, winding their way through Allegheny farm country, and you'll find something special on each one, whether it is an Amish farmer working the fields with a team of draft horses, or an eight-sided schoolhouse (they were built that way so children couldn't be trapped in a corner by the Devil), or a pretty vista from one ridge to the next.

Just a mile or two north of New Paris, you'll pass an attractive covered bridge. Detour on Route 4013 just ahead to find another bridge. It carries a warning sign that you risk a $5 fine for crossing the bridge at a pace any faster than a walk. That can be a real trick on a fully-laden dresser! Route 4013 ends on Route 56 which, if followed to the left will return you to Route 96. You'll find another bridge on your left as you approach Route 56, stranded in the middle of what is now a cornfield.

Pennsylvania's back roads are an odd lot. Somewhere past the hamlet of Weyant, Route 96 becomes Route 896. Following Route 896, there are times when it narrows to practically one lane. You would expect it to turn to dirt at any moment. (Actually, there's a corollary to Murphy's Law that governs this: any unexplored back road between two points will turn to loose gravel and mud one mile past the halfway point.) Fortunately, this one doesn't. The section that threads its way through **Blue Knob State Park** is beautiful. The roadbed is surrounded on both sides by steep hills; moss-covered boulders loom on either side. Towering trees crowd the roadway in places and when the leaves are out fully, you pass through the forest in near twilight even at midday.

After a few miles you leave the state forest area and run through a host of small villages and hamlets. You can start looking for the sign for the Johnstown Flood National Memorial. It doesn't look like what you would expect the entrance to a National Park, Memorial, or anything else to look like. Cross the railroad tracks, go through a campground-trailer park, along a road that has crater-sized potholes (make every effort to avoid those, trust me), and finally, you arrive at the Memorial.

It takes a few minutes to acclimate yourself and determine if there is anything here to see. Perched high on a hillside is a National Park Service facility with a collection of artifacts, articles, and displays related to the flood. Nearby is a perfectly restored wooden frame house above a large open field.

Nothing seems particularly amiss here, until you look to the right side of the field, see the remains of a broken earthen dam, and realize this huge meadow was once a lake. In late

A dramatic reconstruction of the devastation wrought by the May 1889 flood at Johnstown.

May 1889, after several days of soaking rain, that dam gave way and millions of cubic feet of water ran through the Conemaugh Valley like rain down a gutter. All the trees, telegraph poles, houses, barns, businesses, and 50 miles of railroad track with locomotives and trains of cars were dumped in a huge jumble of debris against a large stone bridge in downtown Johnstown. Just as the flood waters began to subside and relief was near, the massive pile caught fire, and those who could not scramble to freedom were consumed by the fire.

After surveying the grounds, be sure to check out the visitor center and the electric map. A ten-minute narrated presentation gives you a clear picture of exactly what happened. One hundred years later, it will still send shivers up your spine.

The easiest way to leave the Memorial is to return on 869, then turn south on Route 160. This route skirts Johnstown and turns almost due south. After a few miles you return to rural Pennsylvania with long straights intermingled with twisty passages and broad sweeping curves. Just below Wellersburg, you reenter Maryland and 160 becomes Route 47. Route 36 follows Jennings Run through the gap between Piney Mountain on your right and Little Allegheny Mountain on your left. Only a few miles remain before your return to Cumberland.

By the standards of some of the other routes, this one is relatively short and won't take you an entire day to complete. For that reason, I would encourage you to explore some of the side roads that are so abundant. Who knows what unexpected pleasures and adventures wait for you down each one. When the road calls, answer. And if you hear the sound of rushing water behind you, run!

In the background, what remains of the lake at South Fork that flooded Johnstown.

Lodging

Maryland Motel
11903 Bedford Rd. NE
Cumberland, MD 21501
Phone 301-722-2836. $$

Rocky Gap State Park
Pleasant Valley Rd.
Cumberland, MD 21501
Phone 301-777-2138. $

Seven Points Marina
R.D. 1
Raystown Lake Rd.
Hesston, PA 16647
Phone 814-658-3074. Houseboat and small craft rentals. Advance reservations and deposits required. From $500 for 3 or 4 days.

Town Hill Hotel
US Scenic 40
Little Orleans, MD 21766
Phone 301-478-2794. $$

Places of Interest

....

Berkeley Springs State Park
121 S. Washington St.
Berkeley Springs, WV 25411
Phone 800-CALL WVA. $

Blue Knob State Park
RD 1, Box 449
Off Route 869, north of the town of Pavia
Imler, PA 16655
Phone 814-276-3576. Seventy-five campsites, twelve miles of hiking trails, fishing and swimming.

Boal Mansion and Museum, and Columbus Chapel
P.O. Box 116
US Route 322
Boalsburg, PA 16827
Phone 814-466-6210. Daily (except Tuesdays), May 1 to October 31. Spring and fall, 1:30 p.m. to 5 p.m.; summer, 10 a.m. to 5 p.m. $2.50.

C&O Canal Museum
326 East Main Street
Hancock, MD 21750
Phone 301-678-5463. Daily, June through Sept., 9 a.m. to 5 p.m.; Oct. through May, 9:30 a.m. to 4 p.m., closed at least two days a week; call ahead. Free.

C&O Canal National Park
Potomac River between Washington, DC and Cumberland, MD
Phone 301-739-4200. Mon. through Fri., 8:30 a.m. to 4 p.m.
Parking $4 per vehicle (only at Great Falls).

C&O Canal Paw Paw Tunnel
WV Route 29
Paw Paw, WV 25431
Phone 301-722-8226.

Fort Bedford Museum
Fort Bedford Park
Bedford, PA 15522
Phone 814-623-8891. Daily, 10 a.m. to 5 p.m., May to October.
Closed Tuesdays in May, September, and October. $

Fort Frederick State Park
Maryland Route 56
Big Pool, MD 21711
Phone 301-842-2155. Open 8 a.m. to sunset year-round.

Fort Necessity National Battlefield
RD 2, Box 528
US Route 40, Old National Rd.
Farmington, PA 15437
Phone 412-329-5512. Daily, 8:30 a.m. to 5 p.m. $

History House
218 Washington St.
Cumberland, MD 21501
Phone 301-777-8678. Tues. through Sat., 9 a.m. to 4 p.m. $3

Indian Caverns
PA Route 45 East
Spruce Creek, PA 16683
Phone 814-632-7578. Daily, 9 a.m. to 6 p.m., May 30 through La-
bor Day. Call for other times. $7 admission to cavern.

Johnstown Flood National Memorial
c/o Allegheny Portage Railroad National Historic Site
P.O. Box 355, Lake Rd.
St. Michael, PA 15951
Phone 814-495-4643. Daily, 9 a.m. to 5 p.m. Film every hour on
the hour from 10 a.m. to 4 p.m. National Park Passport stamp location. Free.

Ohiopyle State Park
PA Route 381 North
Ohiopyle, PA 15470
Phone 412-329-8591. $ - $$ for camping, wading is free . . .

Old Bedford Village
US 220 Business
Bedford, PA 15522
Phone 814-623-1156. Reconstructed village with buildings from
1750 to 1850. Working farm, crafts, and displays of historic arti-
facts, special events. $

Old Petersburg-Addison Toll House
Route 3002
Addison, PA 15411
Phone 814-395-3550. Open three to four days per week from the
third weekend of May through September. Run by the local chap-
ter of the Daughters of the American Revolution.

Pennsylvania Military Museum
P.O. Box 148
US Route 322 West
Boalsburg, PA 16827
Phone 814-466-6263. Tues. through Sat., 9 a.m. to 5 p.m.; Sunday, noon to 5 p.m. $3.50 for adults; $2.50 for seniors over 60; $1.50 for youth ages 6 to 18.

Sideling Hill Exhibit Center
I-68 west of Hancock
Hancock, MD 21750
Phone 301-842-2155. May to Sept., 8:30 a.m. to 6 p.m.; Sept. to May, 9 a.m. to 5 p.m. Free.

Springs Museum
PA Route 669 North
Springs, PA 15562
Phone 814-662-2625 or 814-662-4159. $

Spruce Forest Artisan Village
US Route 40
Penn Alps, MD
Phone 301-895-5985. Open Mon. through Sat., 10 a.m. to 5 p.m.

Western Maryland Scenic Railroad and
Transportation and Industrial Museum
13 Canal St.
Cumberland, MD 21501
Phone 301-759-4400. Schedule varies with special runs; call ahead. $

Restaurants

· ·

Baby's Diner
131 South Garner Street
State College, PA 16801
Phone 814-234-4776. Open 11 a.m. to 10 p.m.; closes at midnight on weekends. Average dinner price $7.

Doctor Willy's Seafood
Rt. 4, Box 5246
178 Quarry Rd.
Deep Creek Lake, MD 21541
Phone 301-387-7380. May through June, 4 days/wk; June through Sept., 7 days/wk; Sept. through Oct., 4 days/wk; Nov. through May, 3 days/wk or closed. Open 5 p.m. to around 8 or 9 p.m. Families welcome. If you're in town, call the restaurant to check on hours. There's also a carry-out store/deli with items like crab cakes and steamed shrimp. $9.95 (surf & turf) to $14.95; beverage extra.

Landmark Restaurant
East Pitt Street
Bedford, PA 15522
Phone 814-623-6762. Sun. through Thurs., 7 a.m. to 10:30 p.m. Closes 11:30 p.m. Fri. and Sat. $

Mason's Barn
Intersection of I-68 & US 220
Cumberland, MD 21501
Phone 301-722-6155. Daily, 7 a.m. to 10 p.m. $$

Old Depot Center and Restaurant
19 Depot St.
Frostburg, MD 21532
Phone 301-689-1221. Restaurant open Mon. through Thurs., 11 a.m. to 10 p.m.; closes at 11 p.m. on Fri. and Sat. and 9 p.m. on Sun.

Park-N-Dine
189 East Main Street
Hancock, MD 21750
Phone 301-678-5242. Mon. through Sat., 6 a.m. to 10 p.m.; Sun., 7 a.m. to 10 p.m. $ - $$

Travel Information

....

Bedford County Tourist Promotion Agency
137 East Pitt Street
Bedford, PA 15522
Phone 800-765-3331.

Boalsburg Village Merchants
P.O. Box 331
Boalsburg, PA 16827
Phone 814-466-6865 or 814-466-6210. Info only. Brochure
available about the wide variety of shops in downtown Boalsburg.

Deep Creek Lake State Park Promotion Council
200 South Third Street
Oakland, MD 21550
Phone 301-334-1948. Mon. through Fri., 8:30 a.m. to 4:30 p.m.

Garrett County Promotion Council
Phone 301-334-1948. Call for a vacation guide. They'll send bro-
chures and pamphlets for sights, lodging, and restaurants for
Garrett County.

Huntingdon County Tourist Promotion Agency
241 Mifflin Street
Huntingdon, PA 16652
Phone 814-643-3577.

Lion Country Visitors Bureau
1402 South Atherton Street
State College, PA 16801
Phone 800-358-5466. Call for visitor's guide to Penn State, State
College, and surrounding area.

Rest & Repast Bed & Breakfast Service
P.O. Box 126
Pine Grove Mills, PA 16868
Phone 814-238-1484. Offers referrals to B&Bs in the region.
Info only.

Washington County Visitors Bureau
1826-C Dual Highway
Hagerstown, MD 21740
Phone 800-228-STAY.

Gateway to Skyline

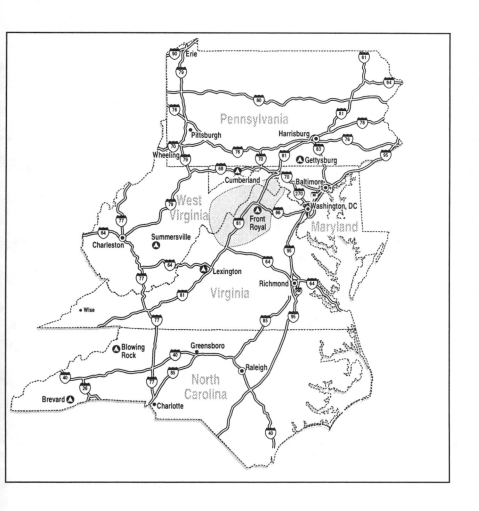

Front Royal, Va.

In Front Royal, you'll find more riders arriving from other areas of the country to ride Skyline Drive than any other spot we'll visit. (Blatant commercial plug coming: be sure to show them your copy of this book so they'll see what they're missing!)

It is said that the name Front Royal is derived from the story of a British field officer who once attempted to mold rough frontier men from this area into a passable militia. They weren't very good soldier material; getting them to march in a straight line was a tall order. Time after time, the officer drilling the troops would shout the same order—"Front the Royal Oak! Front the Royal Oak!"—trying mightily to get his troops to face a large oak tree at the end of the drilling field. He shouted his order so loud and so often, it became a joke among the townspeople. No matter what the topic of conversation was, "Front the Royal Oak!" was the punch line. The joke passed into history, but the label stuck and the town eventually became known as Front Royal.

The hub of activity in Front Royal is around Chester Street. Here you will find the town common area, including the **Warren Rifles Confederate Museum** operated by the local chapter of the United Daughters of the Confederacy. The cottage of Confederate spy Belle Boyd is just down the street. Belle's demeanor and grace were good cover for the work she did, making friends of Federal soldiers and learning their secrets. She would often visit her aunt and uncle who lived in Front Royal and who operated the Fishback Hotel. Once Belle hid in a closet in the hotel over the room where Generals Shields and Banks were discussing tactics in Union maneuvers in the area. The information she gathered helped the Confederate Army win an opening round of the first campaign in the Shenandoah Valley.

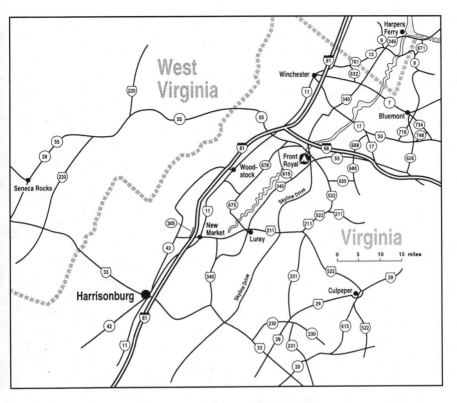

Just outside of town is one of the valley's limestone caverns open for public visits. **Skyline Caverns** are as large as their cousin Luray to the south, but they have an unusual formation called "anthodites" found nowhere else in the world. Anthodites grow from an odd mix of minerals and look like big flowers, with delicate sharp petals that grow in all directions.

Of course the big draw in these parts is the **Shenandoah National Park** and Skyline Drive. If you want to really enjoy Shenandoah at its finest, plan your visit here for either late spring or mid-autumn. In May, the temperatures have warmed enough that nearly all the trees have gained their leaves and spring flowers still carpet the forest floor in abundance. The weather is a bit more settled with fair skies and pleasant temps for touring and hiking. If you plan to come down for the fall foliage season, do not expect to ride on the weekend and have a good time. There are just too many cars,

trucks, and recreational vehicles to make the journey anything more than frustrating. The trick is to go during mid-
week, say Tuesday or Wednesday. And go earlier in the
morning and you'll have the road nearly to yourself.

The big secret that few people know about is riding
Skyline at night. You can witness some spectacular sunsets
here, but when the western sky darkens, the heavens open
before your eyes and you'll understand why Shenandoah
means "daughter of the stars." After about 9 p.m., the ranger
stations close up and you don't pay a dime to ride. There is
one danger involved in riding at night: deer. After a while
you'll have seen so many deer lining the highway you will
lose count. It is best to keep your speed to an absolute
minimum here, no more than 25 mph at the very most. Just
enjoy a very slow, leisurely stroll along the parkway. Once
you get out of the lights of the Front Royal area you can pick
an overlook, park the bike, and enjoy it. Something about the
night air, the darkness, and the sense of isolation makes
conversation with your co-rider or riding buddy seem even
more enjoyable. Savor it. In today's age you don't often have
an opportunity like this to enjoy the company of a friend.

You can't stay in the Front Royal area without paying at
least a half-day visit to neighboring Winchester. By happen-
stance it didn't fall along any of our tour routes in the region,
but leaving it out entirely would be a mistake. By most
definitions, Winchester marks the head of the Shenandoah
Valley, and this position made it an alluring prize for opposing armies during the Civil War. In addition to Civil War era
sites, George Washington's office, the tomb of Lord Fairfax,
and even Patsy Cline's gravesite and memorial are nearby.

The town's location means there are plenty of travel
services to choose from. For campers, the **Front Royal KOA
Campground** just south of town has a great location. After
turning off US Route 340, you ride about half a mile down a
dirt country lane through a pasture to get to the campground.
When you start down the lane you can't help but think, "Gee,
is there really anything back here?" It is a beautiful location
and well off the beaten path.

In the center of town you can find an easy half–dozen
small independent motels and several B&Bs. The **Blue Ridge**

Every year many riders enjoy scenic Skyline Drive near Front Royal.

Motel is a safe choice, or if you have something a little fancier in mind, try the **Chester House Inn.** Although it is outside the immediate area, the restored log building that is the **Inn at Narrow Passage** offers some of the finest accommodations in the area. Still further out are the cabins, lodges and campgrounds along Skyline Drive. All accommodations on Skyline Drive are often booked months in advance, so be sure to call well ahead of time if you plan to stay there. Contact the **ARA Virginia Sky-Line Company** for reservations and information.

Restaurants are all over the place in town. If you're looking for an authentic American dining experience, look no further than the **Fox Diner** on South Street. Owner Loretta Fox Wines will be more than happy to fill you in on what's happening around town, and she gets my vote for the best chocolate milk shake found anywhere. There is another diner on the other end of town called **Sandy's Diner.** It is a beautiful building with more sparkling chrome than any other diner I've ever seen. Your best bet there is breakfast. If you're in the mood for steak, the hottest ticket in town is **Dean's Steak House** on the south end.

Trip 9 Home Country

. . . .

Distance	*140 miles*
Terrain	*Pass through Chester Gap followed by small Piedmont towns and villages, a small mountain ascent, scenic byways, and a valley run*
Highlights	*James Madison's home at Montpelier, Clarks Mountain, Barboursville Ruins, Gayheart's Drug Store*

The Route from Front Royal

→ US 522 south to VA 231
→ VA 231 south to VA 20
→ VA 20 south to Barboursville
→ VA 20 north to Route 615 (East Main Street)
→ VA 615 north to VA 627
→ VA 627 east to VA 697
→ VA 697 north to Moormont Orchard
→ VA 697 south to VA 627
→ VA 627 west to VA 615
→ VA 615 north to US 522
→ US 522 north to Culpeper
→ US 522 north to Front Royal

The route begins following Route 522 south out of Front Royal over Chester Gap. This particular gap should probably be called the "Chester End Run," because it doesn't amount to much of a gap. Route 522 is a wide, smooth and relatively empty road, so take your time as you tour through horse country. Enjoy the wide open vistas, the big green pastures set against the Blue Ridge. In the spring, the fields are awash with yellow buttercups and dandelions, a beautiful setting for our tour. This is Virginia's Piedmont (an Italian term meaning "little mountains") region. The Piedmonts are commonly called the foothills of the Blue Ridge, but the two are actually from different eras. The Piedmonts are the remnants of an older mountain chain that was eventually eroded away, much as the Blue Ridge and Appalachians are worn down compared to the Rockies.

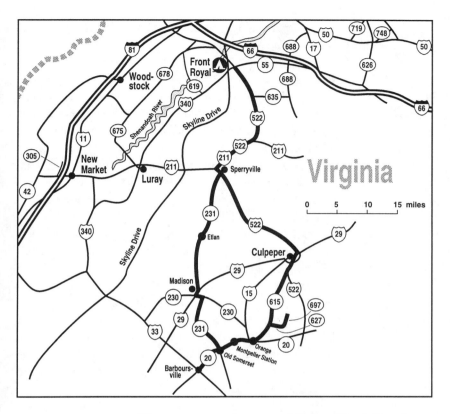

When you enter the town of Sperryville, follow Route 522 through town until you see a sign for Route 231, heading due south. Turn right and follow 231, the Blue Ridge Turnpike. This scenic byway will take you past the entrance for the Old Rag Mountain trail and the Whiteoak Canyon Falls trail in Etlan (see Skyline Loop, Trip 10, for more information about these trails). The riding is easy along this Virginia Byway, and the long fast sweepers will make your bike beg to roll on the throttle and lean a little harder than you might otherwise. There aren't many tricky curves here to fool you, all are well marked and properly banked.

By the time you arrive in Madison, you're probably hungry for more. It comes quickly. Continue following Route 231 through the downtown area (don't panic, this isn't downtown Manhattan) past stately old brick homes and the corner drugstore to join the fast and furious pace of Route 29, but only for a few moments. After just about two miles, Route

231 takes a sharp departure south, splitting from the busy highway and returning to a more genteel pace.

Where Route 231 and Route 20 meet at Old Somerset, turn right and follow Route 20 for a few miles to Barboursville. Follow the Virginia sign for a vineyard, a bunch of grapes, to the **Barboursville Vineyard.** The vineyard is on what was once the estate of James Barbour, governor of Virginia during the early 1800s. Prominently featured on the grounds are the **Barboursville Ruins** of the Barbour mansion, which burned on Christmas Day 1884.

Amaze your fellow touring partners by pointing out the fact that Barbour's mansion was designed by none other than Thomas Jefferson. "Note the remains of the columned portico," you begin, "and the octagonal front room, Jefferson's signature design." Also point out to them that the earthen ramp at the edge of where the portico used to be was built in lieu of steps, a feature not commonly seen. You are free to roam about the outside of the burned out shell, but the interior is closed to visitors. Huge overgrown boxwoods indicate where formal gardens once stood, though standing among them now it is easy to imagine that you have been shrunk to a fraction of your normal size.

Returning to the route, follow Route 20 north toward Orange, James Madison's home town. The roots of the Madison family run deep in this area and this was the fourth President's only home. **Montpelier** is now part of the National Trust for Historic Preservation, a group that restores and preserves important American homes. To tour the home, you need to sign up at Montpelier Station at the general store across the road from the perfectly restored railroad depot. A tour bus will drop you off at the front of the estate, where an ultra–efficient tour guide will escort you through the interior.

The main part of the home dates back to 1760. Through the years different owners have had different ideas about how the house should be configured; your tour guide will show you where some entrances have been blocked over and others added. The house is currently covered with scaffolding while a major restoration project takes place, part of it to replace the all-copper roof. After your tour is finished, you are free to walk around the grounds until the last tour bus runs in the late

Time passes slowly in the formal gardens at Montpelier.

afternoon. One place you must visit is the formal garden at the back of the house. The Garden Club of Virginia has taken care to restore it to its former glory. Here you can get an idea of what the gardens at the Barbour mansion must have looked like in their day. Don't forget to stroll along the front lawn, visit the garden temple, and sit on the front portico. The view of the Blue Ridge is striking, rising like a mighty blue tidal wave on the western skyline and cresting over the Piedmont.

Madison's home and most of his possessions were sold off by his wife, Dolley Todd Madison, to satisfy the debts of her ne'er-do-well son, John Payne Todd. John Todd was often so desperate for money, he would rifle through Madison's papers and tear off his signatures to sell them. As a result, most of Madison's papers were destroyed and his possessions scattered. (I discovered that a square piano that once graced the halls of Montpelier now stands in the front room of the Boal Mansion near State College, Pennsylvania. See Lion Country tour, Trip 5.) Eventually the Madison home and grounds became the property of the DuPont family. It was during this time that it saw its most aggressive expansion, including the show grounds at the front of the estate.

The railroad station was built in front of Montpelier by the DuPonts, who often traveled to New York for business. The only railroad stop was at Orange, some five miles to the east—and though the DuPonts were filthy rich, rules were rules and the engineer would only allow DuPont to get off the train at a railroad station. When you have that much money, though, you don't let a trifling rule stop you from getting what you want. So a station was built at Montpelier to save DuPont the carriage ride.

When you resume the tour, follow Route 20 into the town of Orange. If you'd like to learn more about the fourth President and father of the Constitution, stop by the **James Madison Museum.** When you enter town, turn right on Caroline Street. The museum is on your immediate left. The route returns to Main Street and goes through the small downtown area. On the outskirts of town the road number becomes Route 615.

Ahead and to the right, rising gently on the horizon, is Clarks Mountain. Follow the signs for **Moormont Orchards,** turning right on Route 627, then left on 697. Follow the road to the top until you enter the orchard. Whip out your wide, wide angle lens for this picture.

Clarks Mountain was a popular lookout for scouts during the Civil War, and when you get to the top, it's readily apparent why. On a clear day, the view is not only stunning, it is an excellent vantage point from which to see the three major geological features of Virginia. Turn to the southeast; there lies the coastal plain. The land is broad and flat, a sea of green that stretches to the horizon. Little mountains which characterize the geology of the Piedmont are clearly visible from the northeast to the west. Beyond the Piedmont to the west lies the beginning of the hill and valley escarpment, the third dominant geological feature, the Blue Ridge. Scanning the ridge, when you get to about the middle of the visible range, you can see an area where there are some breaks in the trees. That's Old Rag Mountain, the point we passed much earlier in the day.

If you return to Route 615 and follow it north, you will eventually run into Route 522 again, your ticket home. Route 522 passes through Culpeper, my home town. The downtown area has undergone a recent face-lift which eliminated all the overhead wires, and new lampposts make the streets look positively Mayberry. Hop off your bike at the corner of Main and Davis for a little walking tour of town.

Start at **Gayheart's Drugstore,** the geographical, social, and political center of town. Hop on a vinyl-covered swivel stool for a cup of coffee and a bit of conversation. Also worth a visit is the **Museum of Culpeper History** which chronicles the history of the town from its early origins as Fairfax Courthouse to the present day.

The best place in town for a good hot dog is **Baby Jim's.** It has been in operation for about 40 years now, and has never advertised. It never had to. I don't think they've ever worried too much about the parade of fast food restaurants that have come to town in the last 20 years either. Nobody beats a Baby Jim's hot dog. Nobody. If you want to order like a native, park your bike, walk in to the window and mumble "I'd like two dogs with the works, an order o' fries, and a RC." You can order something else, but no authentic Baby Jim experience is complete without a hot dog. To find Baby Jim's, follow Route 522 all the way through town to the point where it turns left to head west. Go straight through the light instead of turning and Baby Jim's will appear just ahead on your right.

Fountain Hall Bed and Breakfast in the old residential section of town welcomes riders. Otherwise, if you're ready to mount up and move west, follow Route 522 through Sperryville back to Front Royal. As the sun sets over the Blue Ridge, the tall hills cast long shadows across the road, and the sunset is regularly spectacular. I think you will find it a fitting end to a fine day.

Trip 10 Skyline Loop

• •

Distance   *155 miles*

Terrain   *Plenty of curves in the first 40 miles along Skyline Drive, then descending a mountain pass and a Virginia Byway. Another pass at Stanardsville and return via Skyline Drive.*

Highlights   *Skyline Drive, Shenandoah National Park, hiking trails with remnants of old homesteads, Sperryville Emporium, Misty Mountain Vineyard*

The Route from Front Royal

→ US 340 south to Skyline Drive Entrance
→ Skyline Drive to Thornton Gap Entrance at US 211
→ US 211 east to US 522
→ US 522 south to VA 231
→ VA 231 south to US 29
→ US 29 south to VA 230
→ VA 230 west to US 33
→ US 33 west to Swift Run Gap Entrance to Skyline Drive*
→ Skyline Drive to Front Royal

*Alternate Route

→ Continue US 33 west to US 340 north at Elkton to Front Royal

This tour is best suited for a day when you have ridden a lot in days past and want to take a break. There are ample opportunities to get off your bike and explore the dozens of hiking trails along Skyline Drive. We will also pay a visit to a couple of quaint mountain towns and stop off at a vineyard for a personal tour—perhaps by the owner himself. We will then return over the Blue Ridge via Route 33, a popular run for riders.

The tour begins at the north entrance to Skyline Drive in Front Royal, about two miles south of town on Route 340. There has been a tremendous amount of construction in that area to widen the entrance, but it should be complete by the time you read this. Admission to Skyline depends somewhat

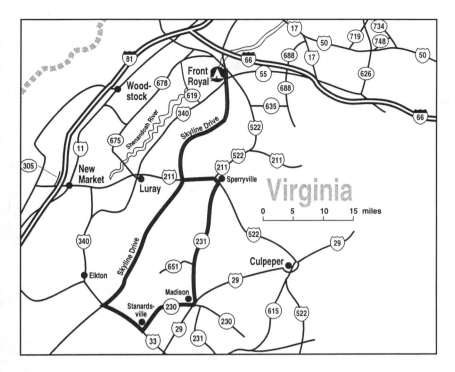

on how the ranger views your mode of transportation. There are different rates for cars and bicycles, and I have been charged both at different times. I think the bigger your smile, the better your chances of getting the bicycle rate!

Be sure to keep your speed at or near the posted limit of 35 mph. Motorcyclists have a mixed reputation on this road, so we should do our best to improve it. It may be tempting to lean into some of the curves, but considering the hiking trails that cross the road and curves you can't see around, 35 is the speed to go. Besides, the purpose of this drive is to relax and enjoy the view.

Skyline Drive is a thin ribbon that traces the length of the 200,000 acres comprising **Shenandoah National Park.** Each year the park attracts hundreds of thousands of visitors, many of whom ride from one end to the other and pronounce themselves satisfied, riders included. Too bad. In addition to the 75 overlooks along the way, there are about 500 miles of hiking trails, waterfalls, black bear, ancient hemlock forests, fern-shrouded pools, and the ruins of pioneer homesteads awaiting your discovery.

Trails range from a few tenths of a mile to dozens. The terrain is gentle so you can hike with a minimum of equipment; sturdy shoes, clothing to suit the season, and a supply of water are adequate for a few hours. Bring lunch or a snack to boost your energy along the trail and you're set for a full day.

If you get an early start, watch out for deer. An estimated 6,000 deer live in the 400 square miles of Shenandoah National Park, so the question is rarely whether you will see deer, but rather how many. The first few miles of the park climb to the crest of the Blue Ridge. The first pullover looks down on the Front Royal area and will give you a hint of what is to come. Next is the **Dickey Ridge Visitor Center,** where the 1.2-mile Fox Hollow Trail begins.

The trail passes through part of the 450 acres once owned by the Fox family. Along the trail are large rock piles, now covered with gray-green moss that makes them look like burial mounds. These stones came out of the fields under cultivation. You will also see the Fox family cemetery, and a low stone wall that ran along the property line between the Foxes and their neighbors, the Merchants.

The Merchants and the Foxes weren't the first to settle this area. It had been a prime hunting ground for Native Americans as far back as 1000 B.C. The first few waves of European settlers washed ashore in the 1600s and used the seemingly limitless supply of wood to build their homes and villages. By the early 20th century, the entire area was a wasteland, stripped of all its resources. Congress designated the area a park in 1924 but didn't authorize any money to be spent. For 12 years the state of Virginia slowly bought land and accepted donations from private individuals until the park was finally established on the day after Christmas 1935. When you gaze up the trunk of a mighty oak, hickory, or black locust that grow here so thick, it is hard to imagine that these trees are only between 50 and 70 years old.

Before you leave the visitor center, be sure to go inside and collect your National Parks Passport stamp.

The rolling contours of the gentle Blue Ridge are the perfect setting for building a world-class scenic parkway, and a heck of a fun motorcycle ride! The Drive itself weaves along the crest of the Blue Ridge joining its kin, the Blue Ridge Parkway, 105 miles south at Afton Mountain. The Civilian Conservation Corps did most of the work, with much of the stonework done by expert Spanish and Italian stone-workers who had just arrived in the United States. The result is an unforgettable mix of flora, fauna, and twisty pavement.

As you sweep through the curves, be sure to stop occasionally at the overlooks to enjoy the view. You can see farthest during the late fall, winter, and early spring when weather patterns move clear northern air through the Shenandoah Valley. On a good day, you can easily see 60 or 70 miles across the valley to the Shenandoah and Allegheny Mountains on the other side. To the east, the Piedmont region is clearly visible, gradually giving way to the coastal plain. Small towns and villages dot the landscape on both sides; those little specks you see moving through the fields are probably tractors.

Motorcycle campers will find campgrounds at Matthews Arm, Lewis Mountain, Loft Mountain and Big Meadows, the latter available by reservation. There are also lodge and cabin rooms available. To camp in the back country, you'll need to get a permit at any entrance to the park. If you want a campsite, my advice is to set up camp early and then go exploring, especially during the summer season. These campgrounds fill up fast. For a room reservation, call well ahead. Many months ahead.

On our tour, exit from Skyline at the Thornton Gap exit. Turn left on Route 211 toward Sperryville. This is a fast five-mile descent with hairpin turns sharp enough that you can really grind the floorboards. Your arrival into the hamlet of Sperryville begins with a collection of roadside stands selling a wide variety of "must haves," including apples, peaches, and cider; lawn ornaments of distinction; furniture; fajitas; "I Love Virginia" toothpick holders; and Elvis commemorative hand towel and bed linen sets.

You can have a fun time just stopping at different stands and looking over the goods. The most impressive collection is at the **Sperryville Emporium.** The Emporium is a converted schoolhouse packed from floor to ceiling. The main building is full of furniture, the annex full of fruits, and the parking lot full of cars. A seasonal flea market operates along the perimeter, and a local barbecue joint operates a stand. In the early fall during apple season, the place is so packed it takes on a carnival atmosphere. You'll often run into other riders here who are passing through on their way to the Drive, and many of the local riders will offer tips on other roads to try.

Modest old homes line the street that is downtown Sperryville, each with its own picket fence and front porch. Some have been converted into shops that sell locally made crafts, antiques, even Native American jewelry. There are plenty of surprises to be found in the antique shops, including pieces and parts of old motorcycles. A rider friend told me he entered a shop one day just as a fellow wheeled an old Indian out the door with a smile on his face as wide as Texas. "Four hundred dollars," the proud new owner told my friend before the question could form in his mouth.

I don't think there are many Indians remaining to be discovered in Sperryville, but it isn't too hard to uncover a tasty meal. You can count on the "expert sandwich mechanics" at the **Appetite Repair Shop** to cure what ails you in a hurry. Owner Cindy Gillies is pleased to report that she has parts to fit all manner of rider, foreign and domestic. There ain't a model they can't fix, she says with authority. Whether you order a simple hamburger or a tasty barbecue, you will go away a satisfied customer.

When you've done all the wandering you want, it's time to suit up and head out. Follow Route 522 south out of Sperryville toward Culpeper and into the lush Piedmont. The right turn for Route 231 comes up just on the outskirts of town. Turn right and follow it. Route 231 is designated a Virginia Byway, and we know what that means—more great riding! Route 231 isn't as curvy as it is scenic. I discovered this road one day by accident, being lost and simply looking for a way to get from one point to another. I quickly discovered that getting lost out here is a good thing. The smooth pavement tempts you to slip into top gear and tilt your head back to smell the air. It's so fresh and sweet you can almost taste it. There's nothing to hear but the drone of your motor

The Appetite Repair Shop works on two-wheelers' hunger as well as four wheelers'.

and the rushing wind. Just make sure you don't relax so much you miss that next curve!

On your right Old Rag Mountain appears from behind the trees, with its bald, rocky top looking somewhat out of place among the tree-covered hills beside it. Old Rag is a little different because geologists say it is an extinct volcano. Old Rag is a popular day trip for weekend warriors who want to test their mettle in the outdoors (and want to be assured a victory). If you decide to conquer it, be sure to bring along the essential gear, plus a little extra food and water. To get to the parking area, turn right on Route 646 and follow this bumpy little cowpath to the foot of the mountain and Route 717, the road which leads to parking. There are often a lot of cars parked at the base, but you shouldn't have too much trouble finding a spot to squeeze your scoot in. Just be sure you have something to place under the kickstand. If there simply isn't any safe place to park, turn around and weigh anchor in the auxiliary lot about a quarter mile from the base. Don't park along the side of the road in between; it'll rile the neighbors.

Further down Route 231 in Madison County a vineyard sign appears next to Route 651; turn right. Route 651 promises to be a great little road with a lot of nip and tuck cornering, but it quickly turns to gravel, and on this day our destination is the vineyard. Follow the vineyard signs and exercise caution as you negotiate the steep gravel lane. It's easily doable though, even loaded two up on a Gold Wing.

Misty Mountain Vineyards is typical of small Virginia vineyards. Most operations are run by just a few people, often a family affair. Misty Mountain owner Dr. Michael Cerceo is an amiable chap who will give you a warm welcome and a personal tour of the vineyard and also serve as your official wine tasting host. There might be a sign on the winery door that says "If you want a tour, come to porch of the house and knock." Right away, you know you are not at the Gallo Brothers' complex. Chances are you'll find Cerceo reading the paper on the screened-in back porch, enjoying the afternoon. Nice work if you can get it, eh? However, this casualness is not an indication of a slack operation—wine making takes a lot of patience and painstaking attention to detail. As he talks about the process, you get the distinct feeling that there is a significant amount of intuition and proper timing involved, kind of like trying to get a Triumph to fire on the first kick.

Finishing out the first leg of Route 231 brings you into the town of Madison. Here the homes are more stately, and the folks are more likely to give you a second look than they would in Sperryville. Don't worry, they don't mean anything by it, they just don't see too many dashing leather-clad figures like yourself darting through town. Madison is another appropriate place to climb off the bike for a look-see. Whether it be this journey or another through the Appalachians, you're always passing some kind of of craft shop of one kind or another, and after awhile they all begin to look alike. If you want to purchase a genuine hand-made souvenir without wondering if it was really "made in the far, far east," check out Madison's own **Little Shop.** You won't find any Elvis towel sets here, just some of the best handiwork anywhere in the region, and at affordable prices.

To depart Madison, continue to follow US Business 29/VA 231 west toward Charlottesville. A few miles west of Madison, make a right turn on Route 230 west. Here the straights are long and the view of the Blue Ridge rising in front of you invites your imagination to speculate what it will

The author's mother demonstrates quilting at the Madison Fall Festival.

be like to attack the ridge. Entering the town of Stanardsville, turn right on Route 33. Your answer will come quickly.

First you enter a series of warm-up curves to get your tires scuffed. Then the road suddenly turns tame and the immediate fun seems over. This doesn't last long; the more serious curves are just ahead. The road widens, giving you two lanes to set up your curves, and you can really give your cornering a good workout. If you have anything left of your footpegs from Route 211, you're liable to wear them out on this stretch. Your ascent is smooth, like you're gliding on some of the low hanging clouds that brush the ridge when they pass. Then all too soon, you've reached the top. The best news is, you've returned to Skyline with another 60 miles of curves to go!

However, time may not be your friend. If it is late in the day or you are tired, I suggest following Route 33 down the mountain, and returning via Route 340 north toward Front Royal. This is an easier ride, one that gives you nice views of the Massanuttens and the Blue Ridge. Route 340 is also a pretty ride, running parallel to the Shenandoah River. You'll also see several long steel truss railroad bridges, some of them a few hundred feet long. The ride is pretty similar to what you experienced on Route 231 and 230, with long straights and an occasional town.

Trip 11   Mosby's Confederacy

• •

Distance   *160 miles*

Terrain   *Route passes through upper Piedmont along twisty back roads, makes a brief excursion into West Virginia, returns over a mountain pass, then travels more Piedmont roads running parallel to Blue Ridge*

Highlights   *The Plains, Middleburg, Summit Point Raceway, Charles Town, Harpers Ferry, Sky Meadows State Park*

The Route from Front Royal

→ VA 55 east to VA 626 (James Madison Highway)
→ VA 626 north to US 50
→ US 50 east to VA 748 (Sam Fred Road) at Middleburg
→ VA 748 north to VA 734 (Snickersville Gap Turnpike)
→ VA 734 west to VA 760
→ VA 760 to VA 7
→ VA 7 west to VA 632 (Crums Church Rd.)
→ VA 632 north to VA 761 (Old Charlestown Pike)
→ VA 761 east becomes WV 13 (Summit Point Road)
→ WV 13 east to W. Washington Street in Charles Town
→ W. Washington Street to WV 9
→ WV 9 east becomes VA 9*
→ VA 9 east to VA 719 in Hillsboro
→ VA 719 south to VA 743
→ VA 743 becomes VA 623 in Willisville
→ VA 623 south to US 50
→ US 50 west to US 17
→ US 17 south to VA 688 (Leeds Manor Rd.)
→ VA 688 south to VA 635 at Hume
→ VA 635 west to US 522
→ US 522 north to Front Royal

*Harpers Ferry Option

→ VA 9 east to VA 671
→ VA 671 north to US 340
→ US 340 south to Harpers Ferry
→ US 340 north to VA 671
→ VA 671 south to VA 9

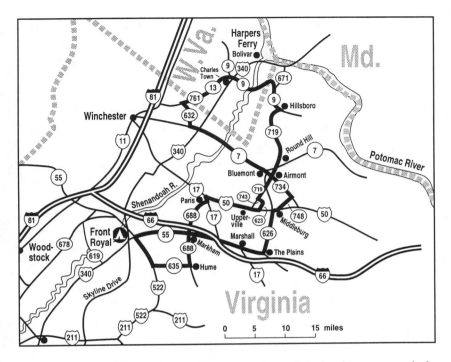

The region we'll venture through today is now popularly known as Horse Country because of the large estate homes and big horse farms that sprawl across it. But during the War Between the States it was known by a more threatening name that sent chills down the spine of many a Union soldier. When a band of renegade Rebel soldiers staged a series of surprise attacks and ambushes, it soon came to be known as Mosby's Confederacy, in honor of their fearless leader, Colonel John S. Mosby.

Route 55 was the primary road through Mosby's Confederacy until it was eclipsed by the interstate in the 1970s. As you motor out of Front Royal through Linden and Markham, what little local traffic is on the road soon disappears. That's your cue to begin power touring mode. In many places your route directly parallels the interstate. It's a good feeling to watch others hurry by while you pursue a little of the good life on your own terms.

When Route 55 intersects with Route 17, you need to make a slight detour to stay off the interstate. Make a right turn on Route 17/55. Just a few tenths of a mile up the road is VA Route 613. Make a left on Route 613 and then a quick right on Route F185. Huh? I don't understand it either, but this is the old alignment of Route 55 and upon entering Marshall, you'll pick it up again. Go figure.

On the other side of town, you'll enter the Confederacy proper. Huge farms are impeccably groomed with impressive manor houses, tree-lined driveways, and miles of stone and white board fence. You really can't make a wrong turn out here, so be sure to venture onto some of the side roads in this area to discover more farms and estates. Route 55 passes through the town of The Plains, where our first stop is at a cozy little restaurant, **The Rail Stop.** You'll always find a wide mix of people at The Rail Stop: local working folks, the horse crowd, tourists, and other motorcyclists. The prestigious **Virginia Gold Cup Races** are run the first of May each year at the Great Meadows Race Course just south of town. Buy your tickets in advance and you too can rub elbows with the well-heeled (the makings of a joke are in there somewhere, but I can't quite catch it).

Just up the street from the restaurant is our exit out. Turn left on Route 626. This road passes through more beautiful country with an occasional glimpse of the Blue Ridge to the west. Curves come at a faster pace here and as you buzz past the lush green pastures, vast homes hidden in large wooded tracts, and the fantastic barns and grounds, a distinct odor registers—yes, out here you can smell money. I don't know about you but I could get used to this lifestyle in a jiffy.

We've arrived by the back door into Middleburg, yet another playground of the rich. And the tourists. If you come through here on a weekend afternoon, this small village is literally crammed with Volvos, Beemers (two- and four-wheeled), and Benzes, and the streets are swarming with activity. The combination of pretty tree-lined streets, quaint shops, and good weather are a powerful lure. Being on two wheels is to your great advantage here in creating a parking spot out of otherwise wasted space.

Follow Route 50 east to the outskirts of town and turn left on Route 748. This little gem takes you through more farming area and connects to Snickersville Gap Turnpike, Route 734. Snickersville Gap is a popular road among area riders, not so much for its curves but for the scenic vistas of the country and the mountains. Snickersville Gap ends at Bluemont, another quaint village nestled at the foot of the Blue Ridge.

Bluemont as a town almost disappeared from the map, like so many other small villages. But growth of the metropolitan area drove people further west to seek relief from the pressures of urban life. New families began moving in during the 1970s, buying old homes and restoring them to their former glory. They not only gave the town a new lease on life, they also gave it a new name, changing it from Snickersville to Bluemont.

In Bluemont, the place to stop for a treat is **Snickersville General Store.** On a cold day, the pot-bellied stove will take the chill out of your leathers in a hurry. You'll often find another rider or two hanging around after a run on the turnpike. The easiest way to continue is to make the right turn on Route 760 across from the store, ending on Route 7. Turn left, head west.

At this point the Blue Ridge is more of a hill than a mountain chain and the road simply plows straight through, making for fast riding. The other side drops you into the northern end of the Shenandoah Valley. About ten miles west of Bluemont you'll make a right turn on Route 632. You'll see a sign for Summit Point. Follow 632 to its end, then make a right on Route 761. Route 761 enters West Virginia and becomes WV 13, Summit Point Road, though there isn't a sign that marks your entrance into the Mountain State except for a change in the color and condition of the pavement. This section of road can be broken up by bad weather and floods easily. The terrain is mostly flat and the road is lined by abandoned farming fields reverting to forest. Then, rounding a curve you see a break in the growth ahead and a large chain link gate appears on the right, the entrance to **Summit Point Raceway.**

During the racing season, which runs from about March through October, Summit Point hosts both two-wheel and four-wheel racing events. Both the American Motorcyclist Association (AMA) and the Western Eastern Racing Association (WERA) sponsor motorcycle races at the track. Motorcycle racing is much more casual than its four-wheel counter-part. All you need to do to be convinced of this is go to the pit area on race day and walk around. If this were a four-wheel event, access to the pits would be strictly controlled. Not so with motorcycling. Walk or ride down to the pits at any time. You can mingle with the riders, eat with them, watch them wrench their bikes. It's an open, carnival-like atmosphere and there is only one topic on the agenda: motorcycles. Even if you personally would never ride on the track, being this close to the action can be a blast.

Although there are grandstands in one or two different parts of the track, you can get even closer, in some places no more than a few feet from the track! It's amazing to stand on a bank overlooking the course and watch riders thunder by on their blazing machines just a few feet from where you stand. You can see every tiny move they make, hear the tires chatter as they grab a handful of brake, and then listen for the telltale "snick" as they ratchet through the gears.

Follow Route 13 east into Charles Town. You enter town on West Washington Street which becomes US 340 north. If you're in the mood to watch the ponies run, you can visit a racetrack of another sort—horse racing. **Charles Town Raceway** is ahead a mile or two on your left. Continuing on Route 340 north will take you to **Harpers Ferry National Historical Park.** However, there is a more scenic, easier way to get there than following heavily traveled 340. Make the right on WV Route 9 heading east out of town. The Blue Ridge is a bit more of a challenge here and several miles of smooth curves will make you think you're in the carousel at Summit Point, making the move on the race leader. About two-thirds of the way up the mountain is a turn out with a nice view of the Shenandoah Valley below, a good spot for a picture. Just a few miles into Virginia, Harpers Ferry Road, Route 671 appears on your left. Following Route 671 to the park is a treat, more smooth pavement and fast traveling.

The road ends on Route 340 just a mile north of town, so turn left and follow 340 south. You can park in the official Harpers Ferry parking lot and take the shuttle down. The small parking fee is also an admission fee to the park. How-ever, since parts of Harpers Ferry are privately owned, you

Which way do
we go?

can drive through the historic section of town and find a spot
on the back side near the train depot and park for free. (Don't
park in the depot lot, it isn't allowed. There are spots along
the street in front of the depot that are blocked by large utility
pole guy wires. Cars can't fit, but you can.)

Harpers Ferry is widely known as one of the flash points
that led to the Civil War. On a chilly October evening in 1859,
22 men led by abolitionist John Brown stormed the federal
arsenal at Harpers Ferry. Their plan was to raid the armory
and pass arms to the slaves, encouraging them to revolt
against their masters. Unfortunately, the plan was ill-con-
ceived and short-lived. In a matter of hours, the armory was
surrounded by Colonel Robert E. Lee and his men. Brown
was captured, tried for treason, and hung. You can tour the
armory where Brown was captured and walk among the other
restored buildings. You can also cross the Potomac River on
a bridge and walk along the river on the C&O Canal towpath
(see Prospect Peak tour, Trip 7, for more information on the
C&O Canal).

While you are in Harpers Ferry, don't miss Bolivar
Heights. Ride through Harpers Ferry and into Bolivar until
you see a sign pointing to Bolivar Heights Park. From here

the view of the Potomac cutting through the Blue Ridge is nothing short of spectacular. Thomas Jefferson had a lot to say about Harpers Ferry in his book *Notes on the State of Virginia.* He probably stood on the same spot as you, noting, "The passage of the Patowmac through the blue ridge is perhaps one of the most stupendous scenes in nature . . . This scene is worth a voyage across the Atlantic."

Return to Virginia via Harpers Ferry Road to the point where we left Route 9. Continue on Route 9 east as we prepare to begin the return journey home. Find Route 719 just outside the village of Hillsboro and turn right heading south. Route 719 runs a long way down the eastern slopes of the Blue Ridge. It is a fine motorcycling road, with a surface that is good throughout, sweeping vistas of the Blue Ridge to the west, and more large estates to the south and east. Within the first few miles on 719 you will encounter the burned out remains of a large stone building. Make a left on Woodgrove Road to continue on the proper course. Your arrival into Round Hill is marked by an intersection with Route 7 again. If you're getting a little low on fuel for yourself, check out the **Round Hill Diner.** They have good food and always treat riders with a friendly smile.

Route 719 remains a plum riding road south of Route 7 and soon intersects with Snickersville Gap Turnpike at Airmont. Just before intersecting with Route 50 near Upperville, Route 719 turns to gravel. It isn't a long stretch and can be managed on almost any rig. If you'd prefer to stay with a hard surface, make a left on Millville Road, Route 743. After about two miles you'll reach the town of Willisville, where the road changes numbers and becomes Route 623. Bear right and continue to follow Route 623 south. At the intersection with Route 50, make a right turn. You'll pass through Upperville, a quaint town with some beautiful old homes. If you're a fan of architecture, be sure to visit the Trinity Episcopal Church. It's on your right as you pass through the village.

The tour turns south on Route 17 for a brief moment. On the right is Paris, home to TV weatherman Willard Scott. Also just ahead on the right is **Sky Meadows State Park.** This is probably one of the best-kept secrets in the Washington, DC, area. If you come through here on a summer afternoon, you'll probably have the entire run of the place. You can tour the manor house or just stroll about the grounds, hike up the Blue Ridge, have a picnic out back in the fully-equipped picnic area, or just enjoy the commanding view of the hunt country from the front yard. What I really enjoy are the rocking chairs on the front porch of a cabin to the side of the main house. Basking in the glow of the late afternoon sun and staring at the gentle slopes of the mountain will make any burden you carry seem a little lighter. In the evening, you'll see deer—not one or two, but herds—in the pastures below the farm.

Just south of Sky Meadows on Route 17 is our next turn, a right onto Route 688, Leeds Manor Road. This historic route once served as a boundary of the Lord Fairfax Proprietary, a grant of land to Lord Fairfax that once encompassed thousands of square miles. The road surface is fair to good (you'll find some broken patches and scattered gravel hazards), but easy going. You literally become lost in a tangle of woods and hills, first climbing then descending, giving you the feeling you're the first one to discover this road. On the back side you descend Naked Mountain, home to **Naked Mountain Vineyards.** Their advertising slogan? "Drink Naked." Suffice it to say their company uniforms draw quite a crowd at local wine festivals.

Route 688 passes under Interstate 66 and crosses Route 55 at Markham. Cross over 55 and follow Route 688 to the right and over the railroad tracks. There are several miles more of good riding with improved pavement but fewer curves. Perhaps the best stretch of pavement of the entire loop is just ahead on Route 635. In Hume, make the right turn on Route 635 and head west. Words are inadequate to describe the serenity and beauty of this road. Route 635 winds gently over high meadows against a backdrop of the Blue Ridge that is also worth a voyage across the Atlantic. The pavement is glass smooth, each curve perfectly banked. You simply couldn't ask for more (other than that it should last longer than it does).

Your arrival at Route 522 marks the conclusion of your reconnaissance in Mosby's Confederacy. Turn right to make your return to Front Royal.

Trip 12 Stonewall's Valley

••

Distance	*125 miles*
Terrain	*Narrow river valley—an exciting, scenic ride, followed by several mountain passes*
Highlights	*Fort Valley, New Market Battlefield, Luray Caverns*

The Route from Front Royal

→ US 340 south to VA 619
→ VA 619 west to VA 678
→ VA 678 south to VA 675
→ VA 675 east to US 340 at Luray
→ US 340 north to US 211
→ US 211 west to VA 305
→ VA 305 north to New Market Battlefield
→ VA 305 south to US 211
→ US 211 east to US 522
→ US 522 north to Front Royal

During the Civil War, the Shenandoah Valley was a much fought-over piece of land because of its strategic location between the warring capitals of Washington and Richmond, and its rich farmland that fed Confederate troops. Lose the valley, and the South would lose the war, but as long as Thomas J. Jackson commanded the Confederate Army of the Shenandoah, this vital region was safe.

Jackson was considered by many to be second only to Robert E. Lee in his ability to achieve victory in battle against superior Union numbers. He had a habit of being found in the thick of the action, rather than safely behind the lines, and this was a source of inspiration for his troops. At the Battle of First Manassas his men rallied around him, with one shouting "There stands Jackson like a stone wall." Soon after, the men simply called him "Stonewall," and the northern Shenandoah came to be known as Stonewall's Valley.

Our trail through Stonewall's Valley begins out of Front Royal following Route 619 west through the outskirts of

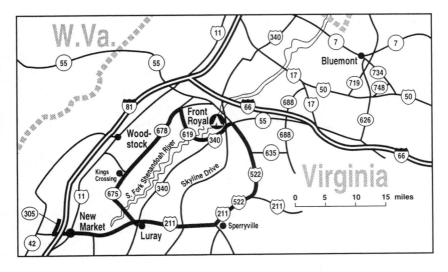

town. The road soon narrows and the Massanutten Mountains loom in the distance, a portent of good riding to come. But even before reaching the mountain, the road begins dipping and twisting, skirting several small hollows. Near the northern base of the mountain, the trailhead of a popular hiking trail is jam packed with cars. This past winter in the Valley has been a hard one and though fully cleared, the roads are still lined with snow, several feet deep in some places. With temperatures reaching into the fifties in March, normally placid Passage Creek has been swollen by the runoff of melting snow, leaving its banks and spilling into the narrow river valley. It still doesn't quite feel like spring here yet. Winter hasn't let go, but it has loosened its grip. March can be a chilly time to make this ride, but it is a rewarding one.

When Route 619 ends, make the left turn on Route 678. This is the entrance to Fort Valley. The first few miles follow the course of the river bend for bend. High sheer cliffs rise on either side, in stark contrast to the time-worn, rounded shoulders of the Blue Ridge. Those who never venture from Skyline will think they have seen everything the Valley has to offer, but having ridden the backside of Massanutten, you will know just how much they missed.

Rounding a curve, I came upon a collection of Forest Service vehicles blocking the road, lights flashing. Had someone fallen in the creek? In the middle of the pack of cars, a large tanker truck was parked with men crawling along the top and removing poles. What the heck is this? I saw that at the end of each pole was actually a net full of anxious trout struggling to get out! Each man carefully walked over to the stream and released his cargo into the roiling waters, stocking Passage Creek for this year's trout fishing season—a sure sign that spring will make its annual appearance after all.

Route 678 continues well into the valley for another twenty-odd miles before arriving at Kings Crossing. Here, follow Route 675 ahead as it veers off to the left. Route 675 crosses the valley and then makes a sudden turn and it's up the mountain! Somewhere I remember reading that only Route 211 crosses directly over the Massanutten Mountains, but that's not true. Route 675 dives directly into the George Washington National Forest and then straight up the side of the mountain without the benefit of a gap to lessen the climb. There are several switchbacks along this section of road, tricky hairpins with a steep ascent in the turn. Gravel wash can make it even more of a challenge, especially on a big rig. When you top out on the ridge, make a stop and climb off the bike. On the side of the road facing the east is a beautiful view of the eastern portion of the Valley with the Blue Ridge in the distance and the town of Luray directly below. The south fork of the Shenandoah River glistens in the foreground. The view alone is reason enough to make this ride—it's something you can take with you that few others will ever see. But wait, there's more! The descent down the eastern face of the mountain is standard fare with a few moderate switchbacks. You will quickly arrive in the town of Luray. When Route 675 ends in town, make a left turn on Route 340 north, then a left on Route 211 west. This is the road to New Market.

Route 211 passes over the Massanuttens again at New Market Gap. The grades are considerably smoother and properly banked for a fast, fun ride. In just a few miles you are deposited into the town of New Market, one of a host of small towns that played a small part in the Civil War. Continue following Route 211 until you pass under Interstate 81. Make a right turn on Route 305 and follow it to the end of the road to the **New Market Battlefield Park.**

*The Battle of
New Market
raged around
this modest
farmhouse.*

Throughout the war, Stonewall's men had repulsed each Union attempt to invade the Valley and destroy the breadbasket of the Confederacy. But in 1863, Stonewall was wounded by friendly fire at Chancellorsville and died. His passing dealt a blow to the Southern forces of Robert E. Lee. Could anyone be as able a protector of the Valley as Stonewall? The test came in 1864 when Ulysses S. Grant began throwing men and munitions at the battered southern ranks in three strategic points across Virginia, including the Valley. General John Breckenridge, though a capable man, had few resources and men to hold off the advancing Union forces. In a desperate attempt to bolster the ranks, he called upon the entire cadet corps at the Virginia Military Institute, 240 boys ages 15 to 18, to join the battle. They marched for four days to supplement the ragged Confederate ranks. It was the first and only time cadet forces in the United States have been pressed into live combat. Though they were hardly prepared for the fight, the cadets accounted well for themselves, capturing an enemy canon and helping the Rebels slam the door once again on the Federal battering ram.

While you are on the grounds, you can tour the museum and walk down to the farmhouse around which the troops rallied before marching into hand-to-hand combat. The entire grounds have been well preserved and you can walk throughout the entire battlefield. It is peaceful, though it is not quiet.

The roar of the cannons has been exchanged for the roar of the interstate which passes by within a few hundred yards—an interstate which, ironically, is a critical link between the two regions of the country which once fought each other to the death on this very spot.

Lunch is an easy choice. Drive back into New Market, make a right turn on Route 11 south. Down the road about three long blocks is the **Southern Kitchen Restaurant.** Do not go to New Market and eat anywhere else. This is the real thing. I don't know anywhere else where you can find peanut soup on the menu as a regular item, and their "Virginia Fried Chicken" puts the Colonel to shame. The decor is strictly fifties, which is part of the charm, but rather than seeming time-worn it looks as clean and fresh as if it opened for business yesterday. I've had a lot of good meals on my journeys through the mountains, but this one was the best.

The route returns over the Massanuttens again via US 211 east with a stop at **Luray Caverns.** The floor of the Shenandoah Valley is predominantly limestone, and over the course of hundreds of thousands of years, underground streams and pools have eroded large caves. Subsequent water dripping through the valley floor caused great limestone formations to grow undisturbed in subterranean isolation. Once settlers moved into the region, folks who began exploring the haunts and hollows would occasionally stumble upon a cave or, in the case of Luray, a truly remarkable cavern. Unlike other caverns I have visited in the course of this writing (we won't mention any names), this one is worth the price of admission. The hour-long tour follows a trail through a vast maze of stunning formations. Many of them are hollow, and if gently tapped (don't actually do this), will make a musical tone. There are so many musical stalactites that the cavern developers created an organ that plays them. It was impressive when I was a wide-eyed eight-year-old and it still is. After you finish the tour of the cavern, you are also invited to take a tour of the transportation museum in the same building. I didn't see any motorcycles, though, just four-wheelers.

*The Southern
Kitchen
Restaurant
serves the best
Virginia
ham—and
peanut soup,
too!*

There are three ways to return to Front Royal from Luray. The easiest way is to follow Route 340 up the western side of the Blue Ridge. Pretty, but no major challenge. You can also return via the Parkway. When you reach the summit of the Blue Ridge on 211, you arrive at the Thornton Gap entrance to Skyline. If you have ridden it within the last seven days and still have your receipt, the trip is free. You can also pass Skyline and continue into Sperryville. When you reach Route 522, follow it north.

Trip 13 Seneca Rocks

· ·

Distance	*210 miles*
Terrain	*Ridges, passes, and river runs characterize this route*
Highlights	*Seneca Rocks, Germany Valley, and curves, curves, curves*

The Route from Front Royal

→ VA 55 west to WV 55 (Wardensville Pike)

→ WV 55 west to US 33 at Seneca Rocks

→ US 33 east to US 11

→ US 11 north to VA 42

→ VA 42 north to US 11 at Woodstock

→ US 11 north to VA 55

→ VA 55 east to Front Royal

You've got to promise you'll keep this one a secret. Well, okay, you can share it with your riding friends, but please don't tell any four-wheelers about this route. Of all the roads I've traveled throughout the Appalachians, this route covers two of my all-time favorites. This is the one route I would recommend to even the most jaded I've-ridden-'em-all rider as a showcase of the best riding the Appalachians have to offer. Let's get to it.

From Front Royal, pick up Route 55 west and make your way through Strasburg and over the Interstate. From this point, Route 55 becomes a pleasure to navigate, with virtually no traffic and perfectly-banked curves that come rapid-fire, over and around the contours of the Shenandoah and Allegheny Mountains. Just before you enter Wardensville, there's a sign along the road indicating the point which was at one time during the mid-1800s the geographic population center of the United States.

First stop on the tour is the **Kac-ka-pon Restaurant** in Wardensville. The Kac-ka-pon offers a great value for any meal, and the prices are as down home as the cooking. If you stop in time for lunch, be sure to save room for a slice from one of their homemade pies.

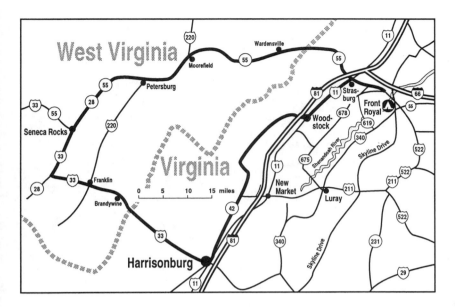

Out of Wardensville you'll find another 25 to 30 miles of even better riding, crossing numerous mountain ridges and following rivers. If you ever held the notion as I once did that nothing good ever came out of West Virginia, you'll find it to be true; they're keeping it all to themselves and this route is the proof. Route 55 joins U.S. Route 220 at Moorefield and follows it south for a few miles before returning on its westerly course at Petersburg. Route 220 is a good road itself, following narrow valleys through West Virginia and well into Virginia. It is often named by motorcycle magazines as one of the best unknown roads in America (obviously they haven't ridden Route 55 and I hope they don't).

Starting somewhere before Petersburg and with increasing frequency you'll notice signs for the Smoke Hole Caverns, Crystal Grottoes, Seneca Caverns, etc., etc. There are probably more attractions of this type in this region than any other because many of the ridges in this area bear limestone caves. Spelunking is a popular pastime. It's not unusual to see a couple of parties of cavers parked by the roadside, headlamps in position, ready to venture into the subterranean passages of the Appalachians.

After Petersburg, Route 55 spends its remaining time chasing a series of rivers before intersecting with US Route

33 at Seneca Rocks National Recreation Area. This is a popular destination for day-trippers who come to climb the rocks. Seneca Rocks' ragged edges stand out from the smooth ridge lines of the hills that surround them. Often in cases like this, the rock that remains was molten rock that was pushed to the surface by geologic forces below. The heat and pressure made it harder than the surface it pushed through and when that surface wore away, the harder rock was exposed.

Next is a great section of Route 33 between Seneca Rocks and Harrisonburg, Virginia. The first ascent you'll make is long by East Coast standards. It will bring you to a fantastic panorama of the Germany Valley. If you're tempted to pull off for a picture, wait until you get to a spot along the road that has a "Germany Valley" marker. It's near the top and offers the best view. This view is a good candidate for your widest lens or a recyclable panoramic camera. To the left and right are the high, imposing ridges of the Alleghenies, while in the valley below, a series of small, uniform ridges punctuate the valley floor.

From Franklin, the route settles for a minute and then makes another ascent before dropping into Brandywine. Brandywine is a cozy little town with a popular recreation area that offers nice campsites and a lake for swimming and fishing. From here, the last great ascent is soon upon you as you trek up the Shenandoah Mountains. After a few miles of switchbacks you can pull off to the side of the road and retrace your path, finding Brandywine in the valley below. Once over the hills, it's another 20 miles or so to Harrisonburg. To avoid the traffic, make a left on Route 42 and head out of town.

When you reach Broadway you face a decision. If you're hungry, follow Route 259 to US 11. On US 11 north at New Market you'll run across the Southern Kitchen Restaurant (see Stonewall's Valley, Trip 12, for details) which is the best place in the area to eat, bar none. You can also continue to follow Route 42 north through Woodstock where you will eventually catch up to Route 11 as well. Route 42 is a more scenic rural ride.

Route 11 crosses paths with Route 55 in Strasburg. If you're inclined, Strasburg is a good place to hop off and walk around for browsing. There are dozens of small shops willing to accept your credit card and to ship. (No space on your bike? Not a problem!) Return to Front Royal on Route 55 east to complete the Seneca Rocks tour.

A view of Germany Valley along US 33. Get out your wide angle lens!

Lodging

· ·

ARA Virginia Sky-Line Co.
P.O. Box 727
Luray, VA 22835
Phone 800-999-4714. Information and reservations for Skyline
cabins and lodges.

Blue Ridge Motel
1370 North Shenandoah Avenue
Front Royal, VA 22630
Phone 703-636-7200. Pool; pets with permission; senior citizen
and AAA discounts available. Large Rolling Thunder group stays
here every Memorial Day weekend. $36 single; $40 two beds.
Prices quoted are for double occupancy. $4 for each additional
person.

Chester House Inn
43 Chester Street
Front Royal, VA 22630
Phone 800-621-0441 or 703-635-3937. $$$

Fountain Hall Bed and Breakfast
609 South East Street
Culpeper, VA 22701-3222
Phone 703-825-8200. All rooms have private baths; three have
private porch. Continental Plus breakfast included. Free off-
street parking in small lot. Walking distance to town restaurants.
$65 for a double to $115 for a 2-room suite. Prices quoted are for
double occupancy.

Front Royal KOA Campground
Two miles south of town on US 340
Front Royal, VA 22630
Phone 703-635-2741. Campsites from $18; cabins from $30.

The Inn at Narrow Passage
US 11 South
Woodstock, VA 22664
Phone 703-459-8000. Singles $50 to 75; doubles $55 to 90.

Places of Interest

....

Barboursville Vineyard and Ruins
VA Route 20 South
Barboursville, VA 22923
Phone 703-832-3824. Mon. through Sat., 10 a.m. to 5 p.m.; Sun., 11 a.m. to 5 p.m. Tours of winery held every Sat. between 10 a.m. and 4 p.m. Tour takes approximately 25 minutes. Free if fewer than 10 people.

Charles Town Raceway
US Route 340
Charles Town, WV 25414
Phone 304-725-7001. Call for post times.

Gayheart's Drug Store
Main and Davis Streets
Culpeper, VA 22701
Phone 703-825-3600. Mon. through Fri., 7 a.m. to 7:30 p.m.; Sat., 7 a.m. to 6 p.m.; closed Sunday.

Harpers Ferry National Historical Park
P.O. Box 65
US 340
Harpers Ferry, WV 25425
Phone 304-535-6115. Park open daily from 8:30 a.m. to 5 p.m.; shuttle buses run every fifteen minutes from 8 a.m. to 6 p.m.

James Madison Museum
129 Caroline Street
Orange, VA 22960
Phone 703-672-1776. Weekdays, 9 a.m. to 4 p.m.; weekends, March through November, 1 p.m. to 4 p.m. $

The Little Shop
West Main Street
Madison, VA 22727
Phone 703-948-4147. Tues. through Sat., 10 a.m. to 4 p.m.

Luray Caverns
US 211 West
Luray, VA 22835
Phone 703-743-6551. 9 a.m. to 6 p.m. One-hour tours start every 20 minutes. $11 adults.

Misty Mountain Vineyards
SR 2, Box 458
VA State Route 638
Madison, VA 22727
Phone 703-923-4738. Mon. through Sat., 11 a.m. to 4 p.m.; Sunday, by appointment only. Tours and wine-tastings available. Call for information. Free.

Montpelier
P.O. Box 67
VA Route 20 South
Montpelier Station, VA 22957
Phone 703-672-2728. Daily, March 16 through December 31. Call for other times. Closed major holidays. $6 adults; $5 senior citizens; $1 children 6 to 12; under 6 free.

Moormont Orchards
6530 Moormont Rd.
Rapidan, VA 22733
Phone 540-672-2730. Open mid-June to early November, 7 a.m. to sunset. Pick your own peaches, nectarines, grapes, plums, apples and pumpkins! Some pre-picked fruit is available from their fruit stand. Say hello to Goodwin Moor while you're there—he's the owner.

Museum of Culpeper History
140 East Davis Street
Culpeper, VA 22701
Phone 703-825-1973. Daily, 11 a.m. to 5 p.m. Closed Sundays. Free.

Naked Mountain Vineyards
P.O. Box 131
VA Route 688 North, near I-66 junction
Markham, VA 22643
Phone 703-364-1609. Wed. through Sun., 11 a.m. to 5 p.m. Free.

New Market Battlefield Park
US Route 211 West
New Market, VA 22844
Phone 703-740-3102. Daily, 9 a.m. to 5 p.m. Free.

Shenandoah National Park and
Dickey Ridge Visitor Center
US Route 340 South
Luray, VA 22835
Phone 703-999-2266.

Sky Meadows State Park
Route 1, Box 540
US Route 17 South
Delaplane, VA 22025
Phone 703-592-3556. Sunrise to sunset. $1.50 per vehicle.

Skyline Caverns
One mile south of Front Royal on US 340
P.O. Box 193
Front Royal, VA 22630
Phone 800-635-4599 or 703-635-4545. Open 9 a.m. to 5 p.m. $9
for adults; $4 for children from 6 to 12; children 5 and under, free.

Snickersville General Store
Snickersville Gap Turnpike
Bluemont, VA 22012
Phone 703-554-8221. Mon. through Sat., 7 a.m. to 7 p.m.; Sundays, 7 a.m. to 5 p.m.

Sperryville Emporium
Intersection of US 211 & US 522
Sperryville, VA 22740
Phone 703-987-8235. Daily, 9 a.m. to 5:30 p.m.

Summit Point Raceway
Summit Point Rd.
Summit Point, WV 25446
Phone 304-725-8444. Call for race schedule information. General Admission $13 to AMA races.

Virginia Gold Cup Races
Great Meadow Race Course
Routes 17 and 245
The Plains, VA 22171
Phone 703-347-2612. Opens the first Saturday in May; first race
at 1:30. Office hours Mon. through Fri., 9 a.m. to 5 p.m. Offices
at 90 Main Street in Warrenton, VA. Friendly folks in the office
and at the races. A unique horse race typical of Virginia. General
subscription/admission is $50 per car with up to six people.

Warren Rifles Confederate Museum
95 Chester Street
Front Royal, VA 22630
Phone 703-636-6982. Open April 15 to November 1. Mon.
through Sat., 9 a.m. to 5 p.m.; Sunday, 12 p.m. to 5 p.m.

Restaurants

··

The Appetite Repair Shop
Main Street
Sperryville, VA 22740
Phone 703-987-9533. Mon. through Wed., 8 a.m. to 4 p.m.;
Thurs. through Sun., 8 a.m. to 8 p.m. Cindy Gillies and crew
have the parts to fix any appetite regardless of make or model.
Breakfast from $2.50; lunch from $3.50; dinner range $7 to
$12.50.

Baby Jim's
North Main Street
Culpeper, VA 22701
Phone 703-825-9212. Mon. through Thurs., 4 a.m. to 10:30 p.m.;
Fri. and Sat., 6 a.m. to 12 p.m.; Sunday, 6 a.m. to 8 p.m. $

Dean's Steak House
708 South Royal Avenue
Front Royal, VA 22630
Phone 703-635-1780. Mon. through Thurs., 11:30 a.m. to 9 p.m.;
Fri. through Sun. 'til 10:30 p.m. $$

Fox Diner
20 South Street
Front Royal, VA 22630
Phone 703-635-3325. Sun. through Thurs., 6 a.m. to 7 p.m.; Fri.
and Sat. 'til 9 p.m. Ask Loretta to mix you a milk shake. Best
anywhere! Sandwiches from $1.50; dinners from $4.

Kac-ka-pon Restaurant
Main St.
Wardensville, WV 26851
Phone 304-874-3232. Sun. and Mon., 7 a.m. to 8 p.m.; Tues.
through Thurs., 7 a.m. to 9 p.m.; Fri. and Sat., 7 a.m. to 10 p.m. $

The Rail Stop
Route 55 - Main Street
The Plains, VA 22171
Phone 703-253-5644. Mon. through Sat., 6 a.m. to 8 p.m.; Sun.,
7 a.m. to 7 p.m. Full meal for $5.

Round Hill Diner
Intersection of Route 719 and Route 7
Round Hill, VA 22141
Phone 703-338-3663. Mon. through Fri., 6:30 a.m. to 2 p.m.; Sat.
and Sun., 7 a.m. to 2 p.m. $

Sandy's Diner
US 340 & US 522
Front Royal, VA 22630
Phone 703-635-2911. Daily, 6 a.m. to 10 p.m. $ - $$

Southern Kitchen Restaurant
Main Street (U.S. Route 11)
New Market, VA 22844
Phone 703-740-3514. Sun. through Thurs., 7 a.m. to 9 p.m.; Fri. and Sat., 7 a.m. to 10 p.m. Let Ruby Newland and her staff serve you up a bowl of peanut soup and a big ol' slab of Virginia cured ham. $ - $$

Travel Information

Fauquier County Chamber of Commerce
P.O. Box 127
Warrenton, VA 22186
Phone 703-347-4414. Information Only.

Front Royal Chamber of Commerce
P. O. Box 568
414 East Main Street
Front Royal, VA 22630
Phone 800-338-2576 or 703-635-3185.

Mid-Atlantic Road Racing Club
P.O. Box 2292
Wheaton, MD 20915
Phone 301-933-2599. Can provide general information on
MARRC schedule at Summit Point. Information only.

Warren County Historical Society
101 Chester Street
Front Royal, VA 22630
Phone 703-636-1446.

Winchester Visitor Center
1360 South Pleasant Valley Road
Winchester, VA 22601
Phone 800-662-4135 or 703-662-4135.

Shrine of the Confederacy

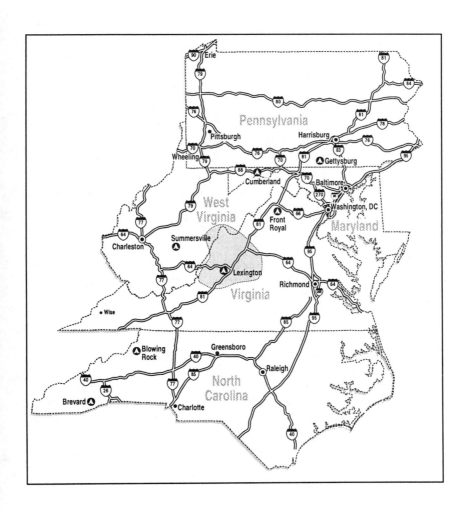

Lexington, Va.

• •

Lexington is a town motorcyclists should find on their maps and circle with a big red marker. It has all the right features to make it a fine destination for a week of exploring the hills and hollows of the Appalachians. Lexington is an old Southern town with a heritage that it displays with great pride. It is located at the intersection of two major interstates, I-81 and I-64, making it a breeze to get to and assuring you of a wide range of travel services. It is a college town, too, which means you can always count on something happening around town.

With all these benefits, it is still relatively small. Somehow, Lexington has managed to hold on to an atmosphere long since lost in many American towns. As you tour the oak-lined avenues and look at the stately old houses, you get a sense of security and serenity, a sense of feeling at home.

Lexington is also in the center of some of the finest, most pleasurable touring I have found anywhere in the region. Five minutes on the road and you are touring the vast Virginia countryside on well-paved, scenic roads with little traffic to contend with at any time of the year.

Few people seem to realize the true value of this area, though. In the time I've spent here over the years, most riders I've spoken with are just passing through, on their way to somewhere else. Too bad. In their rush to make it to their destination, they forget about the journey and miss all that good riding. I did occasionally cross paths with a few riders who were out enjoying themselves. They all had one thing in common: big smiles on their faces.

Accommodations here are inexpensive. The **Colony House Motel** offers a clean, comfortable room for around $30 during the week. Rates go up on weekends when parents are likely to come visiting their little scholars. If you want something a little more upscale, check out **Maple Hall.** Maple Hall is a fully restored plantation home, built in 1850.

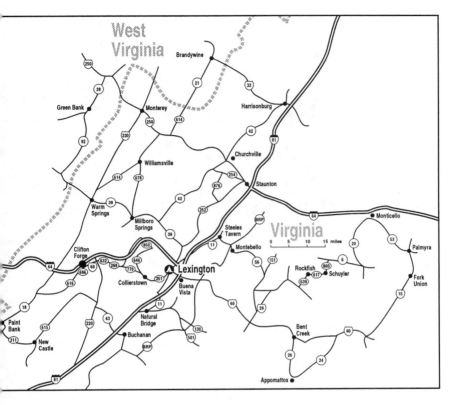

Many of the rooms and suites feature working fireplaces, and all are decorated with antiques.

The **Southern Inn Restaurant** in downtown Lexington is an attractive place to dine, especially when prime rib is on your mind. High backed wooden booths and the huge pocket watch clock on the wall behind the bar are distinctly from an era past. For something satisfying but a little less expensive, try the **Redwood Family Restaurant.** It's on the north end of town near the Colony House.

To the east just a few miles on Route 60 is Buena Vista (pronounced "BYEW-na" Vista; you too can sound just like a native). Buena Vista runs **Glen Maury Park,** a clean campground perched on a hill just outside of town.

Lexington is home to the Virginia Military Institute, a considerable source of Southern pride. VMI was the first state military college in the nation, founded in 1839 on the principle of perpetuating the model of citizen-soldiers. It has a great

Virginia's proud military tradition started here at VMI.

legacy of producing soldiers who have accounted well for themselves in the Civil War and two World Wars.

During the Civil War, 240 cadets at the institute, none older than seventeen, were organized to march against Union forces at New Market (see Stonewall's Valley, Trip 12, for details). The institute also graduated George C. Marshall, who later became Chief of Staff of the Army during World War II, and authored the Marshall Plan for reconstructing Europe after the war. He was awarded the Nobel Peace Prize in 1953, the first professional soldier ever to win the award.

VMI has two museums on campus, the **George C. Marshall Museum and Library** and the **VMI Museum.** Both are free and are well worth taking time to see in order to better understand the role this institute played in shaping world history. Then there is what I can only describe as the Shrine of the Confederacy, the hallmark of the South known as **Lee Chapel and Museum.**

Robert E. Lee spent his final years in Lexington as president of Washington College, a small school which had been nearly destroyed along with VMI after the Battle of New Market. Lee was hesitant to lend his name to the effort for fear that an association with a fallen general might spell final doom for the struggling college. Actually, it was his name that saved the school.

In the reconstruction of the South, Lee's enduring sense of duty to his country elevated his status as a revered leader

Lee Chapel in Lexington, Virginia is considered the Shrine of the Confederacy.

even more. He accepted the position at Washington College for a salary of $1,500 per year, turning down several more lucrative offers. Rather than stir resentment among his fellow countrymen who lost everything in the war, his words and deeds underscored the necessity for Virginia and the rest of the south to put the war behind them and concentrate on the task of rebuilding and looking to the future. (It was a message that needed to be heard too, as it was estimated after the war that Virginia alone had suffered nearly half a billion dollars in losses of private and public property and improvements, a figure that few people could possibly conceive of in that day.)

*General Robert
E. Lee keeps a
watchful eye
over the campus
of Washington
and Lee
University.*

Soon after Lee assumed his duties at the college, students began arriving from both North and South, and enrollment increased from less than a dozen to more than 400. Lee worked hard in his new job despite his declining health. Though he was only 58 when he accepted the position in 1865, he had aged well beyond his years, no doubt a consequence of the great burden he had borne for the past few years. He raised money and had a building constructed on campus which served a great many purposes, including Sunday worship services. If you were a student at Washington College, you were expected to attend Sunday services. Otherwise, you risked raised eyebrows from the General, a subtle but powerful reminder that your absence was noted.

Lee's health finally deteriorated and he died in October 1865. He was interred with other members of his family in the crypt below the chapel he constructed. Out of deep reverence for the General, his office was closed without disturbing a single paper and has remained that way since. It is reported that Lee, like his close companion "Stonewall" Jackson, called on A.P. Hill, another gallant southern general lost during the war, on his deathbed. His final words were "Strike the tent!"

Though he led the forces that threatened to tear apart the fabric of the still-young union of states, Robert E. Lee's unprecedented leadership and supreme valor have secured his place in history and assure that he will forever remain among the most respected leaders in this nation's history.

Did I mention **Stonewall Jackson's House** was here, too? Jackson was a professor at VMI before the Civil War and the only home he ever owned is in Lexington. Jackson is also buried here with his family and many Confederate veterans in the **Jackson Memorial Cemetery** downtown.

Just up the road from Lexington is the **Cyrus McCormick Farm.** In case you were sleeping through sixth grade history, McCormick invented the first mechanical harvester which ushered in the industrial age very nearly by itself. Before the reaper, most folks spent their time growing crops and feeding themselves. The reaper allowed one man to do the work of five and our economy shifted from agriculture to an industrial base. Why should you care? Well, this gave people the time to tinker with things in their spare time such as, oh, fitting crude internal combustion engines in bicycle frames to make them self-powered . . .

Trip 14 Highlander Loop

Distance	*200 miles, plus ten mile extension to Cass Railroad*
Terrain	*Mountain passes, narrow river valleys. A wide variety of high speed sweepers and tight switchbacks.*
Highlights	*Luscious green farm country, Green Bank Observatory, Goshen Pass, Monterey, Warm Springs*

The Route from Lexington

→ VA 39 west to WV 92
→ WV 92 north to WV 28
→ WV 28 north to US 250
→ US 250 east to VA 42
→ VA 42 south to VA 254
→ VA 254 east to VA 876
→ VA 876 east to VA 252
→ VA 252 south to VA 39
→ VA 39 east to Lexington

There may be no finer road for motorcycling in Virginia than Route 39, which opens this trip. I make this bold statement at the risk of being proved wrong someday, but I don't look for that to happen any time soon. Route 39 threads its way through a series of small hills and valleys, passing through the peaceful burg of Rockbridge Baths before entering Goshen Pass. The road is cut into the side of the mountain high above the Goshen River. Near the summit of the pass there is a wayside where you can relax by the river and enjoy a picnic lunch.

The Boy Scouts of America have a large camp near Goshen which you will pass en route. I'm told that the only problem with having the camp in a remote location like this is finding enough old ladies for these spirited young lads to help across the street. There are fewer than 5,000 residents in all of Bath County, and what few candidates there are for street-crossing are likely to be worn out by the time each budding Eagle Scout fills his dance card.

When Route 39 runs into Route 220, turn left and head south for a short distance. Just to your right you will find the **Warm Springs Pools.** The pools here and in Hot Springs have long drawn visitors who wish to relax in the perfect 98.6-degree springs. The Warm Springs pool has separate facilities for men and women. Bring a towel and your swimming trunks.

Follow Route 39 west out of Virginia and into Pocahontas County, West Virginia. The route number does not change. If you happen to be on your way to West Virginia for tours in another section of this book, this is a convenient and scenic route which will pass directly through Summersville, the starting location for those tours.

Shortly after entering West Virginia, Route 92 joins Route 39 for a short distance. When the two separate, turn right and follow Route 92 north. This follows a narrow valley

*"Taking the
waters" at
Warm Springs is
a 300 year-old
tradition.*

bounded by Lockridge Mountain to the east, Brown's Mountain to the west. It's hard to imagine that even in a remote area like this you are still within one day's journey of half the population of the country. Route 28 joins Route 92. After passing the dot on the map called Dunmore, you have an opportunity to visit the **Cass Scenic Railroad.** It's about eight to ten miles west on Route 66 in West Virginia (see The Gable End of Hell tour, Trip 21).

This remote area is good for more than just raising cows and making moonshine, it's also good for star gazing. That's why Green Bank was chosen as the site for the **National Radio Astronomy Observatory** in the mid-fifties. Radio astronomy is different from the traditional optical astronomy in that it examines the many different kinds of particles and phenomena that generate radio waves, a portion of which strike earth. It didn't become a serious science until radio technology developed significantly in the 1940s.

The telescopes require an area free of any sources of electromagnetic interference. One look around Green Bank will tell you why they located here. In fact, this area has been designated something of a radio-free zone and special permission is required before anyone can build a facility that might have an effect on the observatory.

There are four big dishes in service right now, the largest being 140 feet in diameter. In 1995, work will be completed on the ambitious 100-meter telescope called the Green Bank

Telescope (GBT). The new scope will look something like a clamshell. Each of the 2,204 panels which comprise the dish will be independently computer-controlled and adjustable so the accuracy of the surface can be maintained to the smallest fraction.

Visitors are welcome at the facility, so be sure to stop by. Along with a slide show and comments from a guide, you also get a tour among the telescopes. And it's all free.

When you get back on the road, follow Route 28 until it intersects with Route 250 at Bartow. It's time to head east, so make the right turn and follow Route 250 back into Virginia. Route 250 is widely known among area riders for its twists and turns. Things start off pretty gently, but as you approach the Virginia state line the frequency of turns quickens, as will your pulse. As you top Lantz Mountain, one of the most beautiful valleys I have seen anywhere opens before you. This is Blue Grass Valley. To the north and south lies a picture postcard valley with big white farm houses and manicured grounds so perfect they resemble scale models. These are the real thing. All this beauty is framed against a backdrop of Monterey Mountain, a few miles distant. It is a sight I promise will not disappoint.

Highland County lays claim to the highest average elevation east of the Mississippi. The town of Monterey is 3,000 feet above sea level. That kind of elevation means cool summer nights even when the rest of the eastern seaboard is sweltering. It would be pretty darn easy to put the kickstand down in Monterey and set up housekeeping there on a full-time basis. You can really stretch out in these parts—the 1990 census indicated that only a handful over 2,600 people call Highland County home.

If you're of a mind to stop for a bite, you can't go wrong with **High's Restaurant** on Main Street in Monterey. If you're staying for the evening, be sure you arrive before 8 p.m. There aren't any all-night joints in this part of the country. Right across the street is the **Highland Inn,** a frequent retreat for the region's BMW motorcycle clubs. These folks know how to pick all the right places. Not only does the Inn provide superb accommodations, you don't have to go far for your meals. Go no further than downstairs for fine dining.

Highland Inn in Monterey is a favorite of area riders.

After dinner there's no finer relaxing than swinging on the second floor porch swing or whiling away the evening watching no cars go by on Main Street from a comfortable rocking chair.

There aren't many stretches of road on the east coast that cross as many ridges head-on as the section of Route 250 between Monterey and Staunton. The next 30 miles have a generous mix of tight 10 mph switchbacks and double-nickel sweepers. There are three or four main passes interspersed with small valleys, so just as you get tired working the bike from one side to the other, you get a short break, and then another workout. Your trip through George Washington National Forest is like riding an avenue for a king, lined with stately old trees and a brook running on either side. Beautiful!

All too soon you arrive at Churchville. Make the turn south on Route 42 and follow it to Buffalo Gap. Follow Route 254 east to the left at the intersection and after a couple of miles, look for county route 876 on your right. This is a neat little road that at times threatens to turn to gravel but never does. It is so deserted and open, it almost feels like you're riding along a farmer's private driveway or through the field. You'll need to exercise all your navigational skills on this route because it takes unexpected turns at some intersections with other roads. It is clearly marked, though, so at worst you'll simply have to make a U-turn and pick up where you left off.

There are many Appalachian panoramas along US 250 near McDowell, Virginia.

This area is so quiet and unhurried your pace automatically slows. You'll feel a real connection with it—a sense of continuity and stability. Cows march slowly across the field in the evening, keeping their appointment with the farmer as they have day after day, year after year. Folks amble down a back lane, returning from a day at the shop or the office as they have done for the last 30 or 40 years. You could easily fall into the habit of living here yourself.

Eventually Route 876 finds Route 252. Route 252, another well-paved country road, meanders gently through towns with innocent names like Brownsburg, Bustleburg, and Middlebrook. When Route 252 ends on Route 39, turn left to make your way back to Lexington.

Trip 15   Valley Run

· ·

Distance	*195 miles plus mileage into/out of Staunton*
Terrain	*Rolling farm country, river valleys, and mountain passes*
Highlights	*Museum of American Frontier Culture, Woodrow Wilson Birthplace and Museum*

The Route from Lexington

→ VA 39 west to VA 42
→ VA 42 north to US 33
→ US 33 west to WV 21
→ WV 21 south becomes VA 614
→ VA 614 south to US 250
→ US 250 west to VA 678
→ VA 678 south to VA 39
→ VA 39 east to Lexington

Today's tour explores roads of the upper Shenandoah Valley, turning in a counter-clockwise direction. It is difficult to find a road that disappoints, and if your bike is stable on gravel or dirt roads, don't hesitate to explore to the sides. There are surprises around every turn, most of them pleasant ones.

If you didn't get a chance to practice your lines on the seductive pavement that is Route 39 in another tour, today is your day. After following Route 39 through Goshen Pass, turn right on Route 42 in the town of Goshen and follow it north. Route 42 passes through the village of Craigsville and eventually works its way between Great North and North Mountains to Buffalo Gap. Once through the gap you re-enter the Shenandoah Valley with its wide-open views and green pastures.

Churchville is a good place to turn if you want to check out Staunton (pronounced STAN-uhn by the local folks). Follow Route 250 about 12 miles east into downtown Staunton. The **Museum of American Frontier Culture** is on the east side of town and worth a visit. When the European settlers came to this country, they brought their old methods

of living with them and adapted them to a new country. The museum is home to three farmhouses of Scots-Irish, German, and English heritage, each having been carefully disassembled in its home country and then brought to this 180 acres in the Valley where all three cultures began to intermingle in the 1700s. A fourth farm from Botetourt County, Virginia, shows how these European designs were carried over from the Old Country and evolved into an American style.

Downtown is the **Woodrow Wilson Birthplace and Museum.** Wilson, the 28th President of the United States, was born here in 1856. He came from a wealthy family and was well educated, earning a doctorate in political science and rising through the academic ranks to become president of Princeton.

When you've had enough looking around, find your way back out Route 250 west, Churchville Avenue. Turn right and follow Route 42 north to Harrisonburg. The scenery between Churchville and Harrisonburg is nice enough to write home about, and so is the road. What will get you are those occasional straights that give you a chance to look around, and then before you know it, Surprise! The road makes an abrupt turn.

Your route does take you into downtown Harrisonburg, but the traffic is usually pretty moderate. Harrisonburg is an active college town, home to James Madison University. Your next turn comes in the middle of town onto Route 33. Make the left and head west toward the mountains. We've got some dicing to do! Even though U.S. Route 33 is one of just a handful of east-west corridors over the mountains, there isn't much traffic to speak of because, quite frankly, there isn't much to arrive at when you get over the mountain— other than more good riding

Once you enter the **George Washington National Forest** the road unexpectedly straightens for what must be two miles. The Shenandoah Mountains lie directly in front of you, hidden by thick forest, and even with advance warning, the first curve is surprisingly sharp.

The pass over the Shenandoahs begins with some moderate speed switchbacks. The tighter stuff is on the back side when your downhill cant makes it more of a challenge. The view is so enchanting it can be a real distraction, but there are a few turnouts near the summit where you can stop for a look. The road straightens at Brandywine, site of the **Brandywine Recreation Area.** If you're looking for cheap camping in the middle of nowhere, this is a great place. Most of my riding and camping buddies like to come out here to beat the summer heat because you can always count on Brandywine to be about ten to 15 degrees cooler. Camping is $8 per night. If there is a spot along the outside of the loop in the very back of the camp, take it. This gets the least traffic and is also nearer the one full bath facility in the center. The others are pit toilets. 'Nuff said about that!

You can hike an easy trail that leads from the camp to an old sawmill site along the ridge. It isn't uncommon to spot a

*There's a view
around every
curve on US 250
near Monterey,
Virginia.*

lot of wildlife, especially if you hike early in the morning or at dusk. There's even the off chance you might see a black bear. The lake sports a beach (it's a big pond, really, but I suppose if it has a beach it qualifies as a lake) and changing house if you need to cool off.

There isn't much doing in the town of Brandywine, but there is one good place you can stop for a sandwich—**Fat Boys Barbecue Palace.** It's also a good place to catch up on what's happening in Brandywine. The traffic in and out of the combination restaurant/video rental enterprise is everyday folk and the gossip that passes over the lunch counter will bring you up to speed right away.

At the T intersection in Brandywine, make a left turn on County Route 21 toward Propstburg and Sugar Grove —and the Naval Base. Yep, your Navy has seen fit to build a naval base on the South Fork of the Potomac River that has barely enough water to float a canoe. Rumor has it the original purpose for the base was the development of a top secret craft code-named "Waterless," a revolutionary new ship that required no water to float. The secret was to make the boats small enough to hold only a few people and outfit them with tracks like a bulldozer and a big gun on a turret that could spin around in any direction. The project was canceled in 1953 after the Navy discovered the Army had been using a similar device for 40 years, called a "tank." (Actually, the naval base

Your arrival in the Old Dominion goes relatively unnoticed.

is a communications facility. My apologies to my Navy riding buddies . . .)

At Sugar Grove, follow the road to the left to stay on course. Turning right will take you further into West Virginia and eventually you will run into Route 220. Only the cows in the field or a watchful hawk will note your passing. On either side you are surrounded by mountain ridges. Route 21 often looks as though it will run directly over a ridge only to divert at the last possible moment and find a narrow gap through it. The only indication you have returned to the Old Dominion is a small sign which says simply "Virginia." Here the road becomes Route 614.

Route 614 continues to follow the south fork of the Potomac. When Route 614 intersects Route 250, turn right and follow 250 west to stay on paved surfaces and to catch some serious switchbacks. Hug the curves back across Bullpasture Mountain and turn left on Route 678 in the burg of McDowell. In a way I hate to say that you'll soon discover "more of the same," because I don't want you to get the impression you will be bored. You won't! In this case, more of the same is something you could handle all the time!

After passing through Flood, the road draws closer to the Bullpasture River until the two are almost one. Somehow both just manage to squeeze through a tight gap and do an end run around Bullpasture Mountain. There are some places where the river front is privately owned and stopping along the river would be trespassing. However, there are other areas open to the public where you can stop for a breather and enjoy the rushing water.

From here Route 678 ends on Route 39 just above Millboro Springs and the journey home begins. You've still got plenty of good riding left; Goshen Pass is yet to come. And if you happen to run into any Navy fellas, ask them to tell you all about the "Waterless Project." Remember, you heard about it here first.

Trip 16   Hollow Hunting

· ·

Distance   *200 miles*

Terrain   *Mountain roads with sharp turns at odd cambers, main routes mixed with large fast sweepers and tight hairpins*

Highlights *Confederate ironworks ruins, short section of Blue Ridge Parkway, including Peaks of Otter, Natural Bridge*

The Route from Lexington

→ VA 251 west to VA 770
→ VA 770 west to VA 646
→ VA 646 north to VA 850
→ VA 850 west to VA 269
→ VA 269 west to VA 632
→ VA 632 west to US 60
→ US 60 west to VA 696
→ VA 696 west to VA 616
→ VA 616 south to VA 613
→ VA 613 west to VA 616
→ VA 616 south to VA 18
→ VA 18 south to VA 311
→ VA 311 south to VA 615 (Craigs Creek Rd.)
→ VA 615 east to US 220
→ US 220 south to VA 43
→ VA 43 east to Blue Ridge Parkway
→ Blue Ridge Parkway north to US 501
→ US 501 north to VA 130
→ VA 130 west to US 11
→ US 11 north to Lexington

This tour features some of the roads favored by local riders who have guarded them as a closely held secret until now. There are abundant opportunities to explore roads leading in all directions from the planned route—limited only by your time and imagination. Dual sport riders would have a field day with the tracks that take the high road over some of the ridges, rather than skirt around them like the paved roads.

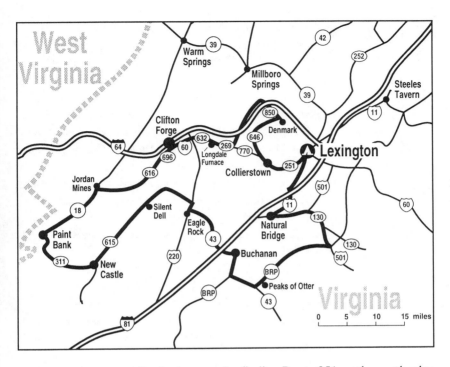

Begin the route by finding Route 251 on the south edge of Lexington. This road will quickly whisk you out of town on broad curves and into rural Virginia. At Collierstown, the road narrows and for a brief period becomes Route 770, changing after Collierstown to Route 646. The front of North Mountain rises before you like a fortress, and though the road looks as though it will make a direct charge on the stronghold, it turns north at the last moment. There is no paved road directly over the summit. Route 770 does cross the mountain but this is a route for dual-sport riders. I am still apologizing to my touring rig for trying to make it across. Routes 770 and 646 are representative of the country lanes that crisscross the landscape throughout the entire Appalachian region in un-ending variety. You could spend weeks in Lexington alone, riding in a different direction each day, tracing each little line on the map. I haven't found a bad road out here yet; there just aren't any people to get in the way. If there is any identifiable danger to riding aggressively on these roads, it would have to be the chance encounter of two pickup trucks stopped in the road, with a couple of old-timers talking to each other. They don't often pick the best place in the road to stop.

The route we follow rides the boundary of the Jefferson National Forest between North Mountain to your left and the twin Big House and Little House Mountains to your right. Route 646 ends at Denmark (passport not required) and then turns left on Route 850 to do an end run and finally find your way around North Mountain. The route that parallels Interstate 64 changes numbers a few times, beginning as 850, then 269, and finally 632. Route 850 begins as a lovely jaunt through the woods; you would never know the interstate is just a few hundred yards to your left. Heck, even the interstate is nice for that matter. It isn't a major east-west route for trucks, so it is actually a nice ride.

Just after you reach Longdale Furnace, look for a pair of tall brick smokestacks on your right. These are what remain of the Lucy-Selina Furnace, a Confederate ironworks built to supply rebel forces during the Civil War. These old stacks stand as defiantly today as they did more than 130 years ago, and they symbolize the pride some Southerners still feel when they speak of the Confederacy.

As you pass through Clifton Forge on Route 60 look for Route 696 and a sign for Selma. A bridge will take you over the track yard and along the foothills of the Rich Patch Mountains. Look for Route 616 on your left. It's one you might easily miss. If you go through a narrow bridge and end up near the interstate, turn around and look for Route 616 on your right. Fortunately the route whisks you away from the industrial section of town quickly and soon you are meandering through a maze of foothills, hollows, and coves. The roadbed is so crooked it seems to turn in on itself sometimes. Route 616 follows an unending series of small creeks and narrow valleys, and when faced with a hill, resigns itself to climbing over it, sometimes meandering back and forth, other times making quick work of it, but never becoming boring. Be sure to watch for roads intersecting Route 616. Sometimes you have to hunt for the road. This is when a good map is indispensable. At the intersection with Route 613, turn right and follow Route 613 for a few tenths of a mile. Route 616 reappears on your left.

On weekdays, views like this along the Parkway are yours alone.

For decades, the early settlers who came from Europe settled on the eastern side of the Appalachians, the mountains acting as a natural barrier separating the seaboard from the rest of the continent. It wasn't until they were hard pressed to find new land that some began following the trails blazed by Daniel Boone and others through the terrifying wilderness deep in the mountains. You may think you live in the sticks in a small town, but even after 400 years of settled history, this area is still sparsely populated. But you know, something is different about this area now. I think it is the advent of the satellite dish. You see them in the yards of even the crummiest houses. They might have a leaky roof, but they can pull in ESPN, by God.

Eventually the road ends near Jordan Mines on Route 18, a wide clean road that follows a narrow valley along Potts Creek. This road ends on Route 311 at Paint Bank; you are now ready to conquer Potts Mountain. Follow Route 311 south. The road gets you warmed up with a few switchbacks and sweepers, then starts to get busy as it climbs the mountain. These are curves familiar to all types of motorcycles, so you'll be assured a good time no matter what you ride. There are some occasional gravel hazards caused by our four-wheeled friends who run a little wide in the curves, a luxury they can afford.

After the fireworks, Route 311 meanders peacefully eastward, passing through the town of New Castle. If lunch is calling, the **Bread Basket Restaurant** is the answer. There aren't many opportunities to grab something to eat out on this route, so lunching at the Bread Basket is one of your few alternatives to packing a picnic lunch. After lunch, you can walk next door into their ice cream parlor for just the right dessert to finish it off.

If you followed Route 311 into town to stop at the restaurant, you'll need to retrace your steps a few tenths of a mile to turn onto Craigs Creek Road, Route 615. This is a beautiful country road which follows Craig Creek for its entire length through dots on the map such as Given, Oriskany, and Silent Dell. At Silent Dell, check out the unusual footbridge crossing the river. Make a right at your intersection with Route 220 and follow it for a short distance, turning left on Route 43 at Eagle Rock. This is a lightly traveled road, easy for making good time. On our ascent of the Blue Ridge, we once again cross paths with the Appalachian Trail. Our entrance to the Blue Ridge Parkway is just a few miles south of Peaks of Otter, a small resort area located directly on the Parkway which takes its name from the two matching formations that rise behind it.

The **Peaks of Otter Lodge** is a popular base for exploring the twin Peaks, so you might time your trip to coincide with an overnight stay here and then set out for some backpacking. If you venture through the area on a fall weekend, be prepared to deal with traffic. The great majority is clustered around the lodge and service center on the Parkway. Some folks just can't move fast enough to get out of their own way, so be patient if you're creeping along. Go during the week or at any time other than peak foliage weekends to avoid the crowd.

After the 45 mph speed limit on the Parkway, you'll probably be wanting a little faster pace. Exit the Parkway at Route 501 and turn left, following it west as it careens down the Blue Ridge. I'll wager you won't go any faster than you did on the Parkway, but it will seem like warp speed! Don't let those fast curves seduce you; there are some tighter surprises lurking ahead, just waiting for you to overcommit yourself.

A place to catch your breath—Peaks of Otter Lodge on the Blue Ridge Parkway.

When Route 130 splits from Route 501, follow 130 into **Natural Bridge.** In 1774, Thomas Jefferson bought Natural Bridge and the surrounding property from King George III for 20 shillings (in today's money about $2.40). Obviously old King George didn't have good advisors working for him; he could easily have gotten twice as much. The natural arch is proclaimed to be one of the seven natural wonders of the world. If you haven't seen it before, it is worth a look. Not wanting a dollar to burn a hole in your pocket, the purveyors of the bridge have thoughtfully erected a few other intellectually stimulating exhibits for your touring pleasure, including a wax museum and a zoo.

The return route follows Route 11 north into Lexington. I like Route 11. I only seem to ride it in small stretches, but I find it rewarding. When you jump on the interstate, you have a tendency to think in miles by the fifties or hundreds. On a road like Route 11, you can anticipate that the next town or village is just a few miles ahead, not 50 or 100. I know I'm not making the same kind of time that I would out on the interstate, but running across those small towns makes me feel like I'm getting somewhere. On the superslab, I'm just lost in the crowd. I think you'll notice this too when you're out there motoring along the highway, this feeling of getting somewhere, of being somewhere. Let's go home.

Trip 17　Surrender at Appomattox

Distance	*220 miles*
Terrain	*Rolling Virginia Piedmont, mountain passes*
Highlights	*Appomattox Court House, Monticello, Ash Lawn, Walton's Mountain Museum, Crabtree Falls*

The Route from Lexington

➜ US 60 east to VA 26
➜ VA 26 south to VA 24
➜ VA 24 east to US 60
➜ US 60 east to US 15
➜ US 15 east to VA 53
➜ VA 53 west to VA 20
➜ VA 20 south to VA 6
➜ VA 6 west to VA 800
➜ VA 800 west to VA 617
➜ VA 617 west to VA 639
➜ VA 639 west to VA 56
➜ VA 56 west to US 11
➜ US 11 south to Lexington

This tour features a good dose of history from three distinct eras. First stop on the tour is the site where the Civil War ended, Appomattox Court House. After that, we will visit Thomas Jefferson's famous home, Monticello, and another home made famous by the TV generation, the boyhood home of Earl Hamner, Jr., creator of the television series *The Waltons.*

The loop begins following Route 60 east over the Blue Ridge Mountains at Buena Vista. This is a good start to the day with a dozen or so miles of smooth, twisty pavement. Once over the Blue Ridge, Route 60 straightens and makes a beeline for Richmond. When you approach the James River, turn right on Route 26 and follow it to Appomattox. A left turn on Route 24 will bring you to the **Appomattox Court House National Historic Park.** On your way to and from

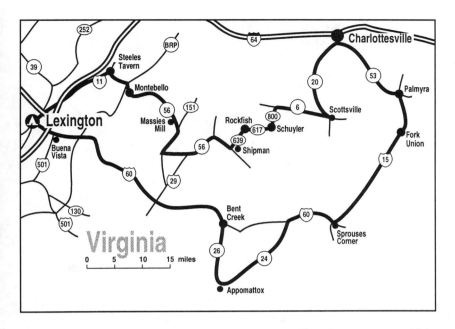

Appomattox, you pass through rolling farm country which, with the exception of a few more houses, looks pretty much the same as it did in April 1865.

The atmosphere at Appomattox Court House is quiet, reverent. A few visitors speak to each other in hushed tones and walk through the courtyard where two armies once met. Here General Robert E. Lee surrendered the Army of Northern Virginia to Union General Ulysses S. Grant, ending the four-year-long Civil War. Though it was finished nearly 130 years ago, the story of the surrender still tugs at the heartstrings.

After a long siege and years of posturing, Grant's army was finally able to sweep through Richmond, the Confederate capital. The Confederate army retreating to the west was cut off from its supplies and stood little chance of gaining reinforcements. Lee's men were nearly starved and poorly clothed. The wounded suffered even more. In his words, "There was nothing left for me to do but go see General Grant." Weary but stone-faced, Lee went to meet the General at the town of Appomattox Court House.

The two men met at the home of Wilmer McLean, a private citizen. Ironically, Grant had occupied McLean's house to use as his headquarters four years earlier at the Battle of Manassas. Wanting to get away from the flying bullets, McLean packed up his family and moved to remote central Virginia. The two generals sat in the parlor of the McLean home where General Grant drafted the surrender. His terms were unusually generous, as an offering to begin the healing process. Word of the surrender spread like wildfire through the ranks. Hardened Southern soldiers, who had suffered so much, openly wept. As Lee returned to his battle-weary men, they swarmed around him, hoping to touch him or his horse, Traveler. Lee's eyes filled with tears as he surveyed his ragtag army. Over and over again, he told his men to go home, plant their crops, and obey the law.

After years of neglect and near ruin, the village of Appomattox Court House has now been restored to its appearance during that era. The home of Wilmer McLean has been fully restored and the reconstructed courthouse holds a museum and visitor center (get your Passport stamped here).

After your visit to the courthouse, continue the loop by following Route 24 until it rejoins Route 60. From here it is a short distance to Route 15 at Sprouses Corner. The touring is easy and wide open with views of the Blue Ridge some 50 miles distant. At the intersection with Route 15, turn left and head north. This section of road is more frequently traveled, but you shouldn't have too much trouble keeping a good pace. At Palmyra, make the left on Route 53, the backdoor entrance to Jefferson's **Monticello** and **Ash Lawn,** James Monroe's home. As you approach Charlottesville, the road regains its playful quality and dark woods hide your approach to the Jefferson estate.

Jefferson's home is probably one of the most widely known and visited of all our American forefathers. Jefferson was a Renaissance man with wide-ranging interests and expertise in many things, including architecture, agriculture, literature, and political science. He secured his place in history by authoring the Declaration of Independence, founding the University of Virginia, and serving as our ambassador to France and as third President of the United States. Jefferson was also an inventor, tinkerer, and wine lover. Monticello is full of the products of his imagination, including a seven-day

The television series "The Waltons" was based on Earl Hamner, Jr.'s life in Schuyler, Virginia.

clock and a writing machine that allowed him to duplicate his correspondence. Strolling the grounds is as much fun as touring the inside. Jefferson planted extensive gardens and you can walk freely among them. Jefferson's horticultural legacy has helped modern gardeners revive old and rare varieties of plants that would have otherwise vanished by now. Thus, the gardens you see are very similar to how they would have appeared in Jefferson's day.

Out of Monticello, follow Route 53 to Route 20 to Scottsville and turn right on Route 6. This road must have been designed by laying a straight edge across a sheet of paper and drawing a line—it's pretty darn straight. However, it is a pretty ride. When you enter a straight-away there is nothing to see ahead but a broad tree-lined avenue. Watch for Route 800 appearing on your left and make the turn. This ends on Route 617 in Schuyler (SKY-ler). Things are abuzz these days in Schuyler, thanks largely to the fame of one native son who wrote stories about his family. They called them "The Waltons" for television, but the real "John Boy" was Earl Hamner, Jr. The enduring popularity of the series brought many people searching for Waltons Mountain and prompted the local community to create the **Waltons Mountain Museum.** The museum includes reproductions of some of the famous scenes in the show, including John Boy's room and the kitchen.

Your route out of Schuyler is probably the same one the Walto . . . , er, Hamners would have taken to get to the main highway, and though it is paved, it isn't any busier today than it was 60 years ago. The hills are small but packed tightly together, and the road busily winds through them, following each small opening between them to trace a path. You might feel tempted to drop a trail of bread crumbs, just in case the particular road you're on should dead end without warning. The easiest way out is to stay on 617 until you intersect 639, a left turn that crosses over a mountain river. When you cross the railroad tracks at Shipman, turn right at the end of the road on Route 56. You are now on your way to another encounter with the Blue Ridge. Stay with Route 56 as it joins Route 29, then splits off again.

Route 56 makes a direct assault on the mountains at the Tye River Gap. This is probably the best crossing of the Blue Ridge and attracts a lot of motorcyclists. The road begins with a long straight aimed right at the mountain, then takes a sharp turn upward. From Massies Mill, it follows the Tye River Gap through the mountains. From this direction your ride is mostly up, so you can take a more aggressive riding posture. The road gets even wilder after you pass the intersection with the Blue Ridge Parkway at the gap. On your descent, watch for broken pavement and gravel hazards. Some of the turns are pitched at incredibly steep angles.

One of the popular watering holes for local riders is the **Country Store** at the Montebello Camping and Fishing Resort. On a sunny day, stop for a sandwich, have a seat on the front porch, and watch the parade of bikes. Feel the need for a stretch? The Crabtree Falls trail near Montebello is an easy hike of about three miles. There are at least five major waterfalls along the trail and many smaller ones. Shack up for the evening at the **Montebello Camping and Fishing Resort** in one of their cabins. A trailer is available for rental, too, in case you want to experience life in a trailer park. The **Crabtree Falls Campground,** located just below Crabtree Falls, features campsites alongside the Tye River.

After descending into the valley, Route 56 meanders through Steeles Tavern and ends on Route 11. Lexington is just a few miles south.

Lodging

Brandywine Recreation Area
US Route 33 East
Brandywine, WV 26802
$8 camping, self-registration.

Colony House Motel
Route 11 North
Lexington, VA 24450
Phone 703-463-2195. Singles from $26 weekdays.

Crabtree Falls Campground
HCR 62, Box 88
VA Route 56 East
Tyro, VA 22976
Phone 703-377-2066. Campsites, $12 per night.

Glen Maury Park
10th Street
Buena Vista, VA 24416
Phone 703-261-7321. Campsites, $9 per night.

Highland Inn
Main Street
Monterey, VA 24465
Phone 703-468-2143. $45 to $64.

Maple Hall
Route 5 Box 223
US 11 South
Lexington, VA 22450
Phone 703-463-6693. $70 to $140 per night, double occupancy.

Montebello Camping and Fishing Resort
P.O. Box 3
VA Route 56 West
Montebello, VA 24464
Phone 703-377-2650. Cabins from $60; trailer $35; campsites
(for tents) $10.00 for two people, each additional person 5 and
older $2.50.

Peaks of Otter Lodge
P.O. Box 489
Milepost 89, Blue Ridge Parkway
Bedford, VA 24523
Phone 703-586-1081. Single, $45 to $50; double, $65 to $90.

Places of Interest

• •

Appomattox Court House National Historical Park
Rt. 24 (approximately 3 miles outside of town)
Appomattox, VA 24522
Phone 804-352-8782. Open 8:30 a.m. to 5 p.m.; June through
Aug., 9 a.m. to 5 p.m. $2 for 17 and up; Golden Age pass honored.

Ash Lawn
Route 6 Box 37
VA Route 53 East
Charlottesville, VA 22901
Phone 804-293-9539. Open daily, Mar. through Oct., 9 a.m. to 6
p.m.; Nov. through Feb., 10 a.m. to 5 p.m. $6 adults; $5.50 senior
citizens; ages 6 to 11, $3.

Cass Scenic Railroad State Park
WV Route 66 West
Cass, WV 24927
Phone 800-CALL WVA. $

The Country Store at the
Montebello Camping and Fishing Resort
P.O. Box 3
VA Route 56 West
Montebello, VA 24464
Phone 703-377-2650. Daily 8 a.m. to 6 p.m. in summer; 8 a.m. to
5 p.m. in winter.

Cyrus McCormick Farm
VPI & SU College of Agriculture and Life Sciences
US Route 11 South
Steeles Tavern, VA 24476
Phone 703-377-2255. Daily, 8:30 a.m. to 5 p.m. Free.

George C. Marshall Museum and Library
P.O. Box 1600
US Route 11 South, Main St.
Lexington, VA 24450-1600
Phone 703-463-7103. Mon. through Sat., 9 a.m. to 5 p.m.; Sun.,
2 p.m. to 5 p.m. On the grounds of the Virginia Military Institute.
Free.

George Washington National Forest
Warm Springs Ranger District
Route 2, Box 30
Hot Springs, VA 24445
Phone 703-839-2521. Information only.

Jackson Memorial Cemetery
Main Street
Lexington, VA 24450
Phone 540-463-2931. Open daily 7 a.m. to 4:30 p.m.

Lee Chapel and Museum
Washington and Lee University
North Main St.
Lexington, VA 24450
Phone 703-463-8768. Mon. through Sat., 9 a.m. to 4 p.m.; Sun.,
2 p.m. to 5 p.m. Free.

Monticello
State Rt. 53
Charlottesville, VA 22901
Phone 804-984-9822. Open 8 a.m. to 5 p.m. Winter hours, 9 a.m.
to 4:30 p.m. $8 per adult; ages 6 to 11, $4; senior citizens, $7.

Museum of American Frontier Culture
P.O. Box 810
US Route 250 & I-64
Staunton, VA 24401
Phone 703-332-7850. Daily, 9 a.m. to 5 p.m. except Christmas
and New Year's. Admission $5.

National Radio Astronomy Observatory
P.O. Box 2
WV Route 28/92
Green Bank, WV 24944
Phone 304-456-2011. Daily tours mid-June through Labor Day.
Weekend tours begin Memorial weekend through mid-June and
Labor Day through mid-October. Call for exact times. Free.

Natural Bridge
P.O. Box 57
US Route 11 South
Natural Bridge, VA 24578
Phone 800-533-1410 or 703-291-2121. Daily, 8 a.m. to 5 p.m.
Call for other times. Adults: $8 for bridge only; $13 for bridge,
wax museum, caverns, and "Drama of Creation" light show and
narration.

Stonewall Jackson House
8 East Washington
Lexington, VA 24450
Phone 703-463-2552. Open daily except New Year's, Easter,
Thanksgiving and Christmas; Mon. through Sat., 9 a.m. to 5 p.m.;
Sun., 1 p.m. to 5 p.m. Tours on the half-hour, beginning at 9 a.m.
Last tour at 4:30 p.m. $4.

Virginia Military Institute Museum
US 11 South, Main St.
Lexington, VA 24450
Phone 703-464-7232. Open daily except Thanksgiving through
New Year's Day; Mon. through Sat., 9 a.m. to 5 p.m.; Sun., 2 p.m.
to 5 p.m. Free.

Waltons Mountain Museum
P.O. Box 124
VA State Route 722
Schuyler, VA 22969
Phone 804-831-2000. Daily, March to November, 10 a.m. to 4
p.m. Adults, $3.

Warm Springs Pools
Intersection of US Route 220 & VA Route 39
Warm Springs, VA 24484
Phone 703-839-5346. Hours vary, call ahead to confirm. $

Woodrow Wilson Birthplace and Museum
24 North Coalter Street
Staunton, VA 24401
Phone 703-885-0897. Daily, 9 a.m. to 5 p.m. Last tour begins at
4 p.m. AAA and senior citizen discounts and student rates available. $6 admission includes home and museum (self-guided).

Restaurants

••

The Bread Basket Restaurant
Main Street
New Castle, VA 24127
Phone 703-864-6372. Mon. through Thurs., 6 a.m. to 9 p.m.; 'til
10 p.m. Fri. and Sat. $

Fat Boys Barbecue Palace
US Route 33 East
Brandywine, VA 26802
Phone 304-249-5591. Mon. through Thurs., 5 a.m. to 9 p.m.; Fri.,
5 a.m. to 10 p.m.; Sat., 6 a.m. to 10 p.m.; Sun., 8 a.m. to 8 p.m. $

High's Restaurant
Main Street
Monterey, VA 24465
Phone 703-468-2330. Mon. through Thurs., 5 a.m. to 8 p.m.; Sundays 'til 3 p.m. $ - $$

Redwood Family Restaurant
US Route 11
Lexington, VA 24450
Phone 540-463-2168. Open daily, 7 a.m. to 10 p.m. $-$$

Southern Inn Restaurant
US 11 North, 37 S. Main St.
Lexington, VA 24450
Phone 703-463-3612. Open daily, 10:30 a.m. to around 9 p.m. $$

Travel Information

• •

Bath County Chamber of Commerce
P.O. Box 718
Hot Springs, VA 24445
Phone 703-468-2550. Information only.

Blue Ridge Parkway
Phone 800-PARKWAY.

Buena Vista Chamber of Commerce
2202 Magnolia Avenue
Buena Vista, VA 24416
Phone 703-261-2880.

Highland County Chamber of Commerce
P.O. Box 223
Monterey, VA 24465
Phone 703-468-2550. Information only.

Lexington Visitors Center
102 East Washington Street
Lexington, VA 24450
Phone 703-463-3777.

Mountaineer Country

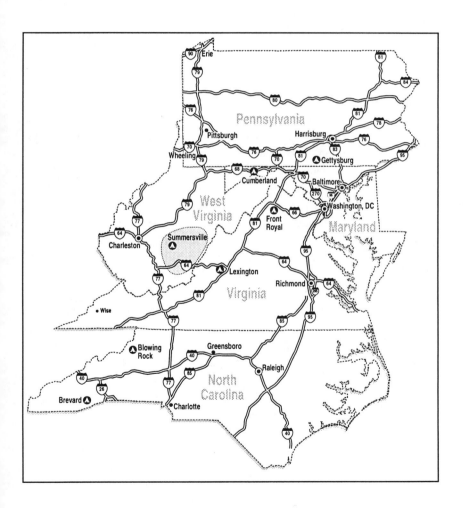

Summersville, W.Va.

●●

Before I started touring by motorcycle a few years ago, the only two points of interest I could recall in West Virginia were the historic town of Harpers Ferry and the Charles Town horse racing track. Thanks to what I heard through the news, I pictured it as a big strip mine that flooded a lot. Why would anyone want to go there? To me, the Mountain State was a 24,282-square-mile question mark.

Motorcycling has erased that question mark for me and has exposed me to more pleasurable experiences in this Appalachian wilderness than by any other means except perhaps hiking or bicycling. I have discovered the dramatic beauty of the New River Gorge, the serenity of the Cranberry Wilderness, the oddity of Beartown State Park. And the people here are as memorable as the landscapes. They don't shy away from conversation. They readily accept you. Touring here is a bit like camping out in your backyard—the experience is new and yet familiar to you at the same time.

When you travel some of the back roads and get deep into the woods, you can easily understand why the first explorers called it a "pleasing tho' dreadful land." At the time they arrived, the woods were full of bears, panthers, and other wild creatures. Records of the first European expeditions seemed to consider it a good day if an expedition didn't lose someone to a wild beast or a slippery incline.

The rest of the state's history is much the same—rough and tumble. Settlers in the area quickly grew uneasy with a colonial Virginia government that was more concerned with events east of the mountains than in their neck of the woods. When civil war broke out, the Union "restored" the government of Virginia in the western part of the state, effectively creating a separate state. Unclear land grants caused many original settlers to sell their claims to enterprising coal magnates for pennies on the dollar, fearing a total loss if their

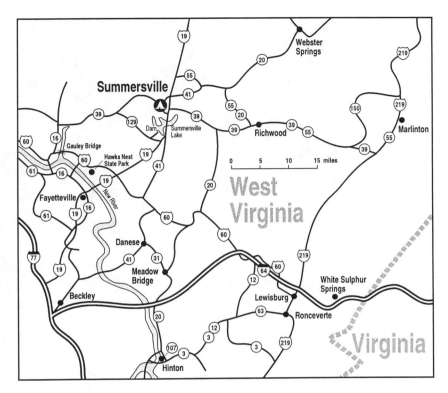

claims were entirely unfounded. And then erupted the much publicized feud between the Hatfields and McCoys that produced the image of the stereotypical drunken, lazy hillbilly.

In a way, the feud began over the matter of who owned a certain razorback hog. After a jury awarded custody of the hog to the Hatfields, things got out of hand. Over a period of 10 or 15 years, the warring clans exchanged gunfire, killing several members of both families. Things really heated up a few years later when a Kentucky deputy began sneaking across the river into West Virginia, capturing Hatfields, and extraditing them the old-fashioned way—tying them up and dragging them across the state line to stand trial. The media got wind of the story and pounced on it. Speculation ran across the country. Would two temperamental backwoods families draw two states to the brink of war? Not really. By that time most of the original parties were dead and the feud just faded away.

Literally, a sign
of times past.

Over the past 20 years, the state has found success in promoting the tourism industry. It has established about two dozen attractive state parks and many miles of unspoiled highway and quiet forest byways to enjoy. I chose Summersville as a starting point for tours in this section because it is centrally located in the heart of the state. In addition to its own share of attractions, it is also close to many other points of interest. It is on the northern edge of **Summersville Lake,** with 4,000 acres of sparkling blue waters just right for attracting boaters, fishermen, and kayakers. (When the Army Corps of Engineers came around to naming the lake's dam, they faced a problem they didn't anticipate in its construction. It was customary to name dams after the towns located closest to them. Summersville wasn't the closest; the town of Gad was. "Gad Dam . . . " Well, you can figure it out for yourself. The Corps no doubt quickly cast aside tradition in this instance and **Summersville Dam** it became.)

Downtown Summersville is like most other American small towns, with a block or two of shops, a courthouse, café, etc., but you don't see any of this by just passing through. US 19 cuts a wide swath to the east of town and it is along this strip that the vast majority of traveler services are located. By turning off the road, though, you'll find some older, quainter establishments such as the **Stonewall Jackson Dining Room.** Just adjacent to the restaurant is the **Mountain State**

Motel, a good place to establish your base camp if you're not camping.

This place looks as though it could have served Stonewall himself. It's a bit of a dive and the decor is, shall we say, mixed. But don't let its looks fool you; it met my three criteria for a good dining experience: a) the silverware and dishes were clean, b) the food was good (great prime rib), and c) it was cheap ($6.95!). Another good bet is **Fran's Family Restaurant** in downtown Summersville. The menu is strictly home cooking, but again, you can eat a tasty meal Mom would approve of for fast-food prices. Out on the strip there are plenty of chain travel services and fast food restaurants. If you're into camping, there are at least two options. Summersville Lake offers camping, as does **Mountain Lake Campground,** a private campground.

The routes I planned fall to the south and east of town, more from circumstance and time than intention. Looking at the places I wanted to visit, most happened to fall in that region. I wouldn't doubt though that the areas north and west aren't equally worth exploring, too. If you have an opportunity to do so, I'd like to hear about what you find.

I hope you take the opportunity to explore West Virginia. When I think of the riding I've done there over the past few years, the old cliché springs to mind: "so many roads . . . so little time."

Trip 18   New River Gorge

••

Distance   *120 miles*

Terrain   *Mostly river valleys and gorges with a small mountain run*

Highlights   *Summersville Dam, Carnifex Ferry, Hawk's Nest State Park, New River Gorge and Bridge, and Five Dollar Frank*

The Route from Summersville

→ WV 39 south to WV 129
→ WV 129 east to Summersville Dam
→ Return WV 129 west to Carnifex Ferry
→ WV 129 west to WV 39
→ WV 39 south joins WV 16
→ WV 16 south and US 60 east at Gauley Bridge
→ US 60 east to Hawks Nest State Park
→ Return US 60 west to WV 16
→ On WV 16 south, turn right at second light after intersection with US 19, 1.5 miles to Fayette Airport
→ Return to WV 16/US 19 intersection
→ US 19 north to New River Gorge Bridge Visitor Center
→ US 19 south to WV 61/16 south
→ Follow WV 61 south at split
→ WV 61 south to WV 41
→ WV 41 north to Summersville

Over the course of researching the routes for this book, I have learned many valuable lessons. On this trip, for example, I learned that riding a motorcycle isn't as much an act of defiance as most people think. Being a rider doesn't mean you are any better prepared to laugh in the face of death or any more eager to meet your maker than those who don't. All of this I learned in the first 30 seconds of a 20-minute plane ride with a fellow everyone knows as Five Dollar Frank.

The road to enlightenment begins in Summersville and follows Route 39 west out of town. Route 39 is fairly typical of most roads in the area: where the valley narrows it follows a creek bed and begins to twist and sway; where the valley

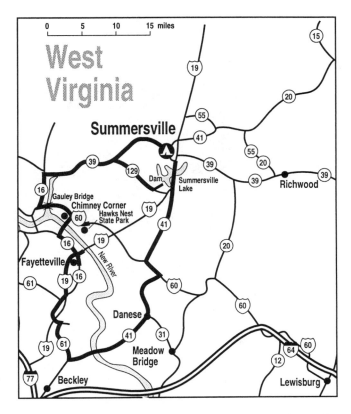

widens, it stretches out and flies straight. You will see the good and the bad of West Virginia along Route 39. Some communities look clean and prosperous, others as though they've been bombed. Hang a left on Route 129 to go out to the **Summersville Dam** and the battlefield at **Carnifex Ferry.** This road isn't heavily traveled. It runs over the hills and along the ridges just south of town near the Summersville Dam.

Summersville Dam holds back the waters of the Gauley River, creating a 4,000-acre lake. Route 129 passes over the top of the dam. Pull off to one side and you can gaze upon the boulder strewn back side. Near the bottom of the dam are two pipes, each about 20 feet in diameter, that allow water to pass through the dam and continue down the river. The pressure exerted is so great the water blows horizontally out of the pipes and about 30 feet downstream before landing in the riverbed. At the put-in point near the base of the dam there's

*Parking is never
a problem at the
Prince, W. Va.
railroad depot.*

a sign warning kayakers that if they hear three short blasts, they can expect a sudden rise in the water level. No kidding.

When you leave the dam, double back toward Route 39. You'll have to look carefully for the turn to Carnifex Ferry Battlefield. It isn't well marked. About two miles west of the dam, Route 129 makes a sharp right. A smaller, unmarked road to the battlefield branches off to the left at the curve. (Watch for a large billboard advertising the Mountain Lake Campground—it's located along Route 129 at the curve in question.) Make the left turn along this pleasant country lane to reach the battlefield.

The battle at Carnifex Ferry was one of dozens of moves and counter moves conducted by both sides during the War Between the States. According to accounts of the battle which took place in September 1861, a contingent of about 6,000 Union soldiers swept through Summersville to re-establish a supply line broken by the rebels in earlier action. The Confederates, outmanned three to one, had time to dig in. They riddled the Union ranks with fire and suffered only 20 casualties themselves.

Despite suffering a rout, the outlook was undimmed for some Union soldiers like Rutherford B. Hayes. According to him, "[West Virginia] is the land of blackberries. We are a great grown-up armed blackberry party and we gather untold

Fill 'er up!

quantities." I'm guessing Hayes, who went on to become the nineteenth U.S. president, didn't see much trench warfare.

Exiting the battlefield, return to WV 129 and head west to WV 39. Turn left and continue south on WV 39, passing though a dozen small villages until you reach Gauley Bridge. Make the left turn on Route 16/60 and head east. You are now following the course the ancient New River has traveled for thousands of years.

Where US 60 and WV 16 split at Chimney Corner, you'll find a good lunch stop at the **Ain't You Et Yet Cafe.** The cafe is filled with decorations from local crafters and shelves stocked with foodstuffs in colorful packages like Shoo Fly Pie mix (featuring real shoos and flies!), licorice, and trail mixes. Meals are good, though hearty eaters might need to order two sandwiches. Their specialty is cheese, made fresh on the premises with nothing artificial added. Pack some along for a snack later, or in a real pinch, to patch a tire (get the semi-soft cheese for patching purposes)!

Follow Route 60 east from the cafe to **Hawk's Nest State Park.** You'll enjoy this section of road as you climb out of the gorge. Rising higher you can see the gorge below and a thin glittering ribbon that is the New River. The best views are from the park. Hawk's Nest has two sections, upper and lower. The upper portion of the park overlooks the New River Gorge at a point where it forms a lake. Down by the lake, there are the usual water diversions such as row boats and

paddle boats. You can also arrange a pontoon boat ride up-river to the New River Gorge Bridge. To navigate the rough terrain between the lake and the lodge above, there is an aerial tramway which is an attraction in itself. At the lodge, ask for a room with a view. There's no extra charge.

The lower area features a hilltop museum constructed by the Civilian Conservation Corps in the early '30s. What looks like a chalet is perched on top of the hill over the gorge. Massive stonework and tremendous wooden beams inside display the craftsmanship of the CCC workers who assembled it. The chalet is filled with a collection of Indian, pioneer, and Civil War artifacts. If you feel in the mood for a hike there are trails which lead to views of the gorge and range from 100 yards to about two miles.

When you leave the park, your best bet for a better ride is to simply retrace your steps to the cafe at Chimney Corner and hang a left, continuing to follow WV 16 and the river into Fayetteville. It was here in this bustling little town that I caught up with a West Virginia legend, Frank K. Thomas, better known to everyone as "Five Dollar Frank" for his $5 airplane rides over the New River Gorge. If you're not sure how to get to Frank's airport, just ask. I stopped at a gas station to ask directions and without hesitation, I was pointed in the right direction. A fella in line heard me asking for directions, though, and said, "You going up with ol' Five Dollar? You're a braver man than me, buddy." How reassuring.

Frank's private airport, **Fayette Airport,** consists of a grass strip runway in his backyard, along with a ragtag collection of buildings cluttered with a variety of flying memorabilia and junk. It is perhaps the only airport in the world with a display of various execution devices. Looking around at the buildings, the planes, and the runway, you might suddenly develop a fear of flying, if you didn't have one already. I was already committed to doing it, so I wasn't going to let anything stop me.

The most exciting part of the trip was taking off. With the precision of an ace fighter pilot, Frank taxied to the end of the runway and whipped the plane, an aging Cessna, around into the prevailing wind. Everything in the plane shook, including the dashboard, which rattled as though it was about to drop out at any moment. We taxied, and taxied, and then taxied some more. I felt like I was riding in The Little Plane That Could. I found myself reciting "I think it can, I think it can" over and over until finally we coasted just clear of the trees at the end of the runway.

Once in the air, the plane settled into a comfortable rhythm and we soared over the beauty of the New River Gorge and the bridge. After seeing the bridge, it was time to land. Frank's approach takes you right over the center of town and through backyards nearly low enough to snag the clothes hanging out to dry. All this is old hat to Frank—he dropped over the neighbor's swimming pool and plopped down on the back forty with ease. A perfect landing. Where did you say the restroom was?

Frank is more than just a pilot, he's also a painter and a writer. I bought a copy of his self-published book, *It Is This Way With Men Who Fly,* and it's all Frank. Here's the preface: "This book—its short stories of the experiences of others and myself—with those that have known flying success, failure, sadness, joy, tension, anger, body pain, mistakes, carelessness, elements of weather, the socialist conspiracy against small business, and worst of all, the harassment of the armchair bureaucrats." (There's a sentence in there somewhere, I just know it.) It too is $5.

Next I visited the **New River Gorge National River Visitor Center** just north of Fayetteville on Route 19 to get another look at the bridge. No sooner had I pulled into the parking lot and gotten my helmet off than I heard the buzz of a certain Cessna and watched as it plotted a familiar course through the sky. Long live Frank Thomas.

The New River Gorge Bridge is the world's largest steel arch bridge, completed in 1977 at a cost of nearly $37 million. It is the highest bridge in the East, standing 876 feet tall. Before the bridge was completed, the trip from one side of the gorge to the other took nearly an hour; now it takes about 30 seconds. You have to see it to believe it—it is impressive. In fact, if you've seen the television commercial where Chevrolet drops a truck over a bridge on a bungee cord, then you've seen it. On the third Saturday in October, the bridge is closed to traffic and a festival is held on the bridge complete with parachutists, bungee jumping (no, no, after you, I insist), and rappelling.

If you carry a National Parks passport, don't forget to get yours stamped at the visitor center. There are several trails from the visitor center, including one which will take you down to the river for great photo opportunities. Just remember, every step you walk down, you have to walk back up!

The other popular diversion here is river running. The New River Gorge is widely recognized as one of the best white water rides anywhere. In many areas, the river is about a mile wide, but it squeezes down to a few hundred feet through the gorge and the result is a ride that promises to be bumpier than even Frank's ten-minute flying tour. In season, the traffic down the river is nearly bumper to bumper. There are a dozen or more companies that organize raft trips on the New. Two of the more established companies are **Class VI River Runners** and **Wildwater Expeditions Unlimited.** Touring the New on a raft will allow you to see the New River Gorge bridge from the best perspective, save perhaps Frank's thrill-a-minute plane ride. Then again, for a couple extra bucks, you could probably get Frank to fly under the bridge, too.

When you are ready to leave the gorge, follow Route 19 south out of the area toward Beckley. Turn left to follow Route 61/16 south away from town. Just a few miles out and you've returned to the peaceful countryside. To return, make

It's a dizzying pleasure to view the New River Gorge from Terra Firma.

a left on Route 41 and follow it north all the way to Summersville. This route also crosses the gorge many miles upstream from the main bridge. It plunges down one side of the gorge, crossing the river on a dilapidated steel bridge near the river, then dutifully climbs the other side of the ridge. The scenery is spectacular on both sides and is a pleasant ride to end the day.

Trip 19   Greenbrier Valley

• •

Distance	*175 miles, 195 with extension*
Terrain	*Moderate hills, mostly valley touring along routes following rivers*
Highlights	*Babcock State Park, White Sulphur Springs, Lewisburg*

The Route from Summersville

→ US 19 south to WV 41
→ WV 41 south to WV 31 (Meadow Bridge Road)
→ Meadow Bridge Road to WV 20
→ WV 20 south to WV 107
→ WV 107 east to WV 3
→ WV 3 east to WV 3/12
→ WV 3/12 east to WV 12
→ WV 12 east to WV 63
→ WV 63 east to US 219*
→ US 219 north to I-64
→ I-64 west to WV 20
→ WV 20 north to WV 20/US 60
→ WV 20/US 60 east to Charmco
→ WV 20 north to WV 39
→ WV 39 west to Summersville

*Alternate Route

→ US 219 north to US 60
→ US 60 west to WV 41
→ WV 41 north to US 19
→ US 19 north to Summersville

The Greenbrier Valley should do much to dispel the notion that West Virginia is one big strip mine. As a touring area, it has much in common with its better known counterpart to the east, the Shenandoah Valley. Large farms stretch across the lowland against a backdrop of the ever-present Alleghenies. Roads meander through the valley, bending where they parallel rivers and cross ridges.

Our route through the Greenbrier begins by following US 19 south to Route 41 south out of Summersville. Route 41 is a beautiful back road that is lightly traveled and an entertaining ride. It intersects with Route 60 and follows that route for a short distance before turning south again.

The first spot you might like to visit along this route is **Babcock State Park.** Located on Route 41 about five miles south of the intersection with US 60, this park is well off the beaten path. It would make a perfect place to set up a base camp for your explorations in this region. In addition to inexpensive campsites, they also rent cabins in standard and economy flavors, the standard having a separate kitchen equipped with appliances and fireplace. All of them feature everything you would need to set up housekeeping. This option will appeal to those who travel by credit card. The park features a number of diversions, including fishing, swimming, boating, and 20 miles of hiking trails.

A grist mill located near the visitor center makes a good photo opportunity. This particular mill is actually reconstructed from several old mills in other parts of the state which had either burned or fallen into disrepair. It continues to grind corn and wheat into products which you can buy at the gift shop. There is a restaurant on the premises which is open for breakfast, making this a promising destination for a morning ride even if you don't want to do the whole loop.

You can easily get lost in your riding and forget about sticking to the route, as I found myself doing throughout my rides in this area. I guess it was a combination of perfectly warm, sunny days that were just right for cruising and the beautiful scenery that caused my to ride 20 miles past my intended turn at Danese. When you're doing this kind of riding, getting lost isn't a big deal; actually it's kind of nice. Realizing my mistake, I made the return to Danese and then turned onto Meadow Ridge Road.

After a stretch of seven miles or so, you'll arrive in the village of Meadow Bridge. Just across the railroad tracks is a general store which is a good spot to stop for a drink and a dime's worth of conversation. An older fellow named Harold joined me on the porch and we started to chat, trading the usual "nice weather" and "where are you from" tidbits. I found that my new acquaintance was not only a good talker, he could often carry both sides of the conversation. Somewhere in the middle of a long tale about his latest fly fishing trip, a train crawled through town with eight engines on the front and three on the rear. The noise was deafening and conversation was impossible, but it didn't matter to my front porch friend. Harold was lost in his remembrance, somewhere in the middle of the river now, casting as he talked. I just kept nodding at the right times and he kept casting. The noise from the train was just beginning to subside when he reached the end of his tale, "Now ain't that the darndest thing you ever heard?"

In Meadow Bridge, pick up Route 20 and follow it south through Elton and Green Sulphur Springs to Sandstone Falls. Route 20 is another road made just for pleasure touring. The ride becomes a bit more dramatic once you cross under the interstate at Sandstone and head toward Hinton. First you make a steep climb as you cross one of the higher ridges in the valley, and the route enters the New River Gorge, paralleling the river all the way to Hinton. Be sure to stop at Sandstone Falls, the largest falls on the river. These falls aren't especially high but their breadth makes them distinct. The entire riverbed looks as though an earthquake tugged at it until it cracked and dropped a few dozen feet.

The outskirts of Hinton arrive long before the town does. When you first see the city limit sign, the only signs of civilization are a few dilapidated buildings and a high school across the river. This, as it turns out, is only the greater Hinton metropolitan area. Downtown is a few miles further south. Hinton is an old company town. You can tell this by the streets lined with nearly identical houses stacked up the side of the hill like rows of dominoes. The older downtown part of Hinton is a cluster of faceless brick buildings with a few scattered tenants. Looking for a place to eat, I caught a glimpse of the now-defunct Hinton Hot Dog Stand and decided it might be as much fun just to see what it was like as it would be to eat there.

Five or six men sat around the lunch counter while a young woman behind the counter chatted with them and simultaneously filled lunch orders with a practiced hand. The dilemma of the day was Larry's. He was having trouble with his brother-in-law, Junior, who had recently borrowed Larry's pickup and bass boat. Having run a little wide in a tight corner, Junior had launched the boat and trailer off a steep cliff and into the tops of the trees a few hundred yards below. Too bad the trailer didn't take the truck and him with it, Larry said.

Across the counter another fellow was complaining about his sister-in-law, Mary Jane, who was getting on his nerves. Someone suggested that maybe they ought to introduce Junior to her. "Let's do that," Larry agreed. "They deserve each other."

Upon cruising through Hinton, I found the other side of town showed a bit more promise than downtown. The activity around a new building being raised on the outskirts of town was furious, and as I passed by a large sign was just being lifted into place. Yep, when the Golden Arches are raised, Hinton will have officially arrived.

Just south of Hinton on Route 20 are the **Bluestone and Pipestem State Resort Parks.** The latter is famous for its Mountain Creek Lodge, which is tucked away in Bluestone Canyon and is only accessible by aerial tram. Both parks offer the usual array of hiking, horseback riding, and water sports. Pipestem also features 27 holes of golf.

Turning east on Route 3, I began following the Greenbrier River. This area is more built up than I had anticipated, with a smattering of little towns and villages along the riverbank. The road is mostly flat and straight because the river valley is wide, giving you ample opportunity to enjoy the sights along the road. You run into the darndest things sometimes, especially when you're not looking for them. I sat in a short line of traffic where some road construction was taking place, waiting to be waved through. When our turn came, we proceeded slowly through the work zone and I saw a statue labeled "John Henry." I dropped out of the line of traffic and stopped for a closer look.

The Big Bend Tunnel nearby was one of many railroad construction projects taking place in this area in the 1870s when the introduction of steam-powered equipment knocked many men out of work. Legend has it that Big John Henry believed that he could outwork any machine and made a bet to prove it. Big John beat the machine at laying track, but like any good tragic hero, he laid down and died, exhausted from the effort.

At Alderson, follow Route 12 when it splits from Route 3. In just a few miles, you'll pick up Route 63 which continues to roughly parallel the river. Five miles later you'll enter the town of Ronceverte (French for Greenbrier) and traffic will increase. It is interesting to note that even though Greenbrier County is a little larger than the state of Rhode Island, its population is only 3.5% of that state's. Turn left on US 219 and follow it north to Lewisburg.

Downtown Lewisburg is an historic district that is worth hopping off the bike for a closer look. The district comprises a few square blocks of stately homes and shops filled with antiques, crafts, and quilts. If you wish to make a two-day trip

John Henry was a steel-drivin' man.

of it, this is a great place to stop for the evening. The whole corridor between White Sulphur Springs and Lewisburg is a traveler's mecca, featuring the majestic **Greenbrier Hotel,** the antique-filled **General Lewis Inn,** and the **Old White Motel.** If you're camping, **Greenbrier State Forest** offers campsites and cabins. Of course, if you want to go all-out, the Greenbrier is it. The Greenbrier has always been an elegant resort and its size and grandeur will utterly amaze you (so will the price). Remember, though, honored guests such as yourself may be able to find a special deal or get a weekend rate. The General Lewis is a good choice when you want more intimate accommodations and service that is on par with the Greenbrier.

For this trip you can return to Summersville in one of two ways. The longer route follows Interstate 64 to Green Sulphur Springs. From here pick up WV 20 again and turn north. You'll pass through Meadow Bridge once again where you're likely to find my buddy Harold at the general store talking to another unsuspecting passerby he's managed to buttonhole.

Continuing north, Route 20 intersects with US 60 just west of Rainelle. Turn right onto WV 20/US 60 east through Rainelle to Charmco. Follow WV 20 north to WV 39 at Nettie, then turn west on WV 39 to Summersville.

A more direct route is to follow US 60 out of Lewisburg. Route 60 is recognized as the scenic corridor through this part of the region. I'd say that's true once you get past Rainelle. Just outside of Rainelle you encounter switchbacks followed by a valley run, and then some more curves. About ten miles out of Rainelle you'll run across WV 41 again. Follow WV 41 north to US 19 to return to Summersville.

While you're in the area, don't forget to keep an eye out for a pickup decorated with tin cans and a "Just Married" sign, towing a patched-up bass boat. You can bet two good ol' boys at the Hot Dog Stand will be grinning from ear to ear.

*"Turn sideways
to enter."*

Trip 20   Cranberry Fields Forever

• •

Distance   *190 miles*

Terrain   *Small mountain passes through national forest then high road through Cranberry Glades. More small passes and back roads through Greenbrier Valley on return.*

Highlights *Cranberry Glades, Falls of Hills Creek, Pearl S. Buck birthplace, Droop Mountain State Park, Beartown State Park*

The Route from Summersville

→ WV 39 east (joined first by WV 20 north and then WV 55 east) to WV 150

→ WV 150 east to WV 55/US 219

→ US 219 south to I-64

→ I-64 west to US 60

→ US 60 west to WV 41

→ WV 41 north to Summersville

The last Ice Age drew to a close some 10,000 to 15,000 years ago and though none of us were around to bid it farewell, we can still see some of the effects of it to this day. On this tour, we will visit the Cranberry Glades, a remnant of that Ice Age heritage, roam the Highland Scenic Highway, and explore the nooks and crannies of Beartown State Park.

This tour is easy to auto-pilot because there are only a few major routes. But there is a lot to see and do. We begin by heading east on West Virginia 39 and pass through the town of Richwood. On passing through, I discovered a couple of interesting tidbits about the town.

For instance, Richwood is the home of the world's largest wooden clothespin factory, surely a fact you will want to readily command as you play Really Trivial Pursuit. Richwood is also known as the Ramp Capital of the World (make that two facts to have on hand). Ramps are actually wild leeks and they are the first growth to appear in the late winter, signaling the arrival of spring.

If you sail into town in early April, you will arrive just in time for the annual Ramp Festival, an old Appalachian tradi-

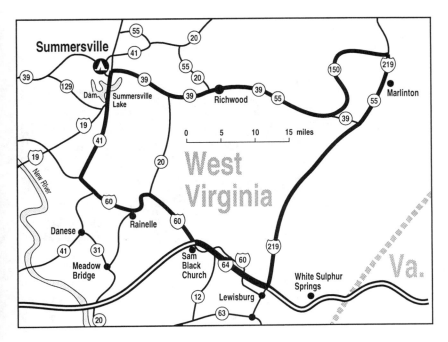

tion dating back to frontier days that heralds the coming of spring. Ramps are gathered in tremendous quantities and served with corn pone, potatoes, and beans. You should be warned though, ramps linger on the breath like garlic. If your riding partner eats any, you had best have some yourself. One other note, there are plenty of opportunities to have a picnic lunch in the quiet solitude of the Monongahela National Forest on this loop, and few chances to pick up the groceries. Richwood is your best bet for that.

East of town you enter the scenic Highland Trace corridor. This is a soothing ride with no competing traffic and those vehicles you do happen upon can be easily dispensed of with a quick twist of the throttle. The first stop you'll want to make is the Falls of Hills Creek. Unfortunately, the trail was closed when I passed by because some portions of the steps were being rebuilt, but it will likely be reopened when you get there. The full trail is about three-quarters of a mile long and descends a steep gorge to a series of falls.

The entrance to the Cranberry Glades Botanical Area is just a little further ahead. It is part of a nearly 53,000-acre wilderness and back country area which is closed to all forms

Cranberry Fields, brought to you by the Ice Age!

of motorized travel. The glades are an unusual feature of the area, dating back to the time when massive sheets of ice moved southward, bringing with them elements of flora more commonly associated with Canadian climates. The bog, a perpetually wet area, became a harbor for cranberries and other plant life uncommon to the surrounding area such as orchids and carnivorous plants like pitcher plants.

The trail through the bog area follows a boardwalk for the entire half-mile route. The chances are good that you will be the only person in the area, especially if you go during the week. The trail begins winding through an area of dense vegetation almost like a jungle. Suddenly, the trail opens into a vast treeless area where the ground is covered by millions of delicate vines. Cranberries, the sign says. I laid down on the boardwalk and got almost close enough to the ground to kiss it and I didn't see a single blessed one. Your luck may vary.

What impressed me as much as the flora was the sense of isolation. No traffic sounds, no jets overhead, no chain saws buzzing. It's a sense easterners of the concrete jungle rarely experience. I guess that's why I felt like there must be at least a dozen pairs of eyes watching me from the thicket. A grasshopper suddenly lunged from its perch and the sound was loud enough to startle me. I had this strange sense that the last remaining undiscovered panther on the east coast would bound out of the forest and devour me.

The boardwalk follows the bog for a few hundred feet, then turns into the forest again. Another small clearing appears, and it is here that you will find the insect-eating pitcher plants. These insidious little plants don't capture their prey in the same dramatic way as the Venus flytrap. The pitcher plant grows in such a way that when an insect ventures inside, it can't get out. The leaves of the pitcher plant excrete a digestive juice that dissolves its prey. What an ugly way to go. These are pretty easy to spot, though I couldn't find any unwitting insects to drop into the plant. Where was that darn grasshopper?

The **Cranberry Mountain Visitor Center,** just east of the botanical area on Route 39, has the standard visitor center stock-in-trade: museum, bookstore, and restrooms. The book selection is specific to West Virginia and includes a section of West Virginia mountain music on cassette. I picked up a copy of some homegrown music by Dwight Diller, a Pocahontas County native whose cover for the album *Hold On* bills his tunes as "Neo-Orthodox Old-Time Mountain Music from West Virginia (without Yodeling)." I should point out that most people would call this "bluegrass," but that term didn't originate until the 1940s. This is authentic mountain music, the kind that leaves a lingering taste of sour mash in your mouth. I popped the cassette into the Wing's tape deck and set off northward on Route 150, the Highland Scenic Highway, adding my own unique vocal talents to some of those tunes in a way Dwight could never have imagined.

The Highland Scenic Highway is touring bliss. The roadway follows a high trace through the mountains, affording long peaceful views with nothing but green all the way to the horizon. If you brought a picnic lunch, you'll find several fine places to stop. I counted traffic on two fingers. This is not a curve-hugging road. It's long and straight and open and the kind of road that makes you slow down to enjoy the ride. Me and Dwight were having a right fine old time traveling down that road together singing "Lizards in the Spring," the "Yew Pine Mountains," and that "Cluck Old Hen." Too bad that road couldn't go on forever. It ended on Route 219 all too soon.

Route 219 is good for some thrills as you work your way down toward Marlinton. If you didn't pack a picnic lunch and you're getting hungry, you can stop by the **Frontier Restaurant** just a mile or two north of town. If it's busy, don't be in a hurry—they'll get around to you sooner or later.

A neat place to get lost is the **Pocahontas County Historical Society Museum,** just a mile or two south of town. The museum houses a collection of antiques and artifacts from Pocahontas County. If you like old gadgets and oddities, this is your place. I spent close to an hour wandering the two stories of goodies and browsing through the special Pearl S. Buck room. One display case features postmarked letters and postcards from all the post offices in Pocahontas County, many of which are now closed. It gives you a sense of how many once-thriving towns and villages ceased to exist when the lumber supply disappeared. Another personal favorite of mine was the table-top flyshooer.

The road that leads to **Watoga State Park** isn't numbered on any maps, but it is clearly marked as a left turn off of US 219 as you head south out of Marlinton. It's off the beaten path by an easy eight to ten miles. At 10,100 acres, Watoga is West Virginia's largest state park. Watoga is a Cherokee word meaning "river of islands," which aptly describes the Greenbrier River. Watoga has 33 cabins for rent in addition to two separate and fully-equipped campgrounds. It is also strategically located along the Greenbrier River Trail.

Returning to US 219, you'll encounter three stops clumped together. First is the **Pearl S. Buck Birthplace Museum.** Buck was born in 1892 in this house built by her great-grandfather. Her missionary parents took her with them to China when she was just six months old. Author of *The Good Earth,* Buck won the Pulitzer Prize for Literature in 1932, followed by the Nobel Prize for Literature in 1938. She is only one of two Americans ever to receive both of these awards.

A little further down the road is the entrance to Droop Mountain State Park. Droop Mountain was the scene of the largest Civil War engagement in West Virginia. The neatest feature of the park is a stacked log tower you can climb for views from an elevation of 3,100 feet.

Scan the ridges at Droop Mountain's wooden tower.

The last stop on the list is also a state park protecting the unusual geology of the area; Beartown State Park, just a few miles south of Droop Mountain. Beartown is noted for its unusual sandstone formations. It looks as though a prehistoric gopher dug a series of interconnecting tunnels along the hillside and over the years the tunnels collapsed, creating alleyways through the rocks. An elaborate boardwalk allows you to explore the area without damaging it.

The remainder of the trip through the Greenbrier Valley is easy touring on the big shoulders of Route 219. Entering Lewisburg, follow Interstate 64 west toward Beckley. This is not potholed, high-volume interstate like I-40 or the Pennsylvania Turnpike, this is more like your own personal concrete ribbon into the heart of the Mountain State. However, you don't want to follow it all the way into Beckley. Your best bet is to pick up Route 60 when it departs from the interstate at Sam Black Church. Route 60 gets twisty when it encounters a sizable ridge; other sections bulldoze straight through the hills. You will encounter some traffic through Rainelle, but once past that, anything that gets in your way can be dusted with a twist of the wrist. To complete the loop, follow WV 41 north to US 19. Turn right on US 19 north to return to Summersville.

Trip 21   The Gable End of Hell

••

Distance   *190 miles*

Terrain   *Small mountain passes through Monongahela National Forest, and farming valleys*

Highlights   *Cass Scenic Railroad*

The Route from Summersville
→ WV 41 east to WV 55
→ WV 55 east to WV 20
→ WV 20 north to WV 15
→ WV 15 east to US 219
→ US 219 south to WV 150
→ WV 150 south to WV 55/39
→ WV 55/39 west to WV 39
→ WV 39 west to Summersville

The lumberjacks who transformed the quiet town of Cass into a wide open Dodge City each payday are gone. The ringing of axes and the thunder of falling timber no longer echo through this part of the eastern Alleghenies. The sawmill—a massive building packed with belts, pulleys, blades, timber, and men—is gone. Cruising through the town of Cass gives little indication of what used to be the essence of this town's existence—until you reach the Cass Scenic Railroad.

Getting to Cass is a simple matter. Follow Route 41 east out of town through suburbia. Pick up Route 55 east when the two routes intersect. Stay on Route 55 until it joins Route 20 north, and then follow that. I was a little surprised at the amount of traffic on the road in the morning (almost a genuine rush hour), but it was heading in the opposite direction. The northern loop of the route runs out of traffic around Camden on Gauley. Despite the harsh weather and heavy use, West Virginia's state roads are in good condition. Except for the occasional speed zone you can keep it at full throttle.

Route 20 passes along the Gauley River on the northern border of the Monongahela National Forest and the Cran-

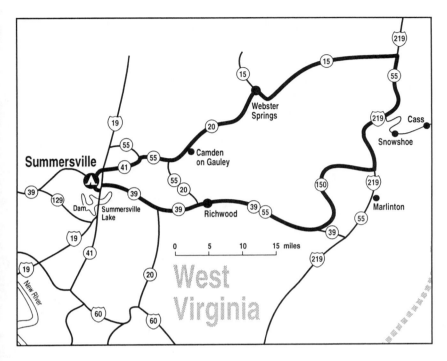

berry Recreation Area (see the Cranberry Fields Forever tour, Trip 20) before intersecting with Route 15 at Webster Springs. Turn right and follow it east until arriving at Route 219. Turn right here and head south, deep into the National Forest. I think Route 219 is perhaps my favorite corridor through this area because the road runs at a tangent to the Appalachians. You get a few miles of mountain passes followed by a scenic valley ride and more mountains. The process repeats itself along the length of US 219, a handy fact to keep in mind if you're planning another ride along this route. The turnoff for Cass is prominently marked as a left off Route 66 near Snowshoe.

The road surface is less refined with some tight, off-camber turns that more aggressive riders will enjoy if only to wear down trailing metal parts. It's hard to believe, but little cow-paths like this were once the main roads through the mountains. They weren't much more than muddy lanes. Can you imagine trying to get through during the spring thaw? Muddy bogs would be more like it.

One of my favorite stories about traveling through this area comes from accounts of two brothers who had more than their share of trouble along this route. The Trotter brothers had the contract to deliver mail from Staunton, Va. to Parkersburg, W. Va. After several complaints about their sporadic service, the Postmaster General sent a reprimand from his cozy little office in Washington, D.C. The brothers had no doubt received some of these complaints in person and this letter was just about the last straw. They responded to the Postmaster's letter, "If you knock the gable end of Hell out and back it up against Cheat Mountain and rain fire and brimstone for forty days and forty nights, it won't melt the snow enough to get your damned mail through on time." The Trotters never heard the Postmaster complain again.

When you roll into the town of Cass, you'll find a quiet, almost sleepy little burg nestled beneath Cheat Mountain. Things were different at the turn of the century when the timber operation was in full swing in Cass. It was by most accounts a large den of sin and iniquity which thrived on the appetites of hard-living lumberjacks. After working from dawn to dusk seven days a week for months on end, these fellas would get their pay and then head into town for some worldly diversions. The town teemed with saloons, women of ill repute, games of chance, and frequent gunplay. By the mid-1900s, the timber gave out and the town was on its way to becoming extinct just like so many other small lumber towns. However, fate intervened when the state bought the railroad and most of the town and set it aside as **Cass Scenic Railroad State Park** in 1963.

The highlight of the park is a ride up the mountain in converted flatbed cars pulled by Shay locomotives. The Shay engine is a wonderfully complex machine and a triumph of engineering which would be tough to match even today. It was designed to reach timber in the higher elevations that couldn't be reached by ordinary engines. It had to handle heavy loads and negotiate frail tracks laid on steep ground, as much as an 11 percent grade. When you're on the road and see a warning about a 9 percent grade, you know the descent will be steep. Imagine descending that kind of grade hauling a few thousand tons of hardwood!

While you can have a good time just gawking at them sitting still, they're even more fun to ride. If you want a really

An engineer lovingly tends a stray locomotive at Cass Railroad State Park.

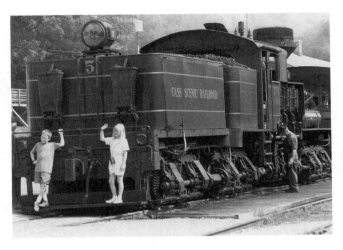

good look at how they work, board the car nearest the engine. The smoke and noise is tremendous when these giant black beasts get underway, but the real work begins on the slopes. Smoke and cinders begin to rain down in tremendous clouds so thick the entire mountain range is obscured until you change directions. The smell of burning coal fills your lungs and permeates your clothing. And you'll nearly jump out of your skin the first time the engineer grabs a handful of steam whistle as he approaches an intersection.

You can take two different runs, depending on the amount of time you have. One train runs three times a day to an intermediate point at Whittaker Station, once a regular stop along the line and now the place where dinner trains stop during the summer season. That ride lasts about an hour and a half. For a longer ride and even more tremendous views, the ride to Bald Knob leaves once a day at noon and requires four and a half hours to make the run. Fall color runs are nothing short of spectacular.

The Whittaker Station run is $9 and Bald Knob is $12. That price also includes admission to the wildlife and histori-cal museums. You can also walk along a footpath that passes by the old sawmill site and eventually leads to the machine shop where you are invited to visit the engineers who keep these remarkable engines running. Once you deboard the train back in the village, take the time to walk around and visit the restored homes and shops. Cass is another company town, with rows of crackerbox homes in varying states of repair. You can rent a restored company home here, and, like at other West Virginia state parks, it comes with everything you need. Be sure to call the 800 number and ask for a current calendar and rate schedule, because there are many special runs and events. Of the many attractions I have visited in West Virginia, Cass has the greatest entertainment value for the dollar.

While you're in the area, you may wish to visit the National Radio Astronomy Observatory (see Highlander Loop tour, Trip 14) or visit the Cranberry Glades (see Cranberry Fields Forever tour, Trip 20). Retrace your steps along Route 66 to Route 219 and follow it south. Turn right and follow the Highland Scenic Highway (Route 150) along the tops of the mountains. When you're touring a route through a remote area like this it's easy to understand why some people in the Appalachians seem to be from a different time. That kind of isolation also breeds superstition and a deep-rooted belief in witches, demons, and past life experiences.

Around here they still tell the tale of a man who had strong flashbacks of something that happened to him in a former life. He could clearly recall a vision of his two brothers in a past life murdering a man. He remembered helping them move the body into a limestone cave and placing it on a shallow ledge in the cave. He never told anyone about it because he thought it wasn't real. Some time later, his son was exploring limestone caves in the Blue Ridge area, and taking photographs of them. One of the pictures looked remarkably like the vision his father kept seeing, prompting him to tell his family about it. His son revisited the cave with the intention of proving to his father that the vision was only imagination. He entered the cave, walked a short distance, and found a ledge. Shining a flashlight over the edge, he discovered a human skeleton, fossilized by water dripping through the limestone. It was later determined that the skeleton was at least 200 years old. Had any visions of a former life lately?

When Route 150 ends, turn right and follow Route 39/55 through Richwood and into Summersville. Pleasant dreams . . .

Lodging

Babcock State Park
Route 1, Box 150
WV Route 41 North
Clifftop, WV 25831
Phone 800-CALL WVA or 304-438-5662. Cabins from $250 per
week; campsites from $10 per night.

Bluestone State Resort Park
WV Route 20 South
Box 3, Athens Star Route
Hinton, WV 25951
Phone 800-CALL WVA. $$$

The General Lewis
301 East Washington Street
Lewisburg, WV 24901
Phone 304-645-2600. Approved by AAA and Mobil Travel
Guide. In the historic district of town. The house is a museum of
West Virginia history in itself; each room is filled with antiques.
From $55 double occupancy.

The Greenbrier
US Route 60 West
White Sulphur Springs, WV 24986
Phone 800-678-8946 or 800-624-6070. One of the oldest and
most prestigious resorts in the United States. 547 guest rooms, 51
suites, and 69 guest houses. Activities include golf, tennis, fine
dining and dancing, conference rooms, and world famous spa and
mineral baths. Singles $158 to $441 per night; doubles $264 to
$478; suites and cabins $238 to $301.

Hawk's Nest State Park
P.O. Box 857
US 60 West
Ansted, WV 25812
Phone 800-CALL WVA or 304-658-5212. Lodging from $50 to
$106 April through October; $10 lower other times.

Mountain Lake Campground
P.O. Box 486
US 19 North
Summersville, WV 26651
Phone 800-624-0440. 200 sites, some with water and electricity;
group sites; rental camping trailers; swimming beach. $

Mountain State Motel
P.O. Box 9
WV Route 41 North, Main St.
Summersville, WV 26651
Phone 304-872-2702. $$

Old White Motel
P.O. Box 58
US 60 West
White Sulphur Springs, WV 24986
Phone 304-536-2441. AAA approved, clean, comfortable, and
considerably less expensive than its better known neighbor. Rates
from $30, double occupancy.

Pipestem Resort State Park
Pipestem, WV 25979
Phone 800-CALL WVA or 304-466-1800. Open year-round.
Cabins and campsites, horseback riding, hiking, watersports, golf
course, group activities, child care facilities. $15 per night with
full hook-up; cabins (2 bedrooms), $196 a week.

Watoga State Park
Marlinton, WV 24954
Phone 800-CALL WVA. $$

Places of Interest

••

Cass Scenic Railroad State Park
WV Route 66 West
Cass, WV 24927
Phone 800-CALL WVA. $

Class VI River Runners, Inc.
P.O. Box 78
US 219 South
Lansing, WV 25862
Phone 800-622-0704. April to October. One of the most established river running companies in the area. Campgrounds, $6 per person. Lower New River trip ranges from $78 weekdays to $90 Sat. Spring/Summer Gauley trip, $81 weekdays, $88 Sun., $98 Sat. Fall Gauley trip for major white water fiends ranges from $90 to $116.

Cranberry Mountain Visitor Center
Intersection of WV 150 & WV 55/39
Hillsboro, WV 24946
Phone 304-653-4826. Call for hours. Free.

Fayette Airport
Frank K. Thomas, Manager
Route 2, Box 480B
Fayetteville, WV 25840
Phone 304-574-1035. Airplane rides from $5 for 10 minutes.

Greenbrier State Forest
HC 30, Box 154
Intersection of US Route 60 & WV 63
Caldwell, WV 24925
Phone 800-CALL WVA or 304-536-1944. Cabins and campsites, hunting, fishing, seasonal nature programs, hiking, muzzle loading rifle range, archery range, near trailhead of the Greenbrier River Trail. Cabin rates from $65 per night for two. Equipped with cots. Sites: $13 with electricity, $10 without; 6 people per site.

New River Gorge National River Visitors Center
US 219 South
P.O. Box 246
Glen Jean, WV 25846-0246
Phone 304-574-2160. Memorial Day through Labor Day, 9 a.m.
to 8 p.m.; other times 9 a.m. to 5 p.m. Whitewater rafting, trails,
interpretive center, New River Gorge Bridge, National Parks Pass-
port stamp location. Free.

Pearl S. Buck Birthplace Museum
Route 219, 1/4 mile north of Hillsboro
Hillsboro, WV 24966
Phone 304-653-4430. Open Mon. through Sat., 9 a.m. to 5 p.m.;
Sun. from 1 p.m. to 5 p.m.

Pocahontas County Historical Society Museum
Route 219 south
Marlinton, WV 24954
Phone 304-799-6659. Open mid-June to Labor Day; Mon.
through Sat., 11 a.m. to 5 p.m.; Sun. from 1 p.m. to 5 p.m.
Admission is $1.00 for adults, 50¢ for students aged 12-18, and
under 12 free.

Wildwater Expeditions Unlimited, Inc.
P.O. Box 155
US 219 South at Glen Jean
Lansing, WV 25862
Phone 800-WVA-RAFT. April through October. Whitewater
river rides. Group discounts on Sun. through Fri. Reservations
required. Expedition: lower New River, $80 per person on Satur-
days.

Restaurants

. . . .

Ain't You Et Yet Cafe
Route 16/US 60 split
Chimney Corner, WV 25812
Phone 304-632-1809. Daily, 9 a.m. to 5 p.m. Fresh cheeses, candies, and sandwiches. $

Fran's Family Restaurant
Broad Street
Summersville, WV 26651
Phone 304-872-6184. Daily, 6 a.m. to 7 p.m. $

Frontier Restaurant
US Route 219, north of Marlinton
Marlinton, WV 24954
Phone 304-799-4134. Daily, 7 a.m. to 10 p.m. $

Stonewall Jackson Dining Room
Route 1, Box 8
WV Route 41 West, Main St.
Summersville, WV 26651
Phone 304-872-9892. Mon. through Sat., 5:30 a.m. to 9 p.m.;
Sun., 7 a.m. to 8 p.m. $

Travel Information

Lewisburg Visitors Center
Carnegie Hall - 105 Church Street
Lewisburg, WV 24901
Phone 800-833-2068.

Summersville Lake and Dam
U.S. Army Corp of Engineers
P.O. Box 2127
Huntington, WV 25721
Phone 304-529-5211. Information only.

Lost in the Mountains

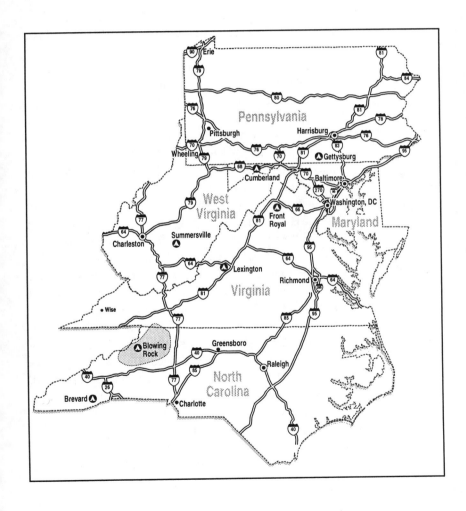

Blowing Rock, N.C.

．．

There are two distinct base camps for tours in Blowing Rock, depending on whether you prefer to camp or motel it during your stay. In either case, you'll fall in love with this area of the country. The pace of life really is slower here, and the folks you meet aren't as concerned about getting ahead or making it big as they are about doing what it takes to get by and enjoying life while they're at it.

For campers, Ferguson is your destination. It's a dot on the map about 20 miles southeast of Blowing Rock and home to a motorcycles-only campground called **Rider's Roost.** If you look at a detailed map, another spot labeled Elkville indicates the precise location of the campground. The Roost is run by brothers Bruce Colburn and Roy Yelverton, "100 percent scooter people" who are serious about their riding. Both are Harley fans with a garage area where they do custom work on their bikes and will also allow campers to do some wrenching. Try finding that at a Kampground of America.

The campground, along the banks of Elk Creek, features a large open grassy area with newly planted ornamental cherries. It is perfect for setting up either tent or camper. Rates are a bargain compared to some larger campgrounds: single riders pay $8 per night and two-up are $10. You can also rent a cabin (reserved in advance) for $18 per night. Hot showers and laundry facilities are located at the campground. Bruce and Roy are working on remodeling the lounge to include a pool table, microwave, and TV area for campers.

You can find breakfast just two miles down the road in Ferguson proper at **The Grocery Basket and Grill.** From the campground, turn left onto 268 east heading into Wilkesboro. Just after the fire station and post office in Ferguson, turn left onto Champion Road. The grill is the second store on the left. My arrival in Ferguson was a source of amusement for some of the fellas at the grill. You see, the grill is the morning

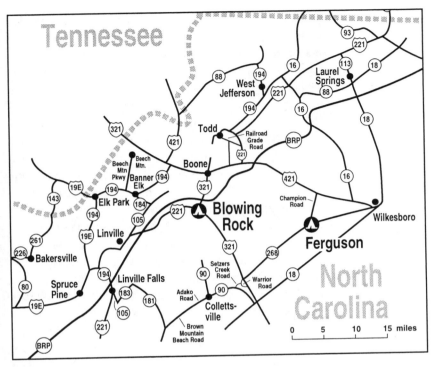

congregating spot for the locals, and when you come tramping in wearing a big red riding suit and carrying a bunch of maps, why, you get the same look Columbus probably got from the first Indians who saw him. Of course they warmed up after a while and pretty soon the stories about bikes remembered and trips taken started flowing like a river.

Joe, the store's owner, is a fella who looks to be in his sixties but has the mischievous blue eyes of a teenager. You can always count on a friendly greeting from Joe, and he can cook up a tasty breakfast. If you're a real southern breakfast aficionado, you can't go wrong with a mush (boiled cornmeal) and scrapple (don't ask) combo.

Blowing Rock is another nice place to stay if you're not into camping. It's a small town that takes its name from a rock formation where a constant wind sweeps up under the rock and returns small items that you throw over the edge. If that sounds kind of insignificant compared to Niagara Falls or Yosemite, well, it is, but that's not the real attraction here. The real draw for me is the town itself.

Main Street is lined with rows of quaint little shops and restaurants. You can walk from one end to the other in 15 minutes and have a grand time sitting in front of the courthouse watching others walk by. It's even better in the evening when a cool breeze sets in and the traffic subsides. At night under the streetlights, Blowing Rock becomes the setting for a Norman Rockwell painting—and you're part of the picture.

The **Blue Ridge Motel** looks like it has seen better years, especially when you compare it to the brand new AAA-rated lodges and inns that surround it. The buildings look a little shaggy and you figure the insides must look the same way. So did I. But when I rolled into town on a Saturday evening, the Blue Ridge was the last motel that hadn't turned on its No Vacancy sign. Was I in trouble? It appeared that I was.

But then, my mother always told me that appearances don't count for everything, and she was right. The Blue Ridge has been in operation under the watchful eye of Kentucky Colonel Glenn Coffey, a Blowing Rock native, since it was first constructed in the mid-fifties. There isn't anything fancy about these units, but they have all the essentials: clean sheets, hot water, air conditioning, and cable TV (well, if you're going to the expense of renting a room, cable is a necessity). Guests in the other lodges were paying upwards of $100 a night while I shacked up for a quarter of that. That made the bed sleep even better. It won't offend the Colonel in the least if you ask to look at the room before you make a commitment. In fact, he usually offers first.

The best feature of the motel is the Colonel himself. Most evenings you can find him sitting out on the front porch reading the local paper. Nothing suits him better than to have you drop by for a little conversation. Any topic will do. Ask him about the early days in Blowing Rock and he can reel off a list a mile long of the well-heeled who have lived in or visited the town. His father was mayor for years, and the Colonel has owned several of the shops in town during the last few decades. Now he spends his time answering the phone for guests and tending the flower beds around the rooms.

In front of the motel is a monument erected to mark the approximate path Daniel Boone took through the area on his way to Cumberland Gap. The marker was originally located

The Rider's Roost in Ferguson, N.C. is your home away from home.

up the street in front of a store the Colonel's brother owned, but redevelopment forced its relocation and the Colonel brought it to his property.

The motel is situated on the north end of town, just a few blocks away from half a dozen eating establishments. You can eat well in Blowing Rock, better than any place I've visited. Earlier in the day, I passed through town and spied a clutch of Gold Wings parked outside **Cheeseburgers In Paradise.** Go figure. This place does serve great cheeseburgers that are huge and cooked to order. Another special place to eat is the **Speckled Trout Cafe,** right next door. They serve the tastiest mountain trout I've ever had. Closer to the motel is **Buchanan's Restaurant,** yet another excellent establishment. Their specialty is Watauga County ham. As difficult as it is for a Virginia boy like me to admit, it's just as good as the ham from the Old Dominion. Out on the Route 321 bypass is **Woodlands Barbeque and Picking Parlor.** The "picking parlor" is for bluegrass music, not a special room for after-dinner toothpick users.

The only other town of any size in the immediate area is Boone, due north of Blowing Rock and easily reachable on Route 321. Boone is home to Appalachian State University which houses the **Appalachian Cultural Center.** A visit to Boone is a good idea for a lazy afternoon when you aren't up to riding too far.

Trip 22   The Lost Provinces

· ·

Distance	*175 miles*
Terrain	*Two mountain passes, low hills and valleys*
Highlights	*Hiking on the Parkway, paddling the New River, small towns and villages*

The Route from Blowing Rock

→ Champion Road north to US 421
→ US 421 west to Old US 421
→ Old US 421 east to NC 16
→ NC 16 north to US 58
→ US 58 east to VA 93
→ VA 93 becomes NC 93
→ NC 93 south to US 221
→ US 221 east to US 21
→ US 21 south to NC 18*
→ NC 18 west to NC 113
→ NC 113 north to US 221
→ US 221 west to NC 16
→ NC 16 south to NC 88
→ NC 88 east to NC 18
→ NC 18 south to Blue Ridge Parkway
→ Blue Ridge Parkway south to US 421
→ US 421 east to Champion Road
→ Champion Road south to Ferguson

*Alternate Route through Wilkesboro:

→ NC 18 south to US 421 Business
→ US 421 Business west to US 421
→ US 421 west to Champion Road
→ Champion Road south to Ferguson

The hills and valleys of the Appalachians have an influence
that goes beyond the manmade boundary lines that separate
one state from another. Many of the roads throughout the
region follow the river valleys that provide the most natural

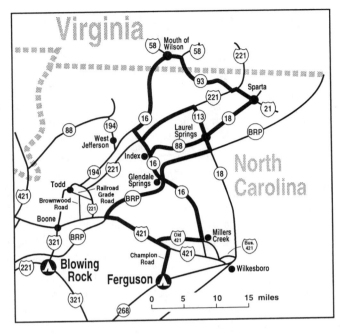

way of getting from one ridge to another. Trading routes in this area ran southeast to northwest and settlers found it most convenient to build commerce with their neighbors in Tennessee and Virginia. In fact, it used to be said that the only way to get to Boone was to be born there. Being isolated from the rest of the state, this area became known as the Lost Provinces. Let's see if we can find them for ourselves.

Begin your search by following Champion Road out of Ferguson to Route 421. At 421, turn left and head west. An old alignment of US 421 appears on your right. I like these older sections of road because they are far less traveled and more varied than the newer section. Old 421 passes through farm country and development is scarce.

Old 421 meets Route 16 in Millers Creek. Turn left to head north on Route 16. Looking at my maps a few weeks after running this route, I discovered that I had been tricked. I somehow missed an older alignment of Route 16 that departs from the main road a few miles north of Millers Creek and continues to the Blue Ridge Parkway at Glendale Springs. Judging from the alignment, it is probably no longer maintained and may not be paved. It looks like a good dual-sport option to the top.

Today's Route 16 makes a direct assault on the Blue Ridge and, after seven or eight miles of relatively straight road, begins to weave across the eastern face of the mountains. Occasionally there is some traffic on this route, but by metropolitan standards the volume is low. The view improves with height but the co-rider benefits the most. There aren't any real places to pull over and stop, so reserve your sightseeing for the Parkway, which will come up soon.

It can be cool anywhere in the highlands and mountains, the Parkway included. My last visit to this area in June was a chilly one, with morning temps on the Parkway in the 40s. On the good side, that brisk Canadian air sweeps away the haze, providing spectacular vistas of the mountains.

While you're at the Parkway, there's a nice short trail you can hike to get the blood pumping on one of those chilly mornings and work off some of that jelly toast Joe so willingly offers at the Grocery Basket. Turn north on the parkway and in about a mile you'll find the Jumping Off Rock Trail. It's a short, easy half-mile hike out to an overlook of the eastern slopes of the Blue Ridge and the North Carolina Piedmont.

They say you learn something every day and my lesson on this particular day was about wildlife. As I made my way down the trail, I stepped through some low brush along the trail. Without warning the brush came alive, and the silence of the forest was shattered by a storm of shrieks, fluttering, and floundering. To be honest, I was scared witless. Turns out I had stepped on the tail feathers of a turkey hen protecting a half-dozen newly hatched chicks. They were pretty darn cute, but each time I stopped to take a peek, she would come after me. The best course of action quickly became apparent—exit stage right.

Route 16 runs across the northwestern corner of the state and ventures briefly into Virginia. This section of the route is mostly wide and straight, with lots of hills to make the scenery interesting. On a clear day along this road, the sky looks like a reflection of the Caribbean. It's so fresh it spar-

*The literal-
minded rider
should think
twice before
acting . . .*

kles. In fact, I got off my bike several times just to marvel at
the sky. Now I know what Carolina Blue looks like.

Route 16 intersects Route 58 at Mouth of Wilson. Turn
right and follow 58 east for a short distance to pick up Route
93 south. Scattered among the signage along the state border
is a telling one: "Motorcycles Must Burn Headlights." Taken
literally, this could cause serious damage to your motorcycle.

Route 93 is like a gentle roller coaster ride, rising up
small hills, banked turns and twists, and rolling gently down
the other side. Photo opportunities abound along this route,
with scenic vistas, old barns, green pastures, and those blue
skies. Wildflowers in season carpet the roadside and the hills
with brilliant yellows, purples, and blues.

Route 93 ends on US 221. Turn left and follow Route
221 to Route 21, then turn right and follow the road to Sparta.
There isn't much fancy about Sparta. It's just a small, clean
town that could easily have been the inspiration for *The Andy
Griffith Show.* You can find a good lunch at **Sparta Restaurant** on Main Street across from the courthouse. The specialty there is chicken livers. That may suit you, but for those
like me who turn green at the thought, try the fried chicken
and homemade pies. After lunch you can stroll the streets to
settle your lunch or just hang out in front of the courthouse
for a little while and watch the cars go by.

Head west out of town on Route 18. Route 18 is more
rolling countryside and fast sweepers bounded by the Blue

Ridge on your left and Peach Bottom Mountain on your right. You'll probably see a lot of space being given to Christmas tree production through this region. The Fraser fir grows well in this climate and has become an important export.

Hang a right on Route 113, which makes an end run on Peach Bottom Mountain, climbing a few hundred feet in the air. This gives you a great view of the mountains in western Ashe County. Turn left on Route 221 to follow this road to the New River. US 221 is a study in contrasts. One section is smooth and seamless pavement with nary a ripple to unsettle your suspension, while other sections are rideable but rough and noisy. In this section, the pavement narrows down to a two-lane country road.

You'll come upon the South Fork of the New River just a few miles ahead. On the other side of the bridge is the **New River General Store.** Out front is a long porch just made for relaxing with a cold soda. Mosey down to the bridge and watch the water pass by. The store is also the headquarters of **New River Outfitters,** where you can rent a canoe and equipment for runs as short as an hour or as long as a day.

You can also enjoy the river from the banks with a picnic lunch. Pick up the fixings at the store, then ride a few tenths of a mile west to **New River State Park.** In addition to a boat launching site, there are trails, a few primitive campsites, and picnic tables with grills. I visited the park in the early afternoon and was alone except for two deer and a park ranger. The ranger said that despite appearances, the parking lot is usually full on weekends, but during the week you have the full run of the place.

From its beginnings here in western North Carolina, the New River runs a course predated only by the Nile. The New is the only river on the North American continent that runs from southeast to northwest. Most rivers east of the Appalachians drain into the Atlantic, but not the New. It has maintained a path that cuts directly through the mountains against the usual flow. It was once the headwaters of the prehistoric Teays River which flowed across most of the continent. The Ice Age disrupted the flow and the only original part that remains is the New. North Carolina has declared a 26-mile portion of the New to be protected from development so it remains free-flowing and unspoiled as it has for thousands of years.

After leaving the park, continue west on 221 to Route 16. If this area looks familiar to you, it should. Our route made a big figure eight and we are near closing the final loop. Follow Route 16 till it picks up Route 88. Turn left at Index to stay on Route 88.

Laurel Springs, at the intersection of Routes 88, 18 and 113, is home to **Linda's General Store**. This one is a bit different than the rest. You get your first clue looking at the assortment of wooden dummies dressed as different members of Linda's family, the Woodies.

There are two recommended routes for your return. One features scenery, the other food. For scenery, follow Route 18 a few tenths of a mile to the Blue Ridge Parkway south. The timing of this route should bring you to the Parkway near time for sunset. Sunsets on the Parkway are a magical experience you never tire of watching. Incurable romantics will be drawn to an overlook to watch in awe as the sun sinks over the infinite ridges to the west. Just remember to ride below posted speeds near dusk and after dark to reduce your chances of an encounter with whitetail deer. You wouldn't fare nearly so well hitting one of those as stepping on a turkey's tail feathers.

If you're headquartered out of Blowing Rock, stay on the Parkway to US 321. To return to Rider's Roost at Ferguson, follow the Parkway to US 421. Follow US 421 east to Champion Road and Champion south to Ferguson.

For more dinner options, follow NC 18 out of Laurel Springs all the way to Wilkesboro. In town, pick up US 421 Business to get to the heart of town, and dinner. One place worth mentioning is the **Santa Fe Restaurant** on Business 421. Despite the southwestern name, the menu is home cooking. To return to Ferguson, follow US 421 Business west to US 421. Route 421 west leads to Champion Road. Turn left on Champion Road and follow it south to Ferguson.

Trip 23   Roan Mountain Mystery

· ·

Distance   *210 miles*

Terrain   *Foothills and lowlands to begin, followed by a mountain ascent to Blue Ridge, a section of wild twisties through the backwoods, then a long, high, twisty pass over Roan Mountain. A valley ride and a short section of the Parkway finish off the day.*

Highlights   *Brown Mountain "lights," Linnville Gorge and Falls, Loafer's Glory, Roan Mountain, and the Linn Cove Viaduct*

The Route from Blowing Rock

→ Route 268 west to Warrior Road
→ Warrior Road to Setzers Creek Road
→ Setzers Creek Road to Route 90
→ Route 90 west to Adako Road
→ Adako Road west to Brown Mountain Beach Road
→ Brown Mountain Beach Road west to NC 181
→ NC 181 north to NC 183
→ NC 183 west to Old NC 105
→ Old NC 105 north to US 221
→ US 221 north to NC 194
→ NC 194 south to US 19E
→ US 19E south to NC 80
→ NC 80 north to NC 226
→ NC 226 east to NC 261
→ NC 261 north to TN 143
→ TN 143 north to US 19E
→ US 19E south to NC 194
→ NC 194 north to NC 184
→ NC 184 south to NC 105
→ NC 105 south to US 221
→ US 221 east to Blue Ridge Parkway
→ Blue Ridge Parkway north to US 321
→ US 321 south to NC 268

Western North Carolina is filled with legends of ghostly figures, strange events, and unexplained phenomena. The strange things which happen in this area aren't as widely

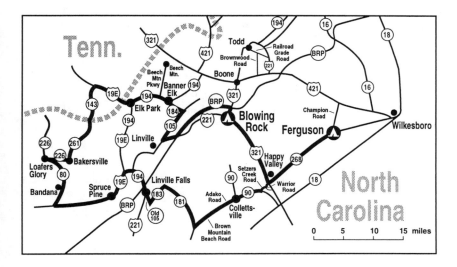

known as sightings of the Loch Ness monster or those unexplained crop circles in England, but they remain well documented events which defy scientific explanation to this day.

Our search to uncover these mountain mysteries begins westbound on Route 268 toward Happy Valley. Here the road hugs one side of the valley in places, perhaps to maximize the amount of land available for farming. This makes the road follow a drunken path with an occasional straight followed by a series of curves. It's a good warm up exercise. It's also part of the Overmountain Victory Trail, marking the route that a band of mountaineers marched to fight the British in the battle of King's Mountain, S.C. It was a decisive victory for the patriots and a turning point in the Revolutionary War.

Route 268 ends on Route 321. Cross the road and you will be on Warriors Road, a dinky little footpath that could be called paved in the loose sense of the word. This leads through the woods to Setzers Creek Road, a right turn. Setzers Creek Road then ends on Route 90. For a state route, 90 isn't much bigger. The road has stood up well to the beating it has taken from lumber trucks. This area is well-suited to dual purpose bikes. There are dozens of side roads to follow, some leading deep into the hollows that see few outsiders. Route 90 turns northward at Collettsville and passes through some beautiful, remote backcountry, bounded by the Johns River on one side and sheer rock walls vibrant green with native ferns and mosses on the other. Suddenly the road becomes dirt. Huh? I thought state primary routes were supposed to be paved, but this one isn't. I made a note to myself: "Get knobbies for Wing." Like General MacArthur, I shall return. Retracing my path to Collettsville, I found the turn I had planned to make. Adako Road crosses the Johns and continues to follow the narrow valley around Brown Mountain. It becomes Brown Mountain Beach Road before intersecting with Route 181.

Brown Mountain has a long history as a source of mysterious lights, reported by Indians well before the first settlers reached the eastern shore. They are seen at night and are reported to roam around the mountain. Dozens of studies and expeditions have been conducted to discover the source of the lights, including some done by departments of the federal gub'ment. Explanations include trains (there are no tracks on the mountain), car headlights (there are no roads on the mountain), swamp gas (no swamps) and a slave searching for his lost master. That one can't be so easily disproved.

Make the right turn on Route 181 to return to the mountains. Soon the road becomes one long, well-banked sweeper after another—a pleasant, fast ride. A left turn on Route 183 will bring you to a parking area for the **Linville Gorge and Falls.** You can easily spend an hour or two here hiking the paths that lead to different views of the waterfalls of the Linn River. The gorge, about 2,000 feet deep, was formed when twisting and shearing forces that built up the mountains caused a weak seam to split, kind of like popping a kernel of corn. (Well, that's how my mind pictures it, a geologist would no doubt take issue with that.) You don't have to walk far to see the falls, just a few tenths of a mile for the upper section, another few tenths for the lower.

You can find a good lunch at **Famous Louise's Rockhouse Restaurant.** Follow Route 183 to Old Route 105, then right on Old 105 to Route 221. You'll find Louise's at the intersection. What's so famous about Famous Louise's? All you have to do is walk inside and look at the ceiling. The restaurant sits on the exact intersection of Avery, Burke and McDowell counties, and signs along the ceiling indicate which county you are in. Your food is prepared in Avery, eaten in Burke, and paid for in McDowell!

Let's see, did I park the bike in Burke County or Avery County??

Return to Route 221 and follow it east to the point where Route 194 enters from your left. Turn on Route 194 to cut across to Route 19E, a busy corridor through upper northwest. Some areas around Spruce Pine are ragged from mining operations. People have been digging holes in the ground around here for a thousand years for minerals. There is a spot somewhere in the hills called Sink Hole Mines, a place where Spanish conquistadors reportedly found silver in great quantities.

Past Spruce Pine is a nice little road, Route 80. The road surface is good in most places, if not smooth, though a few gravel hazards exist at some entrances. The road twists in and out of the North Toe River Valley, making three turns where seemingly one would do. Suits me fine. You'll often find a few other riders out here, as this is a popular spot among locals. About halfway along your route you pass through Bandana, which got its name when a railroad worker tied a bandana to a tree to indicate where a stop was to be made. When route 80 arrives at a T intersection, make a left turn. Route 80 ends in Loafer's Glory on Route 226. There was once a store here which was a popular gathering place for the local men folk to hang around during the day, playing checkers, taking an afternoon snooze, and generally being stinking lazy. Eventually it became known as a "loafer's glory" among the wives of the community and the name stuck.

Enter the town of Bakersville and make the left on Route 261. This section of road is reminiscent of Route 181 in its sweeping curves and great sightlines. It takes its good ol' time winding up the mountains, eventually reaching Roan Mountain State Park on the Tennessee-North Carolina border.

Roan Mountain is the typical southern Appalachian bald. A bald is a treeless area, usually filled with large rhododendron gardens like Roan, although it can be a large grassy area. None of the Appalachians rise above the treeline. There isn't anything inherently different about the soil. So why haven't they been covered with trees like other areas? No one knows. Another unusual feature of Roan Mountain is occasional strange humming or buzzing noises, as though bees are swarming. Sometimes the sound is described as crackling, like high-tension electrical wires. The most likely source, we are told, is the passing of opposing electrical charges between clouds and the ground. Again, no one knows why.

The view from Roan is nothing short of spectacular. The Blue Ridge fills the southern and eastern horizon while the Great Smokies lie to the north and west. You can almost ride right into the gardens. Across from the visitor center is a trail leading to the peak of Roan, a lofty 6,285 feet.

Route 216 becomes Route 143 in Tennessee, making a graceful descent through Cherokee National Forest and **Roan Mountain State Park.** The state park would make a nice night's layover. They have cabins and a lodge, trails, and a swimming pool, but most of all they are in a beautiful location with a relaxing atmosphere. The road through the park

gets twisty and narrow in places. Look well through your
curves before picking an aggressive line. You will encounter
an occasional recreational vehicle on its way to the camping
area and you don't want to be so fully committed to a line that
you can't make an adjustment.

Route 143 ends on Route 19E. We've caught up to the
same road we followed west to get to Spruce Pine, now we'll
follow it south to return to Route 194. I found myself checking and rechecking my map at each intersection on routes
throughout this area. The confused folds and tucks of the
Appalachians have made a mess out of the usual north-south,
east-west corridors. A global positioning receiver would be
more useful than a map.

You'll find Route 194 at Elk Park (No elk, no park.
Hmmm . . .). This brings you back to the Banner Elk area (No
banner, no elk. What's going on here?). A right on 184 and
another on Route 105 puts you in Linville. This is the fastest
way to return to the Parkway. Turn left and follow Route 221
to the Parkway. Just a little way ahead is the **Linn Cove
Information Center** at the head of the Linn Cove Viaduct.
Since its completion in 1987, the viaduct is probably the most
photographed spot on the Parkway.

The Blue Ridge Parkway had been built from both ends
until reaching a difficult area at **Grandfather Mountain.**
The roadway had to be built without attachment to the mountain, and to preserve the delicate ecosystem, no heavy equipment or traditional techniques could be used. In fact, the
means to construct the viaduct had to be invented as there was
no precedent anywhere in the world. The resulting bridge
uses pre-cast concrete and steel beam construction. The
pieces were cast to such tight tolerances there was never more
than a .01-inch variance from the specified fit. No piece of the
bridge is perfectly straight except for the southernmost link.
It's a blast to ride—you feel like you're just hanging in the air
as you glide across the face of Grandfather. For an up-close
look, there is a 300-yard paved trail from the information
center to the underside of the bridge. Your path home can be
traced down the Parkway to Blowing Rock. Here you can
follow Route 321 south to Route 268 to return to Ferguson.

Trip 24   Old As The Hills

Distance	*170 miles*
Terrain	*Slow-paced rural roads with moderately good pavement, some sections with incredibly tight switchbacks, section of US 221 between Linville and Blowing Rock among best in class*
Highlights	*Two unique general stores, Grandfather Mountain, Cone Manor House*

The Route from Blowing Rock

→ Champion Road to US 421
→ US 421 west to Brownwood Road
→ Brownwood Road to Railroad Grade Road
→ Railroad Grade Road to NC 194
→ NC 194 north to NC 88
→ NC 88 west becomes TN 67
→ TN 67 west to US 421
→ US 421 east to Old US 421
→ Old US 421 east to US 321
→ US 321 east to NC 194
→ NC 194 south to NC 184
→ NC 184 north to Beech Mountain Parkway and Beech Mountain
→ Turn around, return to NC 184
→ NC 184 south to NC 105
→ NC 105 south to US 221
→ US 221 east to US 321
→ US 321 south to NC 268
→ NC 268 east to Ferguson

Some areas of the country still evoke a feeling of the glory years of motorcycling. Western North Carolina is one of them. Open country roads are lined with small farms set against a backdrop of low hills. Old road alignments pass buildings that once served as filling stations and country stores that are now converted to another purpose or stand empty and fallen into disrepair, mute testimony to the chang-

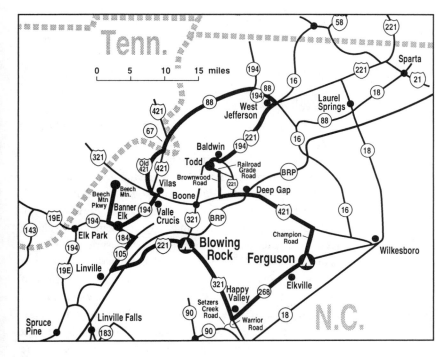

ing times. Surely the next bike you meet will be a '27 Harley or a Henderson.

Our tour begins following Champion Road north out of Ferguson to Route 421. Champion Road is a crooked delight that crosses the foothills just east of the Blue Ridge and is the fastest way to reach Route 421. Turn left and follow 421 west over the Blue Ridge. Your bike will enjoy the fast curves and big pavement that allows you to work up some good lean angles. The ride up is steep and you can drop a gear and crack the throttle hard. When you reach the intersection with the Parkway at Deep Gap, watch for traffic entering from the Parkway.

You can also get to Deep Gap by an even prettier route if you have a dual-sport bike. Follow Elk Creek Road right out of the campground in Elkville and head north. The road turns to gravel a few miles out of camp and then scurries up the side of the Blue Ridge following Elk Creek before ending on the Parkway near Deep Gap. Big pockets of gravel and an uneven grade make this road a hard ride on a big rig.

At Brownwood Road, turn right and follow the sign for the Todd General Store. Where Brownwood Road meets Railroad Grade Road, turn left and follow Railroad Grade. True to its name, this section of road follows an old railroad line. There is at least one bone-jarring dip on this road soon after you make the turn from Brownwood. It just comes out of nowhere and could be a real spring-buster if you hit it at speed. Where are those "Dip" signs when you need them?

Todd was a bustling timber center in its earlier days. As with many towns, it diminished when the timber ran out and many stores closed. **Todd General Store,** built in 1914, continues to serve the community as a tourist draw, museum, and functioning store. You can buy varied items such as brass tacks, beeswax, and Double Yellow Line brand sun-dried canned possum. A fellow riding friend says they make great sandwiches here, too. Just be sure you count the cans of possum on the counter before and after they make your sandwich. Besides the general store, there are a few craft houses and emporiums to knock around in. You just might find an abandoned vintage machine hidden in the back of one of them.

When you arrive at the crossroad with Route 194, you'll need to make a difficult turn uphill and back to the right to get on track. It's a hard trick to do on big bikes and it's easier to take as a left turn, so you might want to follow Railroad Grade across 194, turn around in a flat spot, and return to the intersection to make your turn. Part of Route 194 is known as the Old Buffalo Trail, a route that herds of bison used to follow through the mountains. Biologists tell us that the great beasts would migrate east to spend winters on the coast where temperatures were milder, then return over the mountains during the summers. Some of the trails they left were used by early settlers and eventually incorporated into roads we still use. Nearby is a small village with the gruesome name of Meat Camp. That answers the question of what happened to the buffalo.

NC 194 north is freshly paved and good riding. After leaving Todd it crests a hill and settles down into a small valley dotted with a few small farms. Route 194 intersects with Route 221 at Baldwin and heads north to West Jefferson.

You'll also find an older alignment of the road here that parallels the route into town. Follow the old road for less traffic and more curves.

West Jefferson is home to the **Ashe County Cheese Factory,** the lone survivor of a state-sponsored program from the early 1900s to promote cheese making as a way for dairy farmers to earn extra cash. Soon after the program started, cheese factories popped up all over. Making cheese was easy enough. Getting it to market over tall hills and bad roads was another matter, though, and soon put most would-be cheese kings out of business.

One industry that did thrive during that time was moonshining. And the practice of 'shine running actually formed another industry: stock car racing. The ridge runners who drove souped-up cars with special tanks to hold the whiskey were the forerunners of today's racers. The early members of the National Association of Stock Car Auto Racing (NASCAR) who were the better drivers often started out running corn liquor along the narrow, dark roads of the Lost Provinces.

Mount Jefferson State Park is a good place for a picnic. It's just east of the town on Route 221. A short drive to the top rewards you with a nice view of the Stone Mountains to the west, the Blue Ridge to the east.

Follow Route 88 west out of West Jefferson along the north fork of the New. A few small villages are strung out along the banks of the river, interrupted by farms that manage to squeeze a few acres of crops in the narrow river valley. Eventually Route 88 meanders into Tennessee and becomes Route 67. A small sign announces your arrival into the Volunteer State in a matter-of-fact way. At the junction of Route 67 and 421, turn left, following Route 421 east. Just as you return into North Carolina, look for Old US 421 on your right and follow it.

Along Old 421, buildings that once served the traveling public abound, evoking a nostalgic feeling as you meander along. Around one corner you'll pass an old filling station, now vine-covered and returning to nature, while around the next an old store has been rescued from the same fate, now serving as a craft shop or home. Most of the activity around

*Not a bad way
to start off
a ride . . .*

these buildings is gone, but the shadows they cast in the early morning light are unchanged. If you look into those shadows, you can see and hear images of the past—a tow-headed boy with a white cap putting "fifty cents worth" in a '49 Ford coupe or Joe the mechanic applying incessant banging and verbal torque to a stubborn bolt on a shiny Hudson. As you pass the station, your visions of the past vanish as quickly as they appeared, and the only sound that remains is the throbbing in your engine. If you still hear a banging noise now, it only means your tailbag has gotten caught in your rear wheel. Then again, it might be your stomach clanging the lunch bell.

The old route ends on Route 321 just a few miles west of Vilas. Make a right and continue on Route 321 until you reach Vilas where Route 194 joins. Turn right to follow 194 west. You'll see a sign of things to come: "Warning: Steep winding road . . . not recommended for vehicles over 35 feet in length." They aren't kidding either. Wing drivers with trailers might want to make sure their rigs don't exceed the recommended length! This is more of a paved goatpath than a road, but it is always fun. There are some incredibly tight switchbacks here that have you looking fully back over your shoulder while you are still negotiating the current turn. If you aren't comfortable with looking fully through a turn and counter steering, stay on the interstate and off of this road.

The big twisty stuff lasts for a few miles, then you are deposited into Valle Crucis. Stop at the **Mast General Store,** established in 1883 and the oldest continuously operating general store in the country. The heavy wooden front door displays a plaque indicating the store is on the National Register of Historic Places. The front room is where the groceries and hardware are kept. The center of the room is dominated by a huge pot-bellied stove that looks big enough to burn a cord of wood at a time. Other rooms are filled to the ceiling with crafts and a lot of outdoor gear.

The post office has finally settled at the Mast store. In earlier times, you might have picked up your mail here or down the road at the Farthing's place, depending on whether the local politburo was Republican or Democrat. It moved to the Mast store when a Democrat was elected or to Farthing's Republican stronghold when the GOP won a local election. It went on this way until H.W. Mast married Mary Hazel Farthing near the turn of the century. After that the post office stayed at the Mast store, since it was now in the family.

More twisty road awaits your ride to Banner Elk. Another section of nearly 180-degree switchbacks, then another valley ride. Pavement markings along the way click off the distance in kilometers, remnants of the Tour DuPont bicycle race. Some of the steep uphill climbs on this section will make you rejoice in the fact that your two wheels aren't powered by your two legs alone! In Banner Elk, follow the signs for Beech Mountain to complete your ride to the top. Beech Mountain is a popular ski resort and at 5,506 feet it's also eastern America's highest town.

When you start rolling back down the hill, just imagine what it would be like to blast down this mountain on a bicycle, with contact patches the width of your pinkie finger, wearing no more protective gear than a half-helmet and skin-tight spandex clothing, wheeling through a crowd of others hell-bent on getting down ahead of you. And people think motorcyclists are crazy?

Route 184 south out of Banner Elk has a moderate amount of traffic, mostly the Florida set. It ends on Route 105. Turn right and follow 105 into Linville. In town, turn left on Route 221. You'll find the entrance to Grandfather Mountain just a few miles up the road. **Grandfather Mountain** got its name from Indians who thought the mountain looked like

the face of an old man. Unlike some other natural attractions
where you have to stretch your imagination to see a familiar
shape, this one really does look like the profile of an old man
outlined in the rock. Grandfather Mountain is unique in two
other respects. It is formed of some of the oldest exposed rock
found in the Blue Ridge chain and is the highest summit in
the chain. Grandfather Mountain is privately owned and there
is an admission charge. At the top there are 25 miles of hiking
trails, a nature museum, and the famous mile-high swinging
bridge. If you cross it, you can climb a moderately difficult
trail to get to Linville Peak and 360-degree views of the area.

The route is finished off with a 19-mile dash into Blowing Rock along Route 221. The stretch between Grandfather
Mountain and Blowing Rock is pristine motorcycling road,
mostly flat and very curvy. This section parallels the Blue
Ridge Parkway and was used as a connection during the years
when the Linn Cove Viaduct (the last link in the Parkway)
was being built. The viaduct was finished in 1987 and Route
221 was abandoned by the touring set. Great! It's like having
your own personal section of the Parkway, but with more and
tighter curves and no 45-mph limit!

The last stop of the day is the **Moses H. Cone Flat Top
Manor House** where the Parkway and US 221 meet near
Blowing Rock. Built by textile magnate Cone as a summer
home, the manor house is now home to the **Parkway Craft
Center** and features a wealth of finely-crafted Appalachian
goods. These are several notches above the roadside craft
stands. If you carry a National Parks Passport, you can get a
"Blue Ridge Parkway" passport stamp here. Outside, you
can enjoy the cool breeze on the front porch while you pass
the time in a straight-back rocker. Can't you just picture
yourself living here, glass of lemonade in hand, admiring
your vast estate?

If you're staying in Blowing Rock you have only to
travel a few miles down Route 221 to reach your destination.
If you're returning to camp at Ferguson, follow Route 321
south and then Route 268 east.

Lodging

∙∙∙

Blue Ridge Motel
Main Street
Blowing Rock, NC 28605
Phone 704-295-7341. Singles from $25.

Rider's Roost
100 Elk Creek Road
Ferguson, NC 28624
Phone 910-973-8405. Tent sites $8 single, $12 double; cabins
$20; bunkhouse $10 per person.

Places of Interest

∙∙∙

Appalachian Cultural Center
University Hall
Appalachian State University
Boone, NC 28607
Phone 704-262-3117. Open all year. Tues. through Sat., 10 a.m.
to 5 p.m.; Sun., 1 p.m. to 5 p.m. General admission $2.

Ashe County Cheese Factory
P.O. Box 447
Main and Fourth Streets
West Jefferson, NC 28694
Phone 910-246-2501. Mon. through Sat., 8 a.m. to 5 p.m.

Grandfather Mountain
P.O. Box 995
2050 Hwy 221 North
Linville, NC 28646
Phone 800-468-7325 or 704-733-4337. Open daily all year ex-
cept Thanksgiving and Christmas. Winter, 8 a.m. to 5 p.m.
Spring 'til 6 p.m. Summer 'til 7 p.m. $9

Linda's General Store
Highway 18
Laurel Springs, NC 28644
Phone 910-359-8834. April through October, 9 a.m. to 5 p.m.

Linville Gorge and Falls
U.S. Forest Service
Linville Falls, NC 28647
Phone 704-652-4841. Free permit from Ranger's office required
for backcountry hiking.

Mast General Store
Highway 194
Valle Crucis, NC 28691
Phone 704-963-6511. Mon. through Sat., 6:30 a.m. to 6:30 p.m.;
Sun., 1 p.m. to 6 p.m.

Moses H. Cone Flat Top Manor House
Parkway Craft Center
Blue Ridge Parkway, Milepost 294
Blowing Rock, NC 28605
Phone 704-295-7938. Open May through October. National
Parks Passport stamp for Blue Ridge Parkway. Free.

Mount Jefferson State Park
U.S. Route 221
West Jefferson, NC 28694
Phone 910-246-9653.

New River General Store and
New River Outfitters
10725 Hwy 221 North
Scottville, NC 28672
Phone 800-982-9190 or 910-982-9192. General Store open
Mon. through Sat., 8:30 a.m. to 6 p.m. Closed Sunday. River
trips from $9 including equipment.

New River State Park
U.S. Route 221
Jefferson, NC 28640
Phone 910-982-2587. Sunrise to sunset. Free.

Roan Mountain State Park
Route 1, Box 236
Roan Mountain, TN 37687
Phone 615-772-3303. World's largest natural rhododendron gar-
dens.

Todd General Store
Railroad Grade Road
Todd, NC 28684
Phone 910-877-1067. Summer hours: Mon. through Sat., 7 a.m.
to 7 p.m.; Sun., 12:30 p.m. to 5 p.m. Winter hours: Mon. through
Sat., 8 a.m. to 6 p.m.; Sun., 12:30 p.m. to 5 p.m.

Restaurants

....

Buchanan's Restaurant
Main Street
Blowing Rock, NC 28605
Phone 704-295-3869. Daily, 7 a.m. to 2 p.m. for breakfast and
lunch. Dinner, 5 p.m. to 9 p.m. Full dinners from $9.

Cheeseburgers in Paradise
US 221 & Main St.
Blowing Rock, NC
Phone 704-295-4858. Daily, 11 a.m. to somewhere between 9
and 10 p.m., depending on how they feel!

Famous Louise's Rockhouse Restaurant
Hwy 221 North
Linville Falls, NC 28647
Phone 704-765-2702. Mon. through Thurs., 6 a.m. to 7:30 p.m.;
Fri. and Sat. 'til 8 p.m.; Sun. 'til 7 p.m. $ - $$

The Grocery Basket and Grill
189 Champion Road
Ferguson, NC 28624
Phone 910-973-3114. Mon. through Sat., 6 a.m. to 6 p.m.; Sun., 7
a.m. to 7 p.m. $

Santa Fe Restaurant
U.S. Route 421 Business
Wilkesboro, NC 28697
Phone 910-667-6201. Tues. through Sun., 6 a.m. to 8 p.m. $ - $$

Sparta Restaurant
Main Street
Sparta, NC 28675
Phone 910-372-8016. Mon. through Sat., 6 a.m. to 8 p.m. Closed
Sunday. $

Speckled Trout Cafe
Main Street
Blowing Rock, NC 28605
Phone 704-295-9819. Mon. through Fri.: lunch 11 a.m. to 3 p.m.;
dinner 5 p.m. to 9 p.m. Sat. and Sun.: breakfast and lunch 8 a.m.
to 3 p.m.; dinner 5 p.m. to 9:30 p.m. Specialty is mountain trout
and boy is it tasty! $$ - $$$

Woodlands Barbeque and Picking Parlor
Route 321 Bypass
Blowing Rock, NC 28605
Phone 704-295-3651. Daily, 11 a.m. to 10 p.m. Barbecue and
Mexican specialties. Sandwiches $4; dinners $6.

Travel Information

....

Alleghany County Chamber of Commerce
P.O. Box 1237
348 South Main St.
Sparta, NC 28675
Phone 910-372-5473.

Beech Mountain Chamber of Commerce
403A Beech Mountain Parkway
Beech Mountain, NC 28604
Phone 800-468-5506 or 704-387-9283.

Blowing Rock Chamber of Commerce
Main Street
Blowing Rock, NC 28605
Phone 704-295-7851.

Linn Cove Information Center
Blue Ridge Parkway Headquarters
200 BB&T Building
Asheville, NC 28801
Phone 704-298-0398 (automated info) or 704-271-4779. Daily, 9
a.m. to 5 p.m., May through October. Free.

Southern Appalachian Historical Society
Horn in the West Drive
Boone, NC 28607
Phone 704-264-9089 or 704-264-2120.

The Southern Slopes

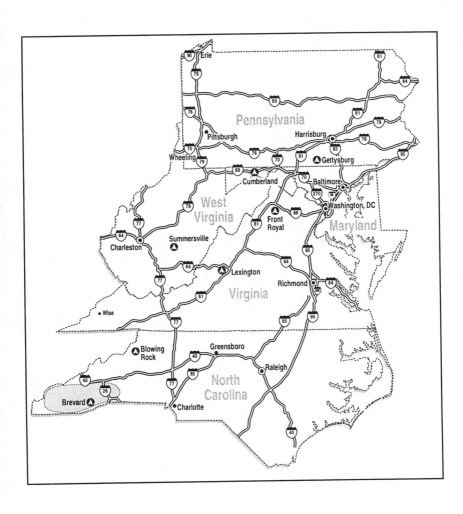

Brevard, N.C.

....

Brevard is a homey little town at the doorstep of Pisgah National Forest. The base camp for the tours in this area is the **Davidson River Campground,** about a mile north of town on Route 276. Davidson River is a popular destination; you may want to make reservations ahead of time using their toll free number (see the listings for details). If you have a pop-up camper, ask for one of the loops that features trailer pads. My campsite featured a special bonus: raspberries! Juicy, red, ripe raspberries. I picked more than two quarts off the vines around my spot. If your plans bring you to the campground in late July, ask for site 101—that's where you'll find them.

As public campgrounds go, Davidson River is clean and quiet. Look around and you'll notice most of the campers bear Florida plates. That's because people have been migrating to western North Carolina for the last two-hundred years to enjoy cool mountain breezes and escape the brutal summer heat of the subtropics. Quiet hour is 11 p.m., but things settle down just after dark. It isn't your normal quiet, though. When the sun goes down, the woods come alive with cicadas, crickets, and a whole host of other noises. An owl joins in for good measure and then, somewhere within the woods, someone plays a hammered dulcimer, the haunting strains of music blending with the forest sounds. The darkness magnifies each sound until your tent practically rocks. As loud as it sounds, it's actually pretty relaxing. You've got to hear it to believe it.

If you prefer a roof over your head, there are plenty to choose from. The **Key Falls Inn** south of town is a quaint country bed and breakfast owned by Clark and Patricia Grosvenor. Their daughter, Janet Fogelman, runs the front desk and manages the inn. I happened to meet Clark, a personable fellow who is pleased to entertain riders in his home. He tells me he has owned bikes at different times in his life and looks

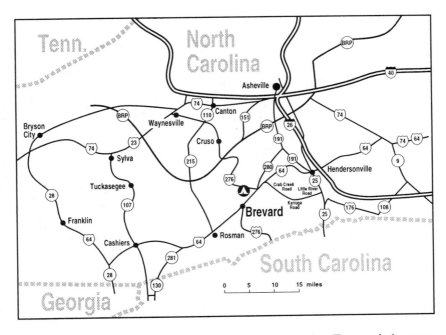

forward to having another one someday. True to their name, there is a small waterfall at the back of the property that you can walk to. The stream runs down by the house under a huge shade tree, making this spot a favorite place to hide from the summer heat. I put the Key Falls at the top of my list for my next visit to the area.

When you have time to spare, downtown Brevard is a comfortable place to park the rig and stroll. Stop by the **Brevard Cafe** for a bite to eat and enjoy browsing the old record albums decorating the walls. The **Brevard Music Center** is open from late June to early August with performances scheduled nearly every evening. You can also have a good time dropping by the softball diamond at Brevard College, where a game is being played most days of the week during the summer.

In case you run out of things to do, Asheville is just 30 minutes away. One place I urge you to visit is **Biltmore Estate,** the home of George Vanderbilt. Its scale and elegance are staggering. When it was finished in 1892 after five years of construction, Biltmore was the largest private residence in America. It still is. Marble, stained glass, gigantic works of

The friendly folks at the Key Falls Inn welcome riders.

art, a gymnasium, bowling alley, pool, the list keeps going. The grounds were designed by the landscape architect Frederick Law Olmsted, whose credits include Central Park in New York. After a tour, you can stroll around and pretend that you are Vanderbilt himself. You could easily spend the better part of a day here—and once you get a taste of the good life, you'll want to stay a lot longer than a day. The estate will validate your ticket for a complimentary second day if you wish to return.

There are hundreds of miles of trails through the national forests in this area, and you can hike for days in the back country. There are dozens of waterfalls, many of which can only be seen by getting off your bike and hiking to them. The **Brevard Information Center** can send you a brochure which locates many of them, and the ranger stations can send detailed information about the hiking trails. Fishing is a certified Big Deal down here because of the hundreds of clear-running streams that are stocked.

As I think back on the time I've spent in the area, I can say without hesitation that hospitality has been a strong point in Brevard, and two-wheeled travelers seem to receive the same warm welcome as anyone else. I found that everyone was eager to please, from the fellas at the corner gas station to the folks at Key Falls. It was even easy to strike up a conversation at the laundromat.

Y'all have a good time, ya hear?

*Route 215 through Pisgah National Forest
offers miles of great riding.*

Trip 25 Taming The Dragon

Distance	*275 miles*
Terrain	*Several mountain passes, valley rides, the "curviest" road in America at Deals Gap, and a long playful stretch of curves along US 64*
Highlights	*Blue Ridge Motorcycle Camping Resort, Nantahala National Forest, Fontana Dam, Franklin gem mines, rafting on the Nantahala*

The Route from Brevard

→ US 276 north to US 23 Business
→ US 23 Business west to US 74
→ US 74 west (joined by US 23 and US 19) to NC 28
→ NC 28 west to US 129
→ US 129 north to Foothills Parkway
→ Turn around and return via US 129
→ US 129 south to US 74
→ US 74 east to NC 28
→ NC 28 south to US 64
→ US 64 east to Brevard

This tour will answer the one question I've fielded more often than any other during the course of working on this book: "What's Deals Gap like?" In case you aren't familiar with the name, Deals Gap is the stretch of US 129 that runs from the Foothills Parkway in Tennessee around the southwestern border of the Great Smoky Mountains and into North Carolina. It's an attractive piece of road. To hear some talk, it's a religious experience. But is one 11-mile stretch of road worth a special pilgrimage, or is it, as one of my left coast riding buddies puts it, "no big deals gap?" Read on, trusted friend, and you shall have your answer.

This is a long one-day ride, and must be broken into two if you desire to spend any time out of the saddle. We begin by following Route 276 through **Pisgah National Forest** along what was once a logging trail. An early morning tour through forest like this is a great way to begin the day. And the further

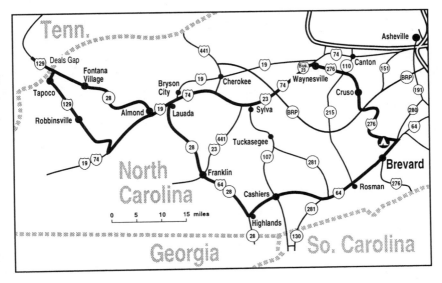

along you get on the road, the more curvy it gets. Sometimes
a little fog settles in during the evening and still hangs in the
trees when you start out. The air is perfumed with the scent
of evergreens so heavy the air is almost green. (Looking
Glass Falls, Sliding Rock and other attractions passed along
this route are discussed in the Pisgah National Forest tour.)

Six miles past the Parkway you pass through Cruso,
home to the **Blue Ridge Motorcycle Camping Resort,** run
by Henry and Dee Hartsfield. Of the four riders-only campgrounds I've visited in North Carolina, this is the finest. The
campground is pleasantly situated along the east fork of the
Pigeon River and has a mix of sunny and shady sites for
camping. A constant breeze helps keep the camp cool, even
on the warmest days of summer. If you stay there overnight,
you'll want to bring a long-sleeved shirt just in case.

Dee runs a kitchen to provide meals for the camp, so you
don't even have to cook. They are completing an expansive
game room and lounge which should be finished by the time
you read this. You could very well make the Resort your
headquarters for the rides outlined in this section. Henry says
that on the highly traveled weekends, they close the gate at
250 bikes. Wow! Most of those riders are repeat customers
who come back year after year, attesting to the quality of the
camp.

Route 276 past Cruso simmers down and becomes a valley road for the duration of your trip. Upon entering Waynesville, look for the intersection with Business 23, follow that west until you join Routes 23 and 74 pointed in the westerly direction, then remain with Route 74 as other roads join and leave it.

Past Waynesville, Route 74 is a delight to ride. It's big, open, and virtually empty. Graceful sweepers are accented by high mountain ridges in the background and quaint towns and villages in the valley below. Before you know it, you've arrived at Almond and you follow Route 28 west. Route 28 gives you a taste of things to come by climbing and dropping and climbing again, curve heaped upon curve. A moderate pace will give you all the work you want and more. An occasional break in the trees gives you an unparalleled view of the Great Smokies in the distance and Fontana Lake below. There are a few picnic tables en route—if you pick something up in Waynesville or Sylva on your way out, you can take advantage of them.

Fontana Dam is the largest on the east coast, 480 feet high and 376 feet wide. This Tennessee Valley Authority (TVA) project was commissioned after the bombing of Pearl Harbor to provide hydroelectric power to aid in the production of atomic energy. Now devoted to a more peaceful purpose—recreation—the 29-mile Fontana Lake seems like a perfect environment for a restful vacation. And unlike other lake resorts I've visited, it doesn't seem overly crowded or busy. Nearby is **Fontana Village Resort,** a good place to make a stopover for the evening, or just a convenient place for lunch. They have a big cafeteria and good food. There's also an ice cream store located next to the cafeteria.

Deals Gap and the answer to the big question lies just a few miles further west. Like many people, I first heard about Deals Gap a few years ago when the motorcycle magazines began hyping the "curviest road in America," a sure-fire attention getter if I've ever heard one. According to everything that has been printed, there are 318 mountain curves in 11 miles. Hmmmmm. It's just 11 miles? Is it really 318 curves? Who counted them? I started thinking that all this hype must be the East Coast rider's way of compensating for

Dee Hartsfield runs a great motorcycles only campground near Cruso, N.C. with her husband, Henry.

not having a few thousand miles of curves in his backyard as do some of our West Coast friends. Sounded like a case of pavement envy to me. Still, as I sat on the front porch of the ice cream parlor at Fontana Village, I could feel my stomach tighten a little and my palms sweat at the prospect of riding what local riders call "The Dragon."

From the direction we're approaching it, the intersection of Route 28 and Route 129 is the ending point for most riders who attack the gap. Most riders begin the run in Tennessee, turn around here and return. The **Crossroads of Time Motel and Motorcycle Campground** is conveniently located here to serve the Ricky Racers and weekend warriors who need to fill up their bikes or their stomachs. The motel would be a convenient place to stay if you arrive late and want to make your trip in the morning, and there is plenty of good company to go around. On the weekends, the place is swarming with full-leather-clad road warriors buzzing around on their 250s and 500s, full dress road sofas like mine, rat bikes, vintage machines, thundering V-twins, and exotic imports. I can't imagine that there would be so many bikes in such a remote location if there weren't something special about this road.

What were the engineers thinking when they laid out the roadbed for US 129 at Deals Gap? We can only be thankful that they didn't use today's blast-and-level road-building techniques which make for fast roads and boring rides. The ride starts off with a quick set of ascending switchbacks almost out of the parking lot at Crossroads and doesn't let up for the next 11 miles. If you're like me, you'll find the road a bit daunting at first, but soon you'll be drawn into the rhythm and find that you're attacking each corner a little harder, hitting each apex with a bit more precision, until soon you are weaving, leaning, braking, accelerating like a pro. After milepost eleven, the road flattens out like someone gave it a yank and you can easily turn around for the return trip. The ride back is even more fun. On your return, the road spends most of its time in ascent, so you can hit it more aggressively. When you get back into North Carolina, you can legitimately buy your "I Survived US 129 at Deals Gap" T-shirt at Crossroads. My conclusion is this: Deals Gap is a nice motorcycling road surrounded by more good motorcycling roads. Don't make a special pilgrimage just for the purpose of running The Dragon, but don't miss it if you're in the area.

The pace slows considerably once you leave the gap and turn south on 129. Following the Cheoah River, the road straightens. There is no development along this section of road, just a series of high cliffs along one side of the road, the river on the other, and forest as far as the eye can see. It's a relaxing ride. To your right is the **Joyce Kilmer National Memorial Forest.** Kilmer, author of the famous poem that begins, "I think that I shall never see a poem as lovely as a tree," was an avid outdoorsman with a deep love for the forest. In his memorial forest is a stand of virgin timber, including a yellow poplar tree eight feet wide, the second largest of its kind in the United States.

The mountains break on your left as you head south out of Robbinsville on 129, revealing the Nantahala River Gorge below. Make the turn onto US 74/US 19 at Topton to continue following the Nantahala River. The length of US 74 from Topton to Beechertown is a popular public access area for river runners and outfitters, so you can anticipate some traffic. On a hot day, this is a great spot to stop and take a ride of a different sort. The **Nantahala Outdoor Center** offers a three and one-half hour trip down the Nantahala River that's tame enough for people like me who aren't as comfortable on the water as they are on two wheels. You will get wet, so you'll either want to plan ahead by bringing a change of clothes or ride until you dry off. On a hot day this can make the difference between an enjoyable ride and a miserable one.

There are also a number of pull-offs along the river where you can just stop for a while, get your T-shirt wet if you wish, and continue on. There are spots along this route with a lot of pedestrian traffic, weekends especially, so be careful.

Route 74 returns to the point where we split to reach Deals Gap. This time, stay with Route 28 when it turns south at Lauada. Here you are treated to another spectacular ten miles of twisting pavement from a high vantage point with scenic vistas and no competition from four-wheelers. Route 28 passes through the famed Cowee Valley, a haven for rock hounds. If you're a gem lover like me, plan to stop at one of the mining camps that dot the landscape, such as the **Mason Mountain Rhodolite and Ruby Mine.** A few dollars buys you a bucket of dirt which you take to a sluice to pan for the one big nugget that will put you on Easy Street. Well, that may be overstating your odds a little, but most places will guarantee that you'll find at least one gem worth mounting.

The town of Franklin is a good place to hole up for the night if you've stretched your one-day trip this far. You can find a good meal any time of the day at the **Sunset Restaurant,** along Route 28 as you enter the town's business district. Their menu features well-prepared, healthy dishes, a nice change of pace from the usual slab–o'–meat and gravy. They make the most refreshing, best–tasting iced tea I have found anywhere. If you'd like to stop over for the night (so you can head back to the gem mine and look for "the big one" again), try the **Downtown Motel** in Franklin.

The return route simply follows Route 64 east. It's a distance of around 60 miles, as I recall. That doesn't sound like much, but when you venture down the road a few miles you'll quickly realize this will be a fun trip. This road is a blast. It follows nearly every contour of the Cullasaja Gorge with an incredibly smooth line of pavement that banks and cambers and pitches like a wild horse. Hold on for this ride!

If you're an advance planner, you can connect this trip with the loops through Pisgah National Forest or with White-water Falls which both explore roads off of Route 64 west of Brevard.

Trip 26 Cradle of Forestry Loop

· ·

Distance   *68 miles, 106 miles with extension*

Terrain   *Two lengthy roads through mountain passes and a small section of the Blue Ridge Parkway*

Highlights *Abundant hiking opportunities around Mount Pisgah, Sliding Rock, Cradle of Forestry, Looking Glass Falls*

The Route from Brevard

→ US 276 south to US 64
→ US 64 west through Brevard to NC 215
→ NC 215 north to NC 110
→ NC 110 north to US 23/74
→ US 23/74 east to NC 151
→ NC 151 south to Blue Ridge Parkway
→ Blue Ridge Parkway west to US 276
→ US 276 south to US 64

The route we're following on this tour constitutes the National Forest Scenic Loop run in reverse. This would be a good day to pack a lunch, because most time is spent within the boundaries of the national forest, and while you might find a stash of wild blueberries to feast on, you might have to share them with a black bear.

Follow Route 64 west out of Brevard to Rosman, then turn north on Route 215 to get the show underway. Within the first mile the forest swallows you up and teases you with a few sweepers that make you hungry for more. Any straggling traffic can be dispensed with a flick of the wrist in some of the straighter stretches. Somewhere within the first few miles, you round a corner and Look Out! Something huge flashes over your head, and instinct forces you to duck. Scanning your rearview mirror you'll discover you've just been bitten by Alligator Rock. There isn't any danger that you'll actually run into it, but the effect is startling.

The route through Pisgah on 215 is a beautiful trek, and the closer you get to the Parkway the more fabulous the view

becomes. And the more twisty. You were just waiting for me
to say that, weren't you? Somewhere within 20 miles of the
Parkway the road begins a steep climb up Tanasee Ridge with
switchbacks galore. Suddenly you break out of the trees and
the entirety of **Pisgah National Forest** unfolds below. There
are several places to pull over for a mile-high photo opportunity. Some have no guard rail or stone retaining wall. You can
walk right to the edge of a sheer cliff and look down a
thousand feet or two feet. Having nearly launched myself off
one of them with an untimely slip of the clutch hand, take my
advice—get off the bike and walk to the cliff!

On the other side of the Blue Ridge Parkway, the road
continues to pass in and out of the trees, allowing you to steal
glimpses of the valley below. It also intermingles with the
Pigeon River which graces your view with waterfalls at
regular intervals. Popular swimming holes are marked by
cars parked along the road.

Route 215 intersects Route 276 at Bethel. Time to make
a decision. If you want to spend a little more time hiking, turn

An unsuspecting driver narrowly misses the massive jaws of "Alligator Rock."

right here and follow Route 276 back to the Parkway. If you need to ride a little more, cross the road and continue on Route 110. This area of the country has a lived-in look and there is some traffic to contend with. I guess you get a little spoiled after spending time with nothing but trees and twis- ties, eh? Route 110 brings you directly into the town of Canton, a nice enough place to visit if the wind is blowing in the right direction. A paper mill in the middle of town makes this a fifty/fifty proposition. Route 110 ends on Routes 23 and 74. Turn right and follow Route 23/74 toward Asheville to Route 151 in New Candler. This section of road is straight and heavily traveled.

The reward for your toils is Route 151 as it approaches the Parkway. The pavement along this road is of an older vintage and broken in places, but it's good enough and I just love the way the curves are stacked together one on top of the other. Part way up the mountain, a waterfall right on the road had attracted the attention of a carload of vacationers who were standing in the middle of the road taking pictures as I rounded the curve. When they saw me they scattered like bowling pins, except for two confused members of the party who stood stock still in the middle of the road like a seven-ten split. I flashed between them before they had a chance to move and picked up the spare.

Upon reaching the Parkway, follow it south. Mount Pisgah is on your right. Reverend James Hall gave the mountain its name because he thought it resembled the mountain Moses stood upon as he viewed the Promised Land. There is a parking area and a 1.5 mile trail that leads to the summit of the mountain. It's a moderate hike with a bit of scrambling involved in places, but a good opportunity to let your legs do some work and let the mind rest from curve chasing. Just down the road from the trailhead is a nice picnic area with large stone tables and grills, plus restroom facilities. Many of the tables rest among the tower oaks and massive rhododendrons, making it the perfect place for a quiet lunch.

As you stand at the overlooks along the Parkway and other scenic back roads, it's amazing to think that at one time all the forest in this area was clear-cut. What looks like a mature forest (climax forest in forestry lingo) is young by comparison to what once stood here. Giant hemlocks, poplars, and other trees hundreds of years old covered these mountains so thickly that you could have probably jumped one branch to another from the eastern seashore to the Mississippi River. All that changed, though, with the landing of the Europeans and the tools they brought with them.

Forestry management was unknown in America until the late 1800s. One tree after another fell for palisades, homesteads, fences, and fire to ward off the wintry chill. Within 200 years, what had once seemed an endless supply of wood was nearing exhaustion. Higher and higher the railroads climbed until some peaks had been cleared entirely, while the steepest ones looked as though they'd been given a bad haircut by a nearsighted barber.

You can thank George Vanderbilt for the lovely view you have today. Vanderbilt became concerned that the destruction of the forest to the west would soon eliminate the vistas from his Asheville estate, Biltmore. He hired Gifford Pinchot to manage the forest around his home. Soon after he added another 100,000 acres, which today approximates the boundaries of Pisgah National Forest. Some people have a knack for making money; Vanderbilt was one of them. When it was discovered that his forest management policy generated greenery in big denominations, interest in managing forests spread across the nation. Pinchot went on to serve as the head of the U.S. Forestry Service and his replacement, Dr. Carl Schenck, established the first forestry school in the United States in Biltmore's Forest.

When you've had enough hiking and picnicking, pack up and follow the Parkway south to Wagon Road Gap, where you'll head south on Route 276. The first few miles feature good riding with a few big switchbacks. You will come up quickly on the next stop. Schenck's forestry school is the setting for the **Cradle of Forestry in America**, an interpretive association dedicated to continuing the work that Schenck did and to educate folks like you and me in the ways of forestry management.

People lived in this area before Vanderbilt bought it, and their empty buildings served as the campus for Schenck's school. Evidently, some of the accommodations were less than luxurious. Students named some of their quarters "Hell Hole," "Little Hell Hole," and my personal favorite, "Rest for the Wicked." The route continues to cascade down Pisgah Ridge, eventually hooking up with Looking Glass River. Route 276 and Route 215 are both old logging trails that were constructed before Vanderbilt bought this land.

You can't mistake the parking area for Sliding Rock. On a hot day it's jammed with cars as everyone seeks an escape from the summer heat. Being on a two-wheeler, you shouldn't have any trouble squeezing your scoot into a small spot. Sliding Rock is a natural waterslide, a gigantic smooth rock face 150 feet in length. About 11,000 gallons of water

*Looking Glass
Falls is a
popular photo
opportunity in
Pisgah National
Forest.*

between 50 and 60 degrees flow over the rock each minute. A lifeguard is on duty during the summer season.

Just a little further down the road and near the end of the loop is Looking Glass Falls, another popular stop. A board-walk lets you climb down to the river for a closer look and better camera angle without tearing up the riverbank. This is one of the most photographed falls in the area.

From here it is just a few miles to Brevard on an easy stretch of road.

Trip 27 Whitewater Falls

• •

Distance   *130 miles*

Terrain   *Lightly-traveled roads between small towns afford a comfortable touring pace. Higher elevations toward end of tour, including a short section of the Blue Ridge Parkway.*

Highlights   *Highest waterfall in eastern U.S., Mountain Heritage Center, Jackson County Courthouse, and highest point of the Parkway*

The Route from Brevard

→ US 64 west to NC 281
→ NC 281 south to SC 130
→ SC 130 west to SC 107
→ SC 107 north to NC 107
→ NC 107 north to US 23/74
→ US 23/74 east to Blue Ridge Parkway
→ Blue Ridge Parkway north to NC 215
→ NC 215 south to US 64
→ US 64 east to Brevard

The first part of the route is wide open dual-laned road following Route 64 west, but somewhere around Rosman things get tight and kinky. I turned right and tried Route 281, finding gravel after a few miles. A side road off of that, Slick Fisher, promised to shortcut across the gravel section, but when it ended, Route 281 remained unpaved. Good for dual sports and smaller bikes you can hold up with your feet. Bad for full dress touring couches. I turned around to remain on sure footing and as I retraced my path, began mentally rearranging my garage, trying to visualize space for a dual sport bike.

The day was growing remarkably hot. The increase in humidity made even my well-ventilated Aerostitch riding suit feel like I was wearing a wet plastic bag. As I returned to Route 64, I determined it was time to shed the suit and find some refreshment. Private enterprise is alive and well along Route 64, guaranteeing that if it is refreshment you seek, you

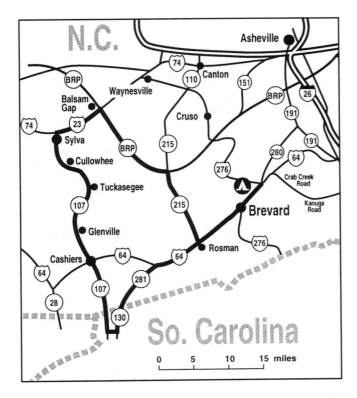

will rarely have to travel far to find it. The Toxaway Falls Stand is everything you'd want in a roadside stand, and more. Plunk down a dollar for a cup of cider and you'll get a hundred dollars worth of conversation and travel advice in return. I mean that in a good way. Having found my first potential route thwarted by unexpected road conditions, I asked the stand owner, a kind country woman in her mid-fifties, what she would recommend I see in the area. She pointed west. "Follow 281 south and you'll find Whitewater Falls. It's the biggest on the East Coast," she said. Who says a dollar won't get you anything these days?

Follow the combined routes 64 and 281 west until they split, then continue to follow Route 281 south. I'll pass along a bit of advice she forgot: bring a bucket. The entire nine miles of the route is covered with blackberry vines, and it didn't look like a single one had been picked. I couldn't help myself, I had to stop a couple of times along the way, whenever a particularly inviting patch came into view, and enjoy

one handful after another. I felt like Rutherford B. Hayes and his "great armed blackberry party." That was the slowest nine miles I've logged on any bike I've owned!

Whitewater Falls is situated on the border between North and South Carolina. At 411 feet, these falls are twice as high as Niagara. Of course, not nearly as much water passes over them, but they are beautiful nonetheless. There is a parking area and a short walk to see the falls from a high and distant view. If you would rather have a closer look, the hike is substantially longer, but there are picnic facilities near the base of the gorge. If you had in mind to ride only a short distance and take a picnic lunch, this would be a great destination.

Out of the lot and a mile later you'll find yourself in the state of South Carolina. Just a mile or two after the South Carolina border, turn right to follow Route 130 through

Sumter National Forest. At the end, turn right and you'll pick up Route 107, our return route north. This route passes through Cashiers (pronounced CASH-ers, rhymes with flashers), a quaint town and another popular summer haunt of the wealthy lowland planters. From the state border to about Glenville, the road is two-lane, a little twisty, and mostly empty. There's a flurry of activity around Cashiers, but north of town you're by yourself. Once you pass the Thorpe Reservoir, the road snuggles up to the west fork of the Tuckasegee River and that means we've got work to do!

Roughly halfway along this section of the route is a rather large and unusual marker, a monument to a woman known locally as **Aunt Sally.** The monument was placed along the roadside by Dr. John Brinkley to honor the memory of a woman who served the community with her knowledge of folk medicine in the days before trained physicians were readily available. Her example inspired Dr. Brinkley to follow in her footsteps and become a doctor himself, returning to the same area to continue her work.

Route 107 continues its trek through the river valley, and begins ascending into the higher elevations, which rewards you with cooler temperatures. Gradually the route straightens as you approach Cullowhee, home of Western Carolina University. The school is located in one of the prettiest natural settings I can recall. Situated in a natural bowl, the Grand Balsam Mountains rise behind it with dramatic effect. On campus is the **Mountain Heritage Center,** a museum which tells the story of the Scots-Irish. It's an interesting story because it demonstrates how the social engineering that takes place on one side of the pond can affect the other.

From the time King James the First of Scotland ascended to the throne of the British Empire, his single greatest desire was to unite the kingdom by bringing the unruly and predominantly Catholic Irish into the Protestant English fold. His idea for accomplishing this was to transplant a colony of loyal Scottish subjects into Ulster, Ireland, and hope that they would have some calming effect on the population. It didn't work. Ultimately the Ulster Scots or Scots-Irish had enough and decided it was time to get out of town while the getting was good. Most of them fled to ports like Philadelphia where

they had trade ties, moved to the interior of Pennsylvania, and slowly worked their way down the Great Valley of Virginia, settling in the hills and hollows of the Appalachians.

The Scots–Irish continue to follow many of the traditions of their former life; you can see and hear them today in the strains of Bluegrass, the annual Gathering of the Scottish Clans at Grandfather Mountain, and the Mountain Heritage Day sponsored each year by the university.

The best place to find a good meal is a few miles north of the museum in Sylva. For a small town, Sylva has a good selection of places to eat. Stop by the **Jackson County Travel Authority** for maps, fliers and more information. After consulting with local gustatory expert Dean Cloer, I followed his recommendation to try **LuLu's Cafe.** Located along Main Street in the heart of downtown, it's an excellent restaurant featuring a wide selection of healthfully-prepared dishes with an "impressive presentation" (that's the only snooty dining term I know so I use it sparingly). I can heartily recommend the chicken served on a bed of wild rice and the excellent gazpacho.

Before you depart Sylva, you might want to take a picture or two of the Jackson County Courthouse, which dominates the landscape. An impressive rotunda crowns the building and the 108 steps which lead to the top make for good photo opportunities.

Follow combined Routes 23 and 74 east out of Sylva toward Waynesville. This is a great stretch of road for its huge sweepers and fantastic view of the mountains. This is one of the prettiest sections of road off the Parkway I've seen. The road through the valley is high enough to get you above the treetops and your view of the Balsam Mountains on either side is unparalleled. You'll find yourself holding the throttle open wider than normal on those big gentle curves, feeling the cool mountain air rush over your body, and buddy— you'll be loving life.

Our route rejoins the Parkway at Balsam Gap. Along the way you'll reach 6,053 feet, the highest elevation on the Parkway and just a few hundred feet shy of the highest elevation in the eastern U.S. In areas above 5,500 feet where the climate remains cool enough throughout the year, flora and fauna of the Canadian forest zone dominate the landscape. Here are the big red spruce and towering fir, making it look for all the world as though you had been transported a thousand miles north.

This section of the Parkway contains some of the most dramatic scenery along its entire length. Most of the mountains you see have summits above 5,000 feet, and on a clear day views can exceed 80 miles. When you reach the vicinity of milepost 425, look for Route 215 and exit following it south. Don't worry, the fun's not over just yet, because Route 215 is one of the finest riding roads in the area. It passes through Pisgah National Forest and in higher elevations it has pullovers with commanding views of its own. About halfway down the mountain, it turns up the heat with switchbacks bunching up together, causing you to reach for the throttle and drop a gear or two. There's a breather, followed by more quick turns, and then Alligator Rock. All too soon you've arrived at the intersection with Route 64 to make the left turn for home base.

Trip 28 Chimney Rock

∙∙∙

Distance   *130 miles*

Terrain   *Hilly to begin, more twists after Hendersonville. Valley ride followed by ascent of Blue Ridge. Route home following Blue Ridge has more curves. Optional shortcut passes through minimum of urban clutter with significantly reduced return time.*

Highlights   *Flat Rock Playhouse, Carl Sandburg's home, Lake Lure, Chimney Rock, the Folk Art Center*

The Route from Brevard
→ US 276 south to US 64
→ US 64 east to Crab Creek Road
→ Crab Creek becomes Kanuga Road
→ Kanuga Road to Little River Road
→ Little River Road to US 25
→ US 25 south to US 25/I-26 Connector
→ US 25/I-26 Connector north to US 176
→ US 176 east to NC 108
→ NC 108 east to NC 9
→ NC 9 north to US 74
→ US 74 west to Blue Ridge Parkway
→ Blue Ridge Parkway north to Folk Art Center*
→ Blue Ridge Parkway south to US 276
→ US 276 south to Davidson River Campground

*Optional route from Folk Art Center
→ Blue Ridge Parkway south to NC 191
→ NC 191 south to NC 280
→ NC 280 west to US 276 at Ecusta
→ US 276 north to Davidson River Campground

The best way to begin this tour is to get into the Flat Rock area from the back door. Out of Brevard, follow Route 64 east to Penrose. Turn right and follow Crab Creek Road to escape from the urban clutter and find a road more suitable to our accustomed style of traveling. The back road is rural, lightly traveled, and offers nice photo opportunities of North Caro-

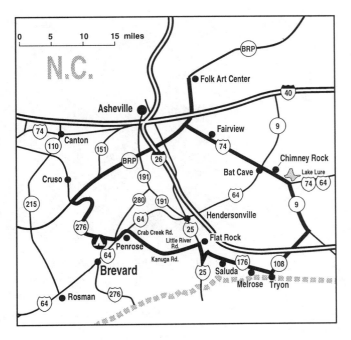

lina's country landscapes. When the road changes counties, it becomes Kanuga Road. To avoid the clutter along US 25 in Hendersonville, make a right turn on Little River Road in Flat Rock. This brings you directly into Flat Rock.

You'll know when you've arrived in Flat Rock by the size of the houses. They're huge. Flat Rock was a summer escape for the well-heeled from the vast estates of the lowlands, which explains the grand designs. Look for Little River Road on your right, make the turn, and follow it to our first two stops. The **Flat Rock Playhouse** and the **Carl Sandburg National Historic Site** are directly opposite one another. The easiest thing to do is find a parking spot in the playhouse lot. There are certain time restrictions when you can park there to visit the home, so check them out.

The Flat Rock Playhouse is the official theater of North Carolina and would make a good night out on the town for one of your free evenings. The schedule includes some well-known titles from Broadway and London. On another note, you'll find the town's namesake resting peacefully in front of the playhouse as it has for thousands of years, a large slab of granite that is just what it looks like: a flat rock.

Carl Sandburg's home offers an interesting insight into the author's life.

Strip out of your riding suit for the hike to the Sandburg Home. It's an uphill walk and if you're covered head to toe with leather you'll be ripe by the time you get to the house. On second thought, I suppose it would be one way to get your own personal tour!

Sandburg's home, Connemara, is an interesting contrast to the big pretentious estates that surround it. Sandburg and his wife Paula were both of conservative Swedish stock, and their simple taste in furnishings is reflected in the practical no-nonsense utility of each room. Paula lived in the home until her death in 1978 and all the rooms are preserved as she left them. Books line the walls in almost all the common rooms except the kitchen, all part of Sandburg's 10,000-volume library. Candid photos of home and family fill the walls where books don't. Paula's brother was Edward Steichen, a world-renowned portrait photographer. He took many of these photographs, including the famous Carl and Paula picture shown in displays in several places throughout the farm.

Sandburg won two Pulitzer Prizes for his writing, one for a history of Abraham Lincoln and another for a collection of poems. He was an amazingly versatile writer who could portray the hard edge of life in his poems and, at the opposite extreme, the funny, nonsense fairy tales that he invented for his daughters, the "Rutabaga Stories." During the summer, members of the playhouse perform his stories for children on the grounds of the home. Be sure to drop by and listen in—his humor was intelligent enough to appeal to all ages.

If you carry a National Parks Passport, collect your stamp downstairs in the converted cellar, now the Park Service's office.

Resume the route out of the parking lot at Sandburg's house by following Little River Road a tenth of a mile east to US 25. Turn right on US 25 south to leave Flat Rock. Route 25 intersects with a connector road to get to Interstate 26. Follow the Route 25 connector road toward the interstate, but exit on US 176 east. This stretch of Route 176 gives you a good mix of straights and sweepers as you pass through a few small villages. Along portions of this route, you can't help but notice the vast areas of trees that are covered by an incredibly dense, broad-leaf vine.

This is the infamous kudzu. It was brought from Asia for ground cover along roadsides to prevent runoff and reduce mowing, but like a science experiment gone wrong, the stuff literally took over. Anything that stands still more than a few days is enveloped by a veil of green. If you stop along the roadside, you'll swear you can almost hear the stuff growing. But remember, don't stand in one place too long!

Towns along the road like Saluda tell you the history of an area in more interesting ways than you will ever read about in this tome or any other. You can see the cycles of boom and bust by looking at the buildings downtown. Things are looking up right now as a new surge in tourism in the area has brought new coats of paint to some old buildings and new businesses to serve the needs of passersby-by.

If your ride is happy in the dirt, you can cut across the route here by following Holbert Cove Road and then pick up Silver Creek Road to come out just a few miles south of Lake Lure, our next destination. A good portion of the roads are gravel and would be slow going on a full dresser. Staying on Route 176 will reward you with a section of twisties that trails off around Melrose. Follow 176 into Tryon, Route 108 east, then Route 9 north. Most of the riding between Tryon and Lake Lure is easy cruising over rolling roads with an occasional glimpse of the Blue Ridge to your west.

The view from the bottom of Chimney Rock is as good as the view from the top—and cheaper, too!

Your entry into the Lake Lure area may be a busy one. This is a stretch where Routes 64 and 74 share the same roadway and the result is often heavy traffic, making your left turn difficult. On a hot day it can be an especially tough stretch to ride. However, a few public beach areas along the lake beckon you to hop off your ride and dip your T-shirt in the sparkling blue waters, a move that will bring instant relief.

When you get to Chimney Rock, you begin to realize what generates so much traffic along this road. All you have to do is look up. Striking a suggestive pose against a backdrop of tree-covered ridges is an outcropping of rock suggesting a chimney (or other devices, depending on your imagination). It's now a part of a private enterprise called **Chimney Rock Park** which includes trails that allow you to climb to the top of Chimney Rock or visit Hickory Nut Falls. An elevator has been installed if you aren't in the mood for hiking. Reaching the top gives you a commanding view of the gorge, falls, and Lake Lure.

Somehow all this climbing and hiking and sightseeing cultivates a pretty sharp appetite. And just as you'd expect, there are a host of restaurants, taverns, and shops waiting to please. Many of the restaurants on the same side as Chimney Rock are built along a sheer cliff with back decks which run well behind the restaurant, putting you near the river which runs through the gorge.

While in town, you had just as well surrender to the bug and browse among the wide variety of tasteless travel gifts found in many of the stores. My sister-in-law was quite pleased with the ceramic spoon holder I bought for her here, featuring an enameled picture of Chimney Rock on it. Every household should have one, I always say.

I thought the store most interesting to visit was **Bubba's General Store,** Bubba being the large golden retriever whose mug is featured prominently on the storefront. I didn't get to meet Bubba, but I did have a chance to stand on the front porch and swill Coca Cola from a genuine deposit bottle, something that disappeared from my hometown years ago. Bubba's also has an upscale brand of merchandise, with more handmade and expensive items than the other stores. Mind you, that's not to take away anything from my spoon holder. Every now and then I had to take it out and admire it. In fact, I liked it so much I went back and bought another for myself.

Route 74 west continues to trace a course through a narrow gorge, often with just enough width carved out of the rock to carry the road. Your route passes through Bat Cave, where you will shed some traffic. True to its name, a cave nearby is home to a large colony of bats.

Between Bat Cave and Fairview, the curves return with a few sections featuring tight, well-graded switchbacks. After crossing the Blue Ridge, the excitement passes and casual touring mode resumes. This course will put you directly in the path of the Blue Ridge Parkway. At this point you are near the **Folk Art Center** run by the Southern Highland Handicraft Guild. The guild is about three miles north on the Parkway (signs point the way). You won't find spoon holders with anything on them here; this is an outlet for Appalachian artisans. Downstairs is a large vendor area where you can buy simple wooden toys or expensive works of art. Upstairs features a museum of more handiwork. Some are available for purchase while others are marked "NFS," not for sale.

A recommendation for the return trip to Brevard depends largely upon the time of day. Since you are so close to Asheville, you might wish to stop in town for dinner. If your return trip is in the dark, the safest return route is to follow the Parkway to Route 191, then pick up Route 280. This leads back to Route 276 where you'll turn north to return to the campground. Whitetail deer are a particular hazard after dark. If you have more time before sundown, a leisurely stroll along the Parkway and a return via US 276 are a fitting end to the day.

Oh, and when you get back, you might check to make sure you didn't pick up any kudzu along the way. Otherwise you might find a mound of green in the morning where your bike had been.

Well, it has to end somewhere . . .

Lodging

· ·

Blue Ridge Motorcycle Camping Resort
Route 2, Box 461
US Highway 276
Canton, NC 28716
Phone 704-235-8350. Season runs April 15 through October 30.
Best motorcycle campground in North Carolina. $8 single, $12
double, $30 cabin double occupancy; includes linens.

The Crossroads of Time Motel & Motorcycle Campground
P.O. Box 58
US Hwy 129 & NC 28
Tapoco, NC 28780
Phone 704-498-2231. Single (with double bed), $22.50. Double
(2 double beds, no TV or AC, fan available), $28.50. Deluxe dou-
ble (two doubles with TV and AC), $32.50. Prices quoted are for
double occupancy. $6.50 for each additional person.

Davidson River Campground
U.S. Route 276
Brevard, NC 28712
Phone 800-280-CAMP or 704-877-4910. Use 800 number for
reservations from ten up to 120 days in advance. Reservations are
accepted for visits between May 1st and October 31st. $10 tent/
trailer sites; limit of 6 per site (they seem flexible).

Downtown Motel
318 East Main Street
Franklin, NC 28734
Phone 704-524-4406. Singles from $22.

Fontana Village Resort
P.O. Box 68
Hwy 28
Fontana Dam, NC 28733
Phone 800-849-2258 or 704-498-2211. Open all year. Camping
from $8; rooms from $29; cottages from $36.

Key Falls Inn
151 Everett Road
Pisgah Forest, NC 28768
Phone 704-884-7559. From $55.

Biltmore Estate
One North Pack Square
Asheville, NC 28801
Phone 800-543-2961. Open daily except Thanksgiving, Christmas, and New Year's, 9 a.m. to 5 p.m. $25 per person.

Brevard Music Center
P.O. Box 592
US Route 64, West Main St.
Brevard, NC 28712
Phone 704-884-2019. Season runs from late June to early August. Tickets from $12.

Bubba's General Store
P.O. Box 193
Hwy 64-74 East
Chimney Rock, NC 28720
Phone 704-625-2479. Daily, 10 a.m. to 7:30 p.m.

Carl Sandburg National Historic Site
P.O. Box 395
US Hwy 25 South
Flat Rock, NC 28731
Phone 704-693-4178. Open 9 a.m. to 5 p.m. every day except Christmas. National Parks Passport stamp location. Guided tours available on weekends at least every hour. $2 per person 17 and older to tour home; free with Golden Age pass.

Chimney Rock Park
P.O. Box 39
Hwy 64-74 East
Chimney Rock, NC 28720
Phone 800-277-9611 or 704-625-9611. 8:30 a.m. to 4:30 p.m. Adults, $9; ages 6 to 15, $4.50; under 6, free.

Cradle of Forestry in America Interpretive Association
1002 Pisgah Highway
Pisgah Forest, NC 28768
Phone 704-884-5713 or 704-877-3130.

Flat Rock Playhouse
P.O. Box 310
2661 Greenville Highway
Flat Rock, NC 28731
Phone 704-693-0731. Season runs Memorial Day to Labor Day.
Box office opens at 10 a.m. Tickets from $18.

Folk Art Center
P.O. Box 9545
Milepost 382, Blue Ridge Parkway
Asheville, NC 28815
Phone 704-298-7928. 9 a.m. to 5 p.m. Free.

Mason Mountain Rhodolite and Ruby Mine
895 Bryson City Road
Franklin, NC 28734
Phone 704-524-4570. Mine is open daily, 8 a.m. to 5 p.m.; gift
shop is open May to Sept. (opens when they get it cleaned up).
$5 per day, includes equipment.

Mountain Heritage Center
Western Carolina University
Cullowhee, NC 28723
Phone 704-227-7211. Weekdays, 8 a.m. to 5 p.m. Free.

Nantahala Outdoor Center
13077 Highway 19 West
Bryson City, NC 28713-9114
Phone 800-232-7238 or 704-488-6900. Trips from $14.

Pisgah National Forest
Pisgah Ranger District
1001 Pisgah Highway
Pisgah Forest, NC 28768
Phone 704-877-3265.

Restaurants

Brevard Cafe
34 South Broad Street
Brevard, NC 28712
Phone 704-884-5060. Sun. through Wed., 7 a.m. to 2:30 p.m.;
also open Thurs. through Sat., 4:30 p.m. to 8 p.m. Full lunch or
dinner, about $5.

Lulu's Cafe
Main Street
Sylva, NC 28779
Phone 704-586-8989. Mon. through Thurs., 11 a.m. to 8:30 p.m.;
Fri. and Sat. 'til 9 p.m. Closed Sunday. $ - $$

Sunset Restaurant
214 Harrison Avenue
Franklin, NC 28734
Phone 704-524-4842. Mon. through Sat., 6 a.m. to 9 p.m. Full
dinners for around $5.

Travel Information

Brevard Information Center
35 West Main Street
Brevard, NC 28712
Phone 800-648-4523 or 704-883-3700. Ask for Esther. Really.

Franklin Area Chamber of Commerce
180 Porter Street
Franklin, NC 28734
Phone 800-336-7829 or 704-524-3161.

Henderson County Travel and Tourism
739 North Main Street
Hendersonville, NC 28792
Phone 800-828-4244.

Jackson County Travel Authority
18 North Central Street
Sylva, NC 28779
Phone 800-962-1911 or 704-586-2155.

Appendix – Motorcycle Dealers

· ·

Following is a list of dealers who sell and service major motorcycle brands in the states covered by this book. While a list of this kind can never be completely accurate, it will nonetheless give you a shot at finding help on the road if you need it.

If you have a Suzuki, you can call their toll-free number to find the location of their current dealers. Call 1-800-255-2550.

DEALER (Alphabetical by state, then numerical by zip code)	BMW	Ducati	Harley-Davidson	Honda	Kawasaki	Moto Guzzi	Suzuki	Yamaha
Delaware								
Honda East Yamaha 620 Pulaski Hwy - Rt. 40 Bear, DE 19701 Phone: 302-322-4120				●				●
Track and Trail BMW 2A King Ave. New Castle, DE 19720 Phone: 302-323-9044	●	●			●		●	
Mike's Famous Harley-Davidson 2102 NE Governor Prince Blvd. Wilmington, DE 19802 Phone: 302-658-1416 Also handles Triumph			●					
Diamond Motor Sports U.S. Route 13 Camden, DE 19934 Phone: 302-697-3222					●	●		●

DEALER (Alphabetical by state, then numerical by zip code)	BMW	Ducati	Harley-Davidson	Honda	Kawasaki	Moto Guzzi	Suzuki	Yamaha
Harley-Davidson of Seaford U.S. 13 North Seaford, DE 19973 Phone: 302-629-6161			•					
Maryland								
Atlantic Cycle & Power 4420 Rt 301 - Crain Hwy White Plains, MD 20695 Phone: 301-705-7278				•	•		•	•
Heyser Cycle Sales U.S. 1 South Laurel, MD 20707 Phone: 301-776-6932				•	•			•
Free State Cycle Corporation 4418 Baltimore Ave. Bladensburg, MD 20710 Phone: 301-779-0800				•			•	
Harley-Davidson of Washington 9407 Livingston Rd. Fort Washington, MD 20744 Phone: 301-248-1200			•					
Otho Williams Inc. 5510 Silver Hill Rd. Forestville, MD 20747 Phone: 301-420-2500				•				
Bob's BMW 10630-Y Riggs Hill Rd. Jessup, MD 20794 Phone: 301-924-5155	•							
Rockville H-D Inc. & Battley-Cycles 7830 Airpark Rd. Gaithersburg, MD 20879 Phone: 301-948-4581 Also handles Triumph, Buell, and Bimota	•	•	•					•
Snavely Service 7820 Airpark Rd. Gaithersburg, MD 20879 Phone: 301-670-9788						•		
Cycles USA 14021 Georgia Ave. Silver Springs, MD 20906 Phone: 301-460-1600				•	•		•	

DEALER (Alphabetical by state, then numerical by zip code)	BMW	Ducati	Harley-Davidson	Honda	Kawasaki	Moto Guzzi	Suzuki	Yamaha
Pete's Cycle Co. 344 Bel Air Rd. Bel Air, MD 21014 Phone: 410-838-8021				•	•		•	•
Garrett's Harley-Davidson Sales 3938 Conowingo Rd. Darlington, MD 21034 Phone: 410-457-4541			•					
Surf N' Turf Cycles 12238 Pulaski Hwy. Joppa, MD 21085 Phone: 410-679-2200					•		•	
Pete's Cycle Co. 800 Ritchie Hwy Severna Park, MD 21146 Phone: 410-647-5880					•			•
Pete's Cycle Co. 5001 Harford Rd. Baltimore, MD 21214 Phone: 410-254-3102 Also handles Triumph	•			•				•
Harley-Davidson of Baltimore 2834 Loch Raven Rd. Baltimore, MD 21218 Phone: 410-366-0616			•					
Cycle World 5810 Ritchie Hwy Baltimore, MD 21225 Phone: 410-636-0600		•		•	•		•	•
Marc's Honda 22 Hammonds Ln. Baltimore, MD 21225 Phone: 410-789-7400				•				
Harley-Davidson of Maryland 6339 Howard Ln. Elkridge, MD 21227 Phone: 410-796-1044			•					
Rosedale Cycle World 7930 Pulaksi Hwy Baltimore, MD 21237 Phone: 410-574-3800		•		•	•		•	•
Annapolis Honda-Polaris 333 Busch's Frontage Rd. Annapolis, MD 21401 Phone: 410-757-1100				•				

DEALER (Alphabetical by state, then numerical by zip code)	BMW	Ducati	Harley-Davidson	Honda	Kawasaki	Moto Guzzi	Suzuki	Yamaha
Harley-Davidson of Annapolis 1929 Lincoln Dr. Annapolis, MD 21401 Phone: 410-263-3345			●					
Cumberland Cycles 10580 Mt. Savage Rd. NW Cumberland, MD 21502 Phone: 301-777-3614							●	●
All Seasons Motorsports 4137 Maryland Hwy Oakland, MD 21550 Phone: 301-334-4558					●		●	●
Fredericktown Yamaha 5800 Urbana Pike Frederick, MD 21701 Phone: 301-663-8333								●
Harley-Davidson of Frederick 5722 Urbana Pike Frederick, MD 21701 Phone: 301-694-8177			●					
JT Motorsports 5708 Urbana Pike Frederick, MD 21701-7202 Phone: 301-846-4318							●	
Dutrows Sales & Service 6949 Baltimore Nat. Pk. Frederick, MD 21702 Phone: 301-473-8117				●				
Honda of Hagerstown 19828 National Pike Hagerstown, MD 21740 Phone: 301-797-7200				●				
Twigg Cycles 34 North Cannon Ave. Hagerstown, MD 21740 Phone: 301-739-2773					●		●	●
C & L Cycle Shop 1526 Liberty Rd. Eldersburg, MD 21784 Phone: 410-795-3780				●			●	
Horner Honda 1135 S. Salisbury Blvd. Salisbury, MD 21801 Phone: 410-749-6661				●				

DEALER (Alphabetical by state, then numerical by zip code)	BMW	Ducati	Harley-Davidson	Honda	Kawasaki	Moto Guzzi	Suzuki	Yamaha
Sundance Cycle 103 S Fruitland Blvd - Box 249 Fruitland, MD 21826-1653 Phone: 410-749-0111						•	•	
North Carolina								
Granite City Yamaha 960 Highway 52 South Mount Airy, NC 27030 Phone: 910-786-5343								•
Worth Honda/Kawasaki 600 W. Pine St. Mt. Airy, NC 27030 Phone: 910-786-5111				•	•			
Curly's Harley-Davidson 3825 Reidsville Rd. at B-I40 Winston-Salem, NC 27101 Phone: 910-722-3106			•					
Honda of Winston-Salem 591 So. Stratford Rd. Winston-Salem, NC 27103 Phone: 910-765-0330				•		•		
Suzuki of Winston-Salem 5658 Country Club Rd. Winston-Salem, NC 27104-3309 Phone: 910-765-9156							•	
Forsyth Motosports Inc. 5599 University Pkwy. Winston-Salem, NC 27105 Phone: 910-767-2020 Also handles Triumph and Bimota	•	•			•			
Carolina Yamaha Polaris 745 Silas Creek Pkwy Winston-Salem, NC 27127 Phone: 910-727-1888								•
Cox's Harley-Davidson 278 Crestview Church Rd. Asheboro, NC 27203 Phone: 910-629-2415			•					
Cycle Center 520 Cox Ave. Asheboro, NC 27203 Phone: 910-629-2092					•			

DEALER (Alphabetical by state, then numerical by zip code)	BMW	Ducati	Harley-Davidson	Honda	Kawasaki	Moto Guzzi	Suzuki	Yamaha
Ace Cycle Sales 2468 N. Church St. Burlington, NC 27215 Phone: 910-227-1491				●				
Jordan's 625 N. Park Ave. Burlington, NC 27217 Phone: 910-227-1261			●					●
Honda of High Point 3037 N. Main St. High Point, NC 27265 Phone: 910-869-2510				●				
Honda Suzuki of Sanford Hwy 87 S - 3128 S. Horner Sanford, NC 27330 Phone: 919-775-3638				●			●	
Lee's Kawasaki 1538 National Hwy. Thomasville, NC 27360 Phone: 910-889-4667					●			
Ray's Cycle Shop Rt. 6 - I-85 Business Loop Thomasville, NC 27360 Phone: 910-475-2397				●				
Midway Yamaha-Suzuki 1335 National Hwy. Thomasville, NC 27360-2317 Phone: 910-885-5796							●	●
Stroud Honda-Suzuki of Greensboro 801 Post St. Greensboro, NC 27405 Phone: 910-272-2661				●			●	
Young Harley-Davidson/Kawasaki 538 Farragut St. Greensboro, NC 27406 Phone: 910-273-1743 Also handles Buell			●		●			
Tri City Honda Yamaha 715 Tri City Blvd. Greensboro, NC 27407 Phone: 910-852-4228				●				●
Honda/Yamaha of Raleigh 222 Hwy 70-E Garner, NC 27529 Phone: 919-772-7866				●				●

DEALER (Alphabetical by state, then numerical by zip code)	BMW	Ducati	Harley-Davidson	Honda	Kawasaki	Moto Guzzi	Suzuki	Yamaha
Shelton's Harley-Davidson 1302 N. William St. Goldsboro, NC 27530 Phone: 919-731-2776			●					
Fun Products 2803 Royal Ave. Goldsboro, NC 27534-9496 Phone: 919-778-7433				●	●		●	●
Brewer Cycles Route 6 - Box 291 - Warrenton Rd. Henderson, NC 27536 Phone: 919-492-8553				●	●			●
Fox's Suzuki-Kawasaki 3146 Durham Rd. Roxboro, NC 27573-6101 Phone: 910-599-3787					●		●	
Kawasaki of Raleigh 1302 Downtown Blvd. Raleigh, NC 27603 Phone: 704-452-5831					●			
Motorcycles Unlimited 2609 S. Saunders St. Raleigh, NC 27603 Phone: 919-834-5111 Also handles Triumph	●			●				
Ray Price Harley-Davidson 1126 S. Saunders St. Raleigh, NC 27603 Phone: 919-832-2261			●					
Barnett Suzuki/Ducati/Moto Guzzi 1509 Lake Wheeler Rd. Raleigh, NC 27603-2325 Phone: 919-833-5575		●				●	●	
Motorcycles Unlimited 2609 S. Saunders Street Raleigh, NC 27603-2839 Phone: 919-834-5111	●							
Durham Harley-Davidson 819 N. Miami Boulevard Durham, NC 27703 Phone: 919-682-2261			●					
Byrd's Motorsports 2715 Cheek Rd. Durham, NC 27704 Phone: 919-688-7999					●			

DEALER (Alphabetical by state, then numerical by zip code)	BMW	Ducati	Harley-Davidson	Honda	Kawasaki	Moto Guzzi	Suzuki	Yamaha
Triangle Cycles 4503 Chapel Hill Blvd. Durham, NC 27707 Phone: 919-489-7478				●				●
Brown's Harley-Davidson 2831 N. Church St. Rocky Mount, NC 27804 Phone: 919-446-7292 Also handles Triumph			●					
Twin County Honda-Suzuki 1720 Wesleyan Blvd. Rocky Mount, NC 27804-6629 Phone: 919-977-2191				●			●	
J & E Harley-Davidson 1008 Dickinson Ave. Greenville, NC 27834 Phone: 919-757-1345			●					
Ron Ayers Motorsports 1918 N. Memorial Dr. Greenville, NC 27834-1135 Phone: 919-758-3084				●	●		●	
Collier Harley-Davidson Rte 5 Box 417 - Highway 158 W Roanoke Rapids, NC 27870 Phone: 919-537-6493			●					
Honda-Kawa-Yama of Roanoke Rapids 97 Roanoke Ave. Roanoke Rapids, NC 27870 Phone: 919-537-5985				●	●			●
Moore's Honda 850 W. 5th St. Washington, NC 27889 Phone: 919-946-2944				●				
Carolina Motorsports 3340 US 301 N. Wilson, NC 27893 Phone: 919-237-7076	●			●	●		●	●
Honda-Kawasaki of Wilson Highway 301 S. Wilson, NC 27893 Phone: 919-291-2121				●	●			

DEALER (Alphabetical by state, then numerical by zip code)	BMW	Ducati	Harley-Davidson	Honda	Kawasaki	Moto Guzzi	Suzuki	Yamaha
Askew's Cycles 1161 US 17 South Elizabeth City, NC 27909 Phone: 919-338-1612					•		•	
Turners Sales 1111 W. Ehringhaus St. Elizabeth City, NC 27909 Phone: 919-335-5489				•				
Shue's Motorcycle Sales & Service PO Box 566 - 1708 Hwy. 52 N. Albemarle, NC 28002 Phone: 704-983-1125					•	•	•	
E & H Motorcycle Sales Highway 74 Bypass Forest City, NC 28043 Phone: 704-248-2971				•				
Carolina Harley-Davidson 1994 Remount Rd. Gastonia, NC 28054 Phone: 704-867-2855			•					
Hamme Honda/Kawasaki/Yamaha 319 North Broad St. Gastonia, NC 28054 Phone: 704-866-4110					•	•		•
Suzuki of Gastonia 501 Cox Rd. Gastonia, NC 28054 Phone: 704-867-1273							•	
Al Lane Kawasaki-Yamaha 3636 E. Hwy. 27 Iron Station, NC 28080 Phone: 704-732-8200					•			•
Excel Motorsports 204 N. Cannon Blvd. Kannapolis, NC 28083 Phone: 704-932-6179					•			•
Harley-Davidson of Charlotte 9205 E. Independence Blvd. Matthews, NC 28105 Phone: 704-847-HOGS			•					
BMW Motorcycles of Charlotte 12999 E. Independence Blvd Matthews, NC 28105-4966 Phone: 704-882-6106	•							

DEALER (Alphabetical by state, then numerical by zip code)	BMW	Ducati	Harley-Davidson	Honda	Kawasaki	Moto Guzzi	Suzuki	Yamaha
The Corral 3608 Highway 74 West Monroe, NC 28110 Phone: 704-283-8586					•		•	•
Iron Horse Motorcycle 1905 Roosevelt Blvd. W. Monroe, NC 28112 Phone: 704-283-9467		•	•					
Piedmont Honda/Kawasaki 1925 South Main St. Salisbury, NC 28144 Phone: 704-637-1680				•	•			
Shelby Motorsports 1715 E. Dixon Blvd. Shelby, NC 28150 Phone: 704-482-5946					•			•
Honda of Shelby 4402 E. Dixon Blvd. Shelby, NC 28152 Phone: 704-487-7261				•				
Charlotte Honda/Yamaha/Kawasaki 3012 Freedom Dr. Charlotte, NC 28208 Phone: 704-394-7301				•	•			•
Suzuki Motorsports of Charlotte 4030 South I 85 Charlotte, NC 28208-9459 Phone: 704-394-6666 Also handles Triumph							•	
Cape Fear Harley-Davidson 3618 Sycamore Dairy Rd. Fayetteville, NC 28303 Phone: 910-864-1200			•					
Cunningham Cycle World 4424 Bragg Blvd. Fayetteville, NC 28303 Phone: 910-864-1101			•		•			•
Meridian Motorcycles 3700 Sycamore Dairy Rd. Fayetteville, NC 28303 Phone: 910-867-7465				•			•	
Dunn Cycle Center 107 S. Sampson Ave. Dunn, NC 28334 Phone: 910-892-6037				•				

DEALER (Alphabetical by state, then numerical by zip code)	BMW	Ducati	Harley-Davidson	Honda	Kawasaki	Moto Guzzi	Suzuki	Yamaha
Kawasaki of Lumberton 1001 W. 5th St Lumberton, NC 28358 Phone: 910-738-2852					●			
Yamaha of Lumberton 1031 W. 5th St. Lumberton, NC 28358 Phone: 910-738-1454								●
Currie Chain Saw 1311 W. 5th Street Lumberton, NC 28358-5423 Phone: 910-739-7538				●			●	
Sandhill Cycle Center U.S. 15-501 North Pinehurst, NC 28374 Phone: 910-692-8191				●				●
Sport Cycles 770 Hwy 74 East Rockingham, NC 28379 Phone: 910-582-4528				●	●		●	
Britt Motorsport 6789 Market Street Wilmington, NC 28405 Phone: 910-791-8321	●	●			●			●
Carolina Coast Harley-Davidson 6515 Market St. - Highway 17 Wilmington, NC 28405 Phone: 910-791-9997			●					
Honda/Suzuki of Wilmington 5725 Market Street Wilmington, NC 28405-3501 Phone: 910-799-6150				●			●	
Lejeune Motor Co. 1009 Lejeune Blvd. Jacksonville, NC 28540 Phone: 910-455-1551				●	●			
Cars Moto Sports 1731 Lejeune Blvd. @ Western Blvd. Jacksonville, NC 28546 Phone: 910-353-2143							●	●
Honda-Kawasaki of New Bern 3317-E Hwy 70 East New Bern, NC 28560 Phone: 919-638-3961				●	●			●

DEALER (Alphabetical by state, then numerical by zip code)	BMW	Ducati	Harley-Davidson	Honda	Kawasaki	Moto Guzzi	Suzuki	Yamaha
Harley-Davidson of New Bern 1613 Highway 70 East New Bern, NC 28564 Phone: 919-633-4060			●					
Cornerstone Honda 633 4th St. SW Hickory, NC 28601 Phone: 704-324-9545				●				
Kawasaki-Yamaha of Hickory 1724 9th Ave. NW Hickory, NC 28601 Phone: 704-328-6303					●			●
Foothills Harley-Davidson 1820 First Ave. SW Hickory, NC 28602 Phone: 704-327-3030			●					
Boone Honda 164 S. Depot St. Boone, NC 28607 Phone: 704-264-9212				●				
Boone Kawasaki 128 Perkinsville Dr. Boone, NC 28607 Phone: 704-262-3424					●			
Central Cycle Sales 102 South Main St. Jefferson, NC 28640 Phone: 910-246-7744								●
Honda/Yamaha of Statesville 1809 W. Front St. Statesville, NC 28677 Phone: 704-872-1658				●				●
Tilley Harley-Davidson U.S. 70 W - 106 Airport Rd. Statesville, NC 28677 Phone: 704-872-3883 Also handles Buell			●					
M & H Suzuki Center 1022 Shelton Ave. Statesville, NC 28677-6729 Phone: 704-872-3529							●	
Crossroads Harley-Davidson 1201 Woodfield Way Wilkesboro, NC 28697 Phone: 910-667-1003			●					

DEALER (Alphabetical by state, then numerical by zip code)	BMW	Ducati	Harley-Davidson	Honda	Kawasaki	Moto Guzzi	Suzuki	Yamaha
Wilkes Honda Shop 1301-E Westwood Ln. Wilkesboro, NC 28697 Phone: 910-667-8151				•				
Payne Power Equipment 912 River St. Wilkesboro, NC 28697-2724 Phone: 910-667-1581							•	
Dal-Kawa Cycle Center 312 Kanuga St. Hendersonville, NC 28739 Phone: 704-692-4035					•		•	
Harper Discount Yamaha 1108 Spartanburg Highway Hendersonville, NC 28739 Phone: 704-692-1124								•
Tipton's Blue Ridge Yamaha 1164 Hwy 221 N. Marion, NC 28752 Phone: 704-652-9403								•
Gene Lummus Harley-Davidson 1000 U.S. 70 Swannanoa, NC 28778 Phone: 704-298-1683			•					
Waynesville Cycle Center Route 1 Box 216 - Haywood Waynesville, NC 28786 Phone: 704-452-5831				•	•		•	•
Schroader's Honda 220 Mitchell Dr. Hendersonville, NC 28792 Phone: 704-693-4101				•				
Myers Ducati Husqvarna & MotoGuzzi 1125 Sweeten Creek Rd. Asheville, NC 28803 Phone: 704-274-4271		•				•		
M.R. Honda Kawasaki Yamaha 996 Patton Ave. Asheville, NC 28806 Phone: 704-253-5646				•	•			•

DEALER (Alphabetical by state, then numerical by zip code)	BMW	Ducati	Harley-Davidson	Honda	Kawasaki	Moto Guzzi	Suzuki	Yamaha
Pennsylvania								
McMahon's Cycle Sales 613 Seventh Ave. Beaver Falls, PA 15010 Phone: 412-846-6251			●	●				
Ernest Cerini 1509 Meldon Ave. Donora, PA 15033 Phone: 412-379-6449				●				
Honda Horizon 1250 Greensburg Rd. - Rte. 366 South New Kensington, PA 15068 Phone: 412-337-6500				●				
Gatto Cycle Shop 139 E. 6th Ave. Tarentum, PA 15084 Phone: 412-224-0500			●		●		●	
Lojak Cycle Sales Rt. 2 Box 526 1/2 - Route 908 Tarentum, PA 15084 Phone: 412-226-3727								●
Northgate Honda Rt 19 Box 425 Warrendale, PA 15086 Phone: 412-935-4612				●				
Gibsonia Cycle Center 4684 Route 8 Allison Park, PA 15101-2439 Phone: 412-487-2803							●	●
Spirit Harley-Davidson 1023 William Flynn Highway Glenshaw, PA 15116 Phone: 412-487-3377			●					
Heritage Harley-Davidson 1661 5th Ave. McKeesport, PA 15132 Phone: 412-672-0780			●					
Bob Tracey's World of Cycles 8070 Ohio River Blvd. Pittsburgh, PA 15202 Phone: 412-766-9211								●

DEALER (Alphabetical by state, then numerical by zip code)	BMW	Ducati	Harley-Davidson	Honda	Kawasaki	Moto Guzzi	Suzuki	Yamaha
M.J. Bohn Cycle Shop 2015 Saw Mill Run Blvd. Pittsburgh, PA 15210-4047 Phone: 412-882-4330							•	•
Kawasaki of Pittsburgh 611 Butler St. Pittsburgh, PA 15223 Phone: 412-781-8611					•			
Honda House 1216 Ensign Ave. Pittsburgh, PA 15226 Phone: 412-431-5872				•				
Heritage BMW Motorcycles 780 H Pine Valley Dr. Pittsburgh, PA 15239-2841 Phone: 412-327-5886	•							
Washington Honda/Harley-Davidson 911 Henderson Ave. Washington, PA 15301 Phone: 412-225-3570			•	•				
Bentley's Yamaha-Suzuki-Kawasaki 589 West Pike St. Canonsburg, PA 15317-1068 Phone: 412-746-7100					•		•	•
Barnhart's Honda Rt. 19 in Ruff Creek (Exit 4 off I-79) Prosperity, PA 15329 Phone: 412-627-5819				•			•	
Rainbow Honda U.S. Route 40 Richeyville, PA 15358 Phone: 412-632-6853				•				
Z & M Cycle Sales 69 Romeo Ln. (Rts. 119 & 51) Uniontown, PA 15401 Phone: 412-439-8888			•	•			•	
Laurel Highlands Kawasaki/Yamaha 84 University Dr. - Old Route 119 Lemont Furnace, PA 15456 Phone: 412-437-0670						•		•

DEALER (Alphabetical by state, then numerical by zip code)	BMW	Ducati	Harley-Davidson	Honda	Kawasaki	Moto Guzzi	Suzuki	Yamaha
Super City Sports Sales Route 31 W - RD 6 Somerset, PA 15501 Phone: 814-445-5050				•				•
Bedford Suzuki-Yamaha RD 7 Box 34 - Rt. 30 Business District Bedford, PA 15522 Phone: 814-623-1387							•	•
Custer's Harley-Davidson 1218 E. Main Street Berlin, PA 15530 Phone: 814-267-4618			•		•			
Westmoreland Triumph Mt. Pleasant Rd - RR 5 Greensburg, PA 15601 Phone: 412-423-3496 Also handles Triumph						•		
Bob Thomas Honda/Kawasaki of Irwin 9571 Rt. 30 East Irwin, PA 15642 Phone: 412-863-0237				•	•			
Z & M Cycle Sales Route 30 Box 193 Latrobe, PA 15650 Phone: 412-837-9404			•	•			•	•
Bentley Yamaha-Suzuki-Kawasaki 4451 William Penn Hwy. Murrysville, PA 15668-1917 Phone: 412-325-2344							•	•
Cycle Sports and Service Aster Dr./Greensburg-Mt. Pleasant Rd. Norvelt, PA 15674 Phone: 412-423-4553					•			
Moto Cycle 401 Jones Mills Rd. Stahlstown, PA 15687 Phone: 412-593-6208 Also handles Bimota		•						
Tom's Cycle 1187 Wayne Ave. Indiana, PA 15701 Phone: 412-349-2211							•	•

DEALER (Alphabetical by state, then numerical by zip code)	BMW	Ducati	Harley-Davidson	Honda	Kawasaki	Moto Guzzi	Suzuki	Yamaha
Beach Ford Mercury Yamaha 11th St. Barnesboro, PA 15714 Phone: 814-948-4856								●
DuBois Motorcycle Plus RD # 3 - Oklahoma Salem Rd. DuBois, PA 15801 Phone: 814-371-5750			●					●
Brockway Honda Rte. 219 - Brockway-DuBois Rd. Brockway, PA 15824 Phone: 814-265-0642				●				
Key's Recreational Vehicles Route 28 North Hazen, PA 15825 Phone: 814-328-2222							●	
Elk Cycle Center 315 S. St. Mary's St. Saint Marys, PA 15857-1623 Phone: 814-834-4744							●	
Denny's Johnstown Cycle Center 32 Walnut St. Johnstown, PA 15901 Phone: 814-539-3154					●			●
Zepka Harley-Davidson 1273 Frankstown Rd. (near airport) Johnstown, PA 15902 Phone: 814-536-3745			●					
Cernic's Suzuki Honda 500 Cooper Ave. Johnstown, PA 15906-1104 Phone: 814-539-4114				●			●	
Zanotti Motor Co. 170 Pittsburgh Rd. Butler, PA 16001 Phone: 412-283-2777			●	●				●
Davis Cycle Sales 701 New Castle Rd. Butler, PA 16001-2501 Phone: 412-287-3052					●		●	
New Castle Harley-Davidson Rt. 422 (3 mi west of I-79) New Castle, PA 16101 Phone: 412-924-2310 Also handles Buell			●					

DEALER (Alphabetical by state, then numerical by zip code)	BMW	Ducati	Harley-Davidson	Honda	Kawasaki	Moto Guzzi	Suzuki	Yamaha
Sanders Yamaha Suzuki Kawasaki RR 224 1400 State St. New Castle, PA 16101-1287 Phone: 412-658-6255					●		●	●
Sharon Cycle Sales and Service 265 Connelly Blvd. - Rt. 62 Bypass Sharon, PA 16146 Phone: 412-342-5378				●				
Thunder Recreation 1344 E. State Street Sharon, PA 16146-3298 Phone: 412-981-7282			●		●		●	
Kibuk Cycle Sales Rt. 422 East Kittanning, PA 16201 Phone: 412-548-7628				●				●
Outdoor Sales & Service Route 422 - 1 mi. east of Kittanning Kittanning, PA 16201 Phone: 412-543-2157					●		●	
Keys Recreational Vehicles II East Main St. - Rt. 322 Clarion, PA 16214-8905 Phone: 814-226-4444							●	
Lineman Cycles RD #2 Box 185A Oil City, PA 16301 Phone: 814-676-8550								●
Street Track 'N Trail RD 3 - Rte. 322 Conneaut Lake, PA 16316 Phone: 814-382-4821			●	●	●			●
Monaco Triumph/Moto Guzzi RD 5 Box 607 - Route 417 Franklin, PA 16323 Phone: 814-432-5888 Also handles Triumph						●		
Suzuki of Meadville RR 4 - Route 322 Meadville, PA 16335 Phone: 814-382-5695							●	
World of Wheels Rt 257 - Salina Dr. Seneca, PA 16346 Phone: 814-676-5721				●	●		●	

DEALER (Alphabetical by state, then numerical by zip code)	BMW	Ducati	Harley-Davidson	Honda	Kawasaki	Moto Guzzi	Suzuki	Yamaha
Leisure Time Honda 729 E. Columbus Ave. Corry, PA 16407 Phone: 814-664-4606				•				
Klick's Suzuki 13360 Route 8 Wattsburg, PA 16442-9801 Phone: 814-739-2334							•	
Chet Aleks Yamaha & Marine 1501 Peninsula Dr. Erie, PA 16505 Phone: 814-833-3861								•
Forest Park Honda 3339 W. Lake Rd. Erie, PA 16505 Phone: 814-833-3051				•				
Harley-Davidson of Erie 4575 West Ridge Rd. - Rt. 20 Erie, PA 16506 Phone: 814-838-1356			•					
Cycle City Hon/Kaw/Suzuki 2814 Buffalo Rd. Wesleyville, PA 16510-1704 Phone: 814-898-3524				•	•		•	•
Barnhart Yamaha RD 5 Box 375 Mill Run Rd. Altoona, PA 16601 Phone: 814-942-9172				•	•		•	•
Dee Bee Sales & Service 800 5th Ave. - Juniata Altoona, PA 16601 Phone: 814-943-0081			•				•	
Suzuki of Altoona 229 E. Pleasant Valley Blvd. Altoona, PA 16602-5511 Phone: 814-944-7435							•	
Apple Harley-Davidson 2860 Rte. 764 N. Duncansville, PA 16635 Phone: 814-696-7433			•					
Keystone Kawasaki-Yamaha 1060 S. Route 220 Duncansville, PA 16635 Phone: 814-696-4252					•			•

DEALER (Alphabetical by state, then numerical by zip code)	BMW	Ducati	Harley-Davidson	Honda	Kawasaki	Moto Guzzi	Suzuki	Yamaha
Race's Honda/Yamaha 590 South Ave. Bradford, PA 16701 Phone: 814-362-7426				•				•
Track 'n' Trail 1246 E College Ave. State College, PA 16801 Phone: 814-237-2581				•			•	
Dunlap Yamaha 784 Benner Pike Bellefonte, PA 16823 Phone: 814-355-5445								•
#1 Cycle Center Harley-Davidson Rt. 322 - East of State College Centre Hall, PA 16828 Phone: 814-364-1340			•					
Catalano Cycle Center 216 N. 3rd St. Clearfield, PA 16830 Phone: 814-765-5553					•		•	•
Larry's Sport Center U.S. 6 West Galeton, PA 16922 Phone: 814-435-6548				•				•
Pat & Son Service Center Rt. 934 South (take Exit 29 off Rt.81) Bellegrove, PA 17003 Phone: 717-867-4406					•			
Yamaha of Camp Hill 1101 Slate Hill Rd. Camp Hill, PA 17011 Phone: 717-761-6192								•
Cumberland Kawasaki 350 East High St. Carlisle, PA 17013 Phone: 717-245-0353					•			
Lebanon Valley Honda/Suzuki R.D. 3 - Route 72 Jonestown, PA 17038 Phone: 717-865-6633				•			•	

DEALER (Alphabetical by state, then numerical by zip code)	BMW	Ducati	Harley-Davidson	Honda	Kawasaki	Moto Guzzi	Suzuki	Yamaha
White's Harley-Davidson Sales 1515 E. Cumberland St. Lebanon, PA 17042 Phone: 717-272-4986 Also handles Buell			●					
Laughlin's 240 Ferguson Valley Rd. Lewistown, PA 17044 Phone: 717-248-0926				●	●			
P & P Cycle Center 351 North Lincoln Ave. Lebanon, PA 17046 Phone: 717-272-7811								●
Honda BMW Moto Sports 6653 Carlisle Pike Mechanicsburg, PA 17055 Phone: 717-766-2523	●			●				
West Shore Suzuki 5203 E. Trindle Rd. Mechanicsburg, PA 17055-3552 Phone: 717-697-3099							●	
Teter Sales & Service RD 1 - Route 209 Millersburg, PA 17061 Phone: 717-362-8501					●			
Kauffman's Sports 22 East Shirley St. Mount Union, PA 17066 Phone: 814-542-7246								●
Howell's Harley-Davidson/Triumph 24 E Main St. - Rte. 11 New Kingstown, PA 17072 Phone: 717-766-9366 Also handles Triumph			●					
Harrisburg Harley-Davidson 2225 Sycamore St. Harrisburg, PA 17111 Phone: 717-233-1993			●					
Koups Cycle Shop Inc. 189 N Harrisburg St. Oberlin, PA 17113 Phone: 717-939-7182		●			●			

DEALER (Alphabetical by state, then numerical by zip code)	BMW	Ducati	Harley-Davidson	Honda	Kawasaki	Moto Guzzi	Suzuki	Yamaha
M & S Cycle 1431 Lincoln Way East Chambersburg, PA 17201 Phone: 717-263-1018			●	●			●	
Roxy's Kawasaki-Yamaha 4515 Lincoln Way East Fayetteville, PA 17222 Phone: 717-352-8270					●			●
Bob's Indian Sales & Service 580 Old York Rd. Etters, PA 17319 Phone: 717-938-2556 Also handles Indian				●				
The Rider's Edge 2490 Emmitsburg Rd. Gettysburg, PA 17325 Phone: 717-334-2518								●
Hanover Kawasaki 910 York St. Hanover, PA 17331 Phone: 717-637-1300					●			
Ray Wilt Honda-Yamaha-Suzuki 1754 Carlisle Pike - Rte. 94 Hanover, PA 17331 Phone: 717-632-8801				●			●	●
Honda/Yamaha/Suzuki of York 1881 Whiteford Rd. York, PA 17402 Phone: 717-757-2688				●			●	●
Laugerman's Harley-Davidson Sales 100 Arsenal Rd. York, PA 17404 Phone: 717-854-3214			●					
Don's Kawasaki Yamaha 20 E. Market St. Hellam, PA 17406 Phone: 717-755-6002					●			●
Lancaster Honda 2350 Dairy Rd. Lancaster, PA 17509-2308 Phone: 717-898-0100				●				
Ephrata Cycle and Sports 878 E. Main St. Ephrata, PA 17522 Phone: 717-738-1184				●				

DEALER (Alphabetical by state, then numerical by zip code)	BMW	Ducati	Harley-Davidson	Honda	Kawasaki	Moto Guzzi	Suzuki	Yamaha
Trans-Am Cycle Sales 933 Lititz Pike Lititz, PA 17543 Phone: 717-626-4765	●				●		●	
Fred Heistand Motors 734 Conestoga Ave. Manheim, PA 17545 Phone: 717-665-7100						●		
M & S Sales & Service 1690 Division Highway New Holland, PA 17557 Phone: 717-354-4726							●	
Lancaster Harley-Davidson 308 Beaver Valley Pike Willow Street, PA 17584 Phone: 717-464-2703 Also handles Buell			●					
B & B Sales & Service 791 Flory Mill Rd. Lancaster, PA 17601 Phone: 717-569-5764		●						●
Bob Logue Motor Sports 2091 Lycoming Creek Rd. Williamsport, PA 17701 Phone: 717-323-9959				●				
Suzuki Joe's Sport Center RR 1 - Rt. 414 E. Canton, PA 17724-9801 Phone: 717-673-8562							●	
Country Cycle 4450 Lycoming Creek Rd. Cogan Station, PA 17728 Phone: 717-494-2026	●	●	●	●	●	●	●	●
Ye Olde Cycle Barn RR #3 - Box 2 - on Rte. 405 Hughesville, PA 17737 Phone: 717-584-3842							●	
Preferred Harley-Davidson 3649 US Highway 220 Linden, PA 17744 Phone: 717-320-0630			●					

DEALER (Alphabetical by state, then numerical by zip code)	BMW	Ducati	Harley-Davidson	Honda	Kawasaki	Moto Guzzi	Suzuki	Yamaha
Brinker Outdoor Adventures 4 miles South of Lock Haven on Rte. 64 Lock Haven, PA 17751 Phone: 717-726-3882					●			
Peter's Sporting Goods Route 150 Mill Hall, PA 17751 Phone: 717-726-4066								●
Williamson Honda Suzuki Exit 25 - I-80 Mill Hall, PA 17751-9801 Phone: 717-726-3343				●			●	
Wheels of Williamsport Take Fairfield exit off I-80 Montoursville, PA 17754 Phone: 717-368-1204					●		●	●
Kurtz Kawasaki RD #1 Box 260 Watsontown, PA 17777 Phone: 717-538-2160					●			
J and B Honda Motor Sales 816 Old Berwick Rd. Bloomsburg, PA 17815 Phone: 717-784-1376				●				
Speed & Sport 305 Montour Blvd. - US-11 South Bloomsburg, PA 17815 Phone: 717-784-6831								●
Vreeland's Harley-Davidson 317 Montour Boulevard (Rte. 11 South) Bloomsburg, PA 17815 Phone: 717-784-2453			●					
B & B Sno*Jet Main Street Hartleton, PA 17829 Phone: 717-922-1270					●			
Buttorff's Yamaha Box 32 - Route 45 Hartleton, PA 17829 Phone: 717-922-1151								●

DEALER (Alphabetical by state, then numerical by zip code)	BMW	Ducati	Harley-Davidson	Honda	Kawasaki	Moto Guzzi	Suzuki	Yamaha
Yocum's Motor Sport Shop 325 S. Front - Box 438 Milton, PA 17847-1005 Phone: 717-742-4706							•	
Mikmar Motor Service RR 1 Box 232 Paxinos, PA 17860 Phone: 717-672-9110 Also handles Bimota	•					•		
Road Track & Trail RD 4 - Box 127G - Rte 11&15 Selinsgrove, PA 17870 Phone: 717-374-1197				•	•		•	
Matto Cycle 634 Prt. Carbon-St. Clair-Hwy. Pottsville, PA 17901 Phone: 717-429-0678				•				
Harry's Sales & Service 617 West Oak St. Frackville, PA 17931 Phone: 717-874-1522					•		•	
Schaeffer's Harley-Davidson RR 1 Box 1558 - just off Rte. 61 Orwigsburg, PA 17961 Phone: 717-366-0143			•					
Zechman Cycle Center RD 4 - Box 430 - Route 125 Pine Grove, PA 17963 Phone: 717-345-8918								•
Warren's Honda 1230 Illicks Mill Rd. Bethlehem, PA 18017 Phone: 610-865-0071				•				
Link Cycle Service 303-321 S. 3rd. St. - Route 309 Coopersburg, PA 18036 Phone: 610-282-4800			•	•				•
Honda of Easton 707-709 Wood Ave. Easton, PA 18042 Phone: 610-258-4852				•				

DEALER (Alphabetical by state, then numerical by zip code)	BMW	Ducati	Harley-Davidson	Honda	Kawasaki	Moto Guzzi	Suzuki	Yamaha
Blackman's Cycle Shop 4911 Buckeye Rd. Emmaus, PA 18049-1004 Phone: 610-965-9865 Also handles Triumph	•	•		•			•	•
Bushkill Cycle Suzuki 354 W. Moorestown Rd. Nazareth, PA 18064-9567 Phone: 610-759-3826							•	
Millers Cycle Shop 439 State Rd. Palmerton, PA 18071 Phone: 610-826-5842				•				
Pen Argyl Cycles 506 East Main St. Pen Argyl, PA 18072 Phone: 610-863-5000				•				•
Kawasaki of the Lehigh Valley 1410 Tilghman St. Allentown, PA 18102 Phone: 610-435-1555					•			
Blocker Enterprises PO Box 204 Route 248 Parryville, PA 18244 Phone: 215-377-0440			•					•
Horn's Outdoor Center Rte. 512 Mt. Bethel, PA 18343 Phone: 215-588-6614					•			
Horizon Yamaha 636 Pocono Blvd. - Rte. 611 Mt. Pocono, PA 18344 Phone: 717-839-7950								•
Schoch's Harley-Davidson Rt. 33 & Rt. 209 (Snydersville Exit) Snydersville, PA 18360 Phone: 717-992-7500			•					
Parts is Parts Stadden Rd. Tannersville, PA 18372 Phone: 717-629-1940						•		
Baer Sport Center Rte. 6 East Honesdale, PA 18431 Phone: 717-253-2000			•					

DEALER (Alphabetical by state, then numerical by zip code)	BMW	Ducati	Harley-Davidson	Honda	Kawasaki	Moto Guzzi	Suzuki	Yamaha
Rusty Palmer's RD 4 - U.S. Route 6 East Honesdale, PA 18431 Phone: 717-253-4507				•	•			•
Tri-State Sports Center RD 4 - Route 6 Honesdale, PA 18431 Phone: 717-253-6323							•	
Electric City Harley-Davidson/Buell 215 Hickory St. Scranton, PA 18505 Phone: 717-961-2126 Also handles Buell			•					
Honda Northeast Rt. 6 Scranton Carbondale Highway Scranton, PA 18508 Phone: 717-383-0944				•	•		•	•
Lo-Jan Travel Center Route 6 Scranton, PA 18508-1184 Phone: 717-489-9302				•	•		•	•
Jim Murray's Kawasaki 310 Larch St. Scranton, PA 18509 Phone: 717-342-6752					•			
Pocono R.V./Suzuki Route 940 - PO Box 270 Blakeslee, PA 18610 Phone: 717-646-3664							•	
Kunkle Motors RD 1 Box 386 Dallas, PA 18612 Phone: 717-675-1546								•
Russ Major's Sales 14 Hillside Road - Rt. 309 Shavertown, PA 18708 Phone: 717-696-3893				•				•
Bob's Cycle Shop 607 N. Elmira St. - off Rt. 220 North Sayre, PA 18840 Phone: 717-888-7748				•				

DEALER (Alphabetical by state, then numerical by zip code)	BMW	Ducati	Harley-Davidson	Honda	Kawasaki	Moto Guzzi	Suzuki	Yamaha
The New Montgomeryville Cycle Ctr. 980 Route 309 Montgomeryville, PA 18936 Phone: 215-699-7511	●	●		●	●		●	●
Dean's Harley-Davidson 3353 Bethlehem Pike Souderton, PA 18964 Phone: 215-723-2907			●					
Cycle City Yamaha/Suzuki 2555 West Chester Pike Broomall, PA 19008 Phone: 610-356-2662							●	●
Watkins Suzuki 1100 Township Line Rd. Chester, PA 19013-1446 Phone: 610-485-7950							●	
East Coast Cycle Center 2800 Bristol Pike Bensalem, PA 19020 Phone: 215-639-3100				●				
Suzuki Fun Center 2639 Bristol Pike Bensalem, PA 19020 Phone: 215-638-7878							●	●
Brian's Harley-Davidson and Buell 1223 W. Lincoln Hwy. - U.S. 1 Langhorne, PA 19047 Phone: 215-752-9400 Also handles Buell			●					
Bromley Motorcycle Sales 635 Somers Ave. Feasterville-Trevose, PA 19053-3450 Phone: 215-357-1534							●	
East Coast Kawasaki 208 Levittown Parkway Levittown, PA 19054 Phone: 215-547-5444					●			
Hannum's Harley-Davidson/Kawasaki US Rt. 1 & Rt. 352 Media, PA 19063 Phone: 215-566-5562			●		●			

DEALER (Alphabetical by state, then numerical by zip code)	BMW	Ducati	Harley-Davidson	Honda	Kawasaki	Moto Guzzi	Suzuki	Yamaha
The Spare Parts Co. 406 Vine St. Philadelphia, PA 19106 Phone: 215-922-2214 Also handles MZ bikes	●					●		
Philadelphia Suzuki-Kawasaki-Honda 2450 Castor Avenue Philadelphia, PA 19134-4604 Phone: 215-533-5200				●	●		●	
Devon Honda 860 Lancaster Ave. Devon, PA 19333 Phone: 610-687-3500 Also handles Triumph				●				
Fisher's Cycles RD 2 - US Rte. 30 right before Rte. 10 Parkesburg, PA 19365 Phone: 610-857-9616				●				●
Montgomery County Harley-Davidson Rte. 363 & Bypass 422 - 1217 S. Trooper Valley Forge, PA 19403 Phone: 610-666-5122			●					
Leisure Equipment 2568 Route 724 - P.O. Box 1010 Parker Ford, PA 19457-1010 Phone: 610-495-7122						●		
Frank Kiss & Co. 18 High St. Pottstown, PA 19464 Phone: 610-326-1260				●				
Penn State Motorcycle Corp. 1486 S Hanover St. Pottstown, PA 19464-7465 Phone: 610-323-0525							●	●
Smaltz's Harley-Davidson Rt. 100 & Township Line Rd. Eagle, PA 19480 Phone: 610-458-9004			●					
Hermy's Tire & Cycle Shop Rt. 61 Box 65 Port Clinton, PA 19549 Phone: 610-562-7303		●						

DEALER (Alphabetical by state, then numerical by zip code)	BMW	Ducati	Harley-Davidson	Honda	Kawasaki	Moto Guzzi	Suzuki	Yamaha
Honda Kawasaki of Berks 5306 5th St. HWY. Temple, PA 19560 Phone: 610-921-9256				•	•			
Adams Yamaha World 2225 North 5th St. Reading, PA 19605 Phone: 610-921-3149					·			•
Ray's Motor Service 5560 Philadelphia Pike - US Rt 422 East Reading, PA 19606 Phone: 610-582-2700								•
Sport-Cycle Suzuki Rt. 222 South - RD #6 - Lancaster Pike Reading, PA 19608 Phone: 610-775-3327							•	
Terreson's Harley-Davidson Rt. 222 5 mi. North of Ex 21 - PA Tpk Sinking Spring, PA 19608 Phone: 610-777-9731			•					
Virginia								
East Coast Harley 222 Fraley Blvd. Dumfries, VA 22026 Phone: 703-221-3757			•					
Fairfax Kawasaki 3160 B Spring St. Fairfax, VA 22031 Phone: 703-591-8556					•			
Coleman Power Sport 435 S. Washington St. Falls Church, VA 22046 Phone: 703-237-3400				•	•		•	•
Cycle Sport Unlimited 632 Grant St. Herndon, VA 22070-4702 Phone: 703-471-6990					•		•	•
Hall's Honda 17 Catoctin Circle S.E. Leesburg, VA 22075 Phone: 703-777-1652				•				

DEALER (Alphabetical by state, then numerical by zip code)	BMW	Ducati	Harley-Davidson	Honda	Kawasaki	Moto Guzzi	Suzuki	Yamaha
Manassas Honda 9105 Mathis Ave. Manassas, VA 22110 Phone: 703-361-2233				•				
Whitt's Harley-Davidson Sales 8790 Commerce Ct. Manassas, VA 22110 Phone: 703-631-3750			•					
Cycle Sport 6603 Backlick Rd. Springfield, VA 22150 Phone: 703-451-9330								•
Blalock Cycle 170 Lee Highway Warrenton, VA 22186 Phone: 703-347-4591				•				•
Cycles Woodbridge 2575 Hanco Center Dr. Woodbridge, VA 22191-4015 Phone: 703-670-6196				•	•		•	•
Fredricksburg Motor Sports 390 King's Hwy Fredricksburg, VA 22405 Phone: 703-899-9100				•	•			•
Moto-East 248 Warrenton Rd. - Rt. 17 Fredericksburg, VA 22405 Phone: 703-373-6806								
Morton-Massey 9810 Courthouse Road - Rte. 208 Spotsylvania, VA 22553-9139 Phone: 703-898-8738	•							
Valley Cycle Center 112 South Kent St. Winchester, VA 22601 Phone: 703-667-1893		•			•		•	•
Winchester Harley-Davidson 1160 Milwood Pike Winchester, VA 22602 Phone: 713-662-4468			•					
The Cycle Center 13388 Lovers Ln. Culpeper, VA 22701 Phone: 703-825-5544								•

DEALER (Alphabetical by state, then numerical by zip code)	BMW	Ducati	Harley-Davidson	Honda	Kawasaki	Moto Guzzi	Suzuki	Yamaha
Early's Cycle Center 1921 South High St. Harrisonburg, VA 22801 Phone: 703-433-2585								•
Shenk Honda/Triumph/Moto Guzzi Intersection of I-81 & Rt. 33 East Harrisonburg, VA 22801 Phone: 703-434-7345 Also handles Triumph				•	•	•	•	•
Valley Kawasaki-Suzuki 162 E. Mosby Rd. Harrisonburg, VA 22801-2619 Phone: 703-433-0232					•		•	
Jarman's Sportcycles 114 10th Street NW Charlottesville, VA 22902 Phone: 804-293-4406				•	•		•	•
Schafer Motor Company 333 Madison Rd. So. Orange, VA 22960 Phone: 703-672-5555				•	•		•	•
Waugh Enterprises Harley-Davidson 385 Byrd St. - Rt. 20 N. Orange, VA 22960 Phone: 703-672-5550 Also handles Buell			•					
Shenandoah Harley-Davidson 2800C West Main St. Waynesboro, VA 22980 Phone: 703-942-1340			•					
Wayne Cycle Shop Route 3 - Box 463 - Rt. 340 North Waynesboro, VA 22980 Phone: 703-943-1111					•			•
Ken's Cycle Center 1825 East Nine Mile Rd. Highland Springs, VA 23075-2309 Phone: 804-737-7803						•	•	
R & S Sport Vehicles 5527 Mechanicsville Pike Mechanicsville, VA 23111 Phone: 804-559-4282 Also handles Triumph					•			

DEALER (Alphabetical by state, then numerical by zip code)	BMW	Ducati	Harley-Davidson	Honda	Kawasaki	Moto Guzzi	Suzuki	Yamaha
Cliff's Honda Yamaha 2416 W. Cary St. Richmond, VA 23220 Phone: 804-353-3242				●				●
Richmond Harley-Davidson 7015 Brook Road Richmond, VA 23227 Phone: 804-262-2381			●					
Powersports 11225 Midlothian Turnpike Richmond, VA 23235-4713 Phone: 804-794-9646					●		●	
Honda House Marine 7906 W. Broad St. Richmond, VA 23294 Phone: 804-270-0123				●				
Honda of Virginia Beach 2970 Virginia Beach Blvd. Virginia Beach, VA 23452 Phone: 804-340-6161				●				
Cycle World 4972 Virginia Beach Blvd. Virginia Beach, VA 23462 Phone: 804-499-4146				●	●		●	●
Southside Harley-Davidson 385 N. Witchduck Rd. Virginia Beach, VA 23462 Phone: 804-499-8964 Also handles Triumph and Buell			●					
Honda of Norfolk 6955 Tidewater Dr. Norfolk, VA 23509 Phone: 804-857-0107				●				
Sunrise Auto & Cycle Sales 1559 E. Little Creek Rd. Norfolk, VA 23518 Phone: 804-583-2223					●		●	●
Casey Cycle City 634 J. Clyde Morris Blvd. Newport News, VA 23601 Phone: 804-595-9721	●			●	●		●	●
Hampton Roads Harley-Davidson 7204 Warwick Blvd. Newport News, VA 23607 Phone: 804-245-5221			●					

DEALER (Alphabetical by state, then numerical by zip code)	BMW	Ducati	Harley-Davidson	Honda	Kawasaki	Moto Guzzi	Suzuki	Yamaha
Honda of Portsmouth 1201 London Blvd. Portsmouth, VA 23704 Phone: 804-397-8884				•				
Burcham Cycles 1500 Boulevard Colonial Heights, VA 23834 Phone: 804-526-2300		•			•		•	•
Gios Cycle Sales 2126 Williamson Rd. Roanoke, VA 24012-7928 Phone: 703-563-0301					•	•		
Roanoke Valley Harley-Davidson 2450 Center Ave. NW Roanoke, VA 24017 Phone: 703-343-0705			•					
Jimmy's Cycle Sales 341 Virginia Ave. Collinsville, VA 24078 Phone: 703-647-7711				•				•
Motor Imports 746 Virginia Ave. Collinsville, VA 24078 Phone: 703-647-1121						•	•	
Cycle Center 406 E. 4th St. Salem, VA 24153 Phone: 703-389-5385				•				•
Atlas Honda/Yamaha 2377 Lee Highway Bristol, VA 24201 Phone: 703-669-6666				•				•
Bare Brothers 3101 Lee Hwy. Bristol, VA 24201 Phone: 703-669-1000						•	•	
Lilly Harley-Davidson 17353 Lee Highway Abingdon, VA 24210-7831 Phone: 703-628-5822			•					
Mountain Suzuki Route 80 - PO Box 457 Honaker, VA 24260 Phone: 703-873-4811							•	

DEALER (Alphabetical by state, then numerical by zip code)	BMW	Ducati	Harley-Davidson	Honda	Kawasaki	Moto Guzzi	Suzuki	Yamaha
Southwest Kawasaki and Suzuki Route 2 - Box 569 Pound, VA 24279-9655 Phone: 703-796-4244					●		●	
Patton Motorcycle Sales South 89 Route 2 - Box 20 Galax, VA 24333 Phone: 703-236-3167								●
Mark IV Motorcycles Rt. 2 Box 65 - I-81 & I-77 Wytheville, VA 24382 Phone: 703-228-3118				●	●		●	●
Honda/Suzuki of Lynchburg 2210 12th St. Lynchburg, VA 24501 Phone: 804-847-1276				●			●	
Lynchburg Kawasaki-Yamaha 1805 Twelfth St. Lynchburg, VA 24501 Phone: 804-846-4906					●			●
Harley-Davidson of Lynchburg 8506 Timberlake Rd. Lynchburg, VA 24502 Phone: 804-237-2381			●					
Olde Dominion Motorsports 2104 Riverside Dr. Danville, VA 24540 Phone: 804-799-8000				●	●		●	●
Ed's Honda-Yamaha Rte. 58 East South Boston, VA 24592 Phone: 804-572-6901				●				●
Evergreen of Halifax Intersection 360/58 South Boston, VA 24592-1117 Phone: 804-572-4769							●	
Grundy Honda Riverside Dr. Grundy, VA 24614 Phone: 703-935-2447				●				

DEALER (Alphabetical by state, then numerical by zip code)	BMW	Ducati	Harley-Davidson	Honda	Kawasaki	Moto Guzzi	Suzuki	Yamaha
West Virginia								
Hillbilly Cycle 317 Mercer St. Princeton, WV 24740 Phone: 304-425-4321			•	•	•		•	•
Dohm Cycles 616 Broad St. at Piedmont Rd. Charleston, WV 25301 Phone: 304-342-5148				•	•			•
Harley-Davidson/Kawasaki of W.V. 4924 MacCorkle Avenue SW South Charleston, WV 25309 Phone: 304-768-4211			•		•			
Logan Motorcycle Sales Rt 44 South - Omar Rd. Logan, WV 25601 Phone: 304-752-4145					•			•
Logan Suzuki and Kawasaki PO Box 155 - 3 Mile Curve Yolyn, WV 25654 Phone: 304-752-2313					•		•	
Logan Motorcycle Sales 101 W. 3rd. St. Williamson, WV 25661 Phone: 304-235-5084				•				•
Mike's Harley-Davidson Sales U.S. 52 - 4 miles outside of Delbarton Delbarton, WV 25670 Phone: 304-426-4241			•					
Benjy's Harley-Davidson 408 4th St. Huntington, WV 25701 Phone: 304-523-1340			•					
East End Cycle Sales 2402 3rd. Ave. Huntington, WV 25703 Phone: 304-529-3309					•		•	
Cycle Center 4431 U.S. Route 60 E. Huntington, WV 25705 Phone: 304-736-8911				•				•

DEALER (Alphabetical by state, then numerical by zip code)	BMW	Ducati	Harley-Davidson	Honda	Kawasaki	Moto Guzzi	Suzuki	Yamaha
Beckley Honda 3413 Robert C. Byrd Dr. Beckley, WV 25801 Phone: 304-252-4101				●				
United Cycle 3797 Robert C. Byrd Dr. Beckley, WV 25801 Phone: 304-252-9775					●		●	
Bub's Cycle Center Route 16 South Crab Orchard, WV 25827 Phone: 304-252-4662								●
Wheeling Cycle & Marine 134 17th St. Wheeling, WV 26003 Phone: 304-233-BIKE					●			●
Smitty's Harley-Davidson Sales 100 Lafayette Ave. Moundsville, WV 26041 Phone: 304-845-3304			●					
DeVol's Cycle Center 1117 Broadway Ave. Parkersburg, WV 26101 Phone: 800-433-1559				●				●
Larry's Cycle/Tractor Sales 2706 Pike St. Parkersburg, WV 26101 Phone: 304-428-7102					●		●	
Bridgeman Honda 711 Third St. New Martinsville, WV 26155 Phone: 304-455-1303				●				
DeMotto Honda and Yamaha Route 33 and 250 - 1 mile W of Elkins Elkins, WV 26241 Phone: 304-636-5489				●				●
B & B Harley-Davidson Cycle Sales 100 Alexander Ave. Nutter Fort, WV 26301 Phone: 304-623-0484			●					
R.G. Honda-Yamaha 1619 Buckhannon Pike Nutter Fort, WV 26301 Phone: 304-624-5420				●				●

DEALER (Alphabetical by state, then numerical by zip code)	BMW	Ducati	Harley-Davidson	Honda	Kawasaki	Moto Guzzi	Suzuki	Yamaha
Leeson's Import Motors 320 West Main Bridgeport, WV 26330 Phone: 304-842-5469					•		•	
Four Seasons Recreation 1511 Fairmont Ave. Fairmont, WV 26554 Phone: 304-363-3613					•		•	
Lasobek Harley-Davidson 46 Middletown Rd. Fairmont, WV 26554 Phone: 304-363-8557			•					
Mid-State Marina Route 19 & 4 North Sutton, WV 26601 Phone: 304-765-7325				•			•	•
Lockards Kawasaki Route 19 - Box 38 Flatwoods, WV 26621 Phone: 304-765-5295					•			
Summersville Cycles 1137 Broad St. Summersville, WV 26651 Phone: 304-872-6626					•	•		
Skip's Honda Center Rte. 220 South Keyser,.WV 26726 Phone: 304-788-1615				•				
Romney Cycle Center HC 74 Box 35A - Rt. 50 East Romney, WV 26757 Phone: 304-822-3933					•		•	•

Index

Other Books From Whitehorse Press

Motorcycle Journeys Through New England

by Marty Berke

New England is undoubtedly one of the best areas of the United States for motorcycle touring. Owing to the great variety of terrain, roads in New England often seem haphazard in design and direction, but for motorcyclists seeking adventure travel through beautiful countryside, they are the stuff dream trips are made of.

This handy guide contains suggestions to help you find the best roads in six major riding regions. Altogether, Berke has carefully plotted 19 trips for you (that's less than 90 cents a trip), most of them taking one day to complete. Each trip is detailed by a map and route directions.

Berke brings the region alive with his quick wit and sharp eye for the off-beat, adding his recommendations for restaurants, diners, roadhouses, places to stay, interesting places to visit, and the locations of emergency facilities. Berke's narrative gives you a handlebar view of this unique part of our country.

In addition, the book contains a listing of all major motorcycle dealers in New England. If you have mechanical trouble on the road, the motorcycle dealer listing alone is worth the price of the book.

Berke's interesting commentary and tips let you make the most of your travel time and budget. The trips are designed to accommodate various riding styles, from two-up travelers looking at every nook and cranny, to sport riders chasing more curves than a day's worth of hourglasses. Either way, this book makes it easy to find some great riding.

With over 25 years of riding experience and 15 years of world travel, Marty Berke is a knowledgeable host for your travels through New England.

Contents: • Introduction • Goin' Downeast (Maine, including Acadia National Park) • Cutting the White Mountain Notches (New Hampshire) • Closing the Green Mountain Gaps (Vermont) • Circumnavigating the Lakes (New York) • Cruisin' the Berkshires (Massachusetts) • The Southern Coastline (Connecticut and Rhode Island) • Motorcycle Service Facilities in New England • Index

Paper, 4 x 7-1/2 in., 224 pp., 128 illus.
BERK $16.95

Motorcycle Journeys Through the Alps

by John Hermann

A journey through the Alps is a once-in-a-lifetime adventure, and with this invaluable guidebook you can be sure not to miss any of the roads, mountain passes, or valleys that this awe-inspiring region has to offer. The book contains detailed route descriptions and useful advice that will help you avoid hassles and inconveniences, so that not a precious moment of your vacation is wasted.

You'll be prepared for situations the average Alps traveler might never anticipate, such as how to deal with automated European gas stations, and how to decipher European road signs. You'll know which hotels are must-visits and which ones should be avoided. You'll even know where the police like to hide to nab overzealous motorcyclists. This book makes sure that nothing is left to chance.

All of the region's important roads and passes are described and critiqued (two stars indicates a "must-ride" road). The book contains 49 individual riding trips, each lasting about a day. Hermann covers every region of the Alps, so that whether you want to focus on Switzerland, Germany, Austria, Italy, or France (or Liechtenstein, for that matter), you'll find trips that appeal to you. From the Grossglockner to the Dolomites to the Lauterbrunnen Valley ("The Yellowstone of Switzerland") to King Ludwig's Palace, every important road, pass, and scenic landmark is described with an astounding attention to detail. You'll find information on everything from villages to shops and restaurants, to little-known spots where the views are particularly spectacular.

Hermann's informed, witty prose is dotted with local customs, history, and amusing travelling anecdotes that are sure to enrich your journey. Read this book before your trip (and be sure to pack it with you) and you won't miss any of what makes the Alps a motorcycling paradise.

Known in many touring circles as "Mr. Alps," John Hermann has over 20 years of riding experience and 27 Alpine tours to his credit. He is an acknowledged authority on Alps touring, having travelled alone and with tour groups. His wisdom and experience make this book an essential resource for anyone planning—or even considering—an Alps adventure.

Paper, 5-1/2 x 8-1/2 in., 223 pp., 126 illus.
HERM $19.95

Other Books From Whitehorse Press

• •

ther Books From Whitehorse Press

. . . .

otorcycle Touring and Travel:
Handbook of Travel by Motorcycle
Bill Stermer

arn the fine points of motorcycle touring with
Stermer as your guide. Bill is former Edito-
Director of *Rider* Magazine and a contribu-
to numerous other motorcycling publications.
This is THE handbook for anyone interested
ravel by motorcycle, written by one of Amer-
's foremost riding journalists. Every aspect
planning and executing a trip by motorcycle
covered: picking the proper motorcycle and
uipment, packing the right gear, dressing
art for various weather conditions, tips on ac-
nmodating co-riders and other motorcyclists,
mping, safety — and just plain having fun.
Building on the success of his best-selling
83 book, *Motorcycle Touring*, Bill Stermer
s completely rewritten his touring standard.
otorcycle Touring and Travel contains com-
tely new information about tires, lubricants,
spension enhancements, routine mainte-
nce and safety checks, clothing, and travel
ar.
With over 30 years of riding experience and
re than a dozen years testing and writing
out motorcycles, Bill Stermer is the perfect
ide for motorcycle travelers — novices and
terans alike. You are certain to learn some-
ng new from this book, even if you started rid-
in 1950.
cording to *Road Rider* magazine, **"I wish I**
d a copy of this book when I first started
uring—it certainly would have saved me a
of headaches. Even now, 20 years and
If a million miles later, there are things in
re worth taking serious note of. I highly
commend *Motorcycle Touring and Travel.*"

ntents: • Introduction • Motorcycle Tour-
and Travel • Choosing Your Motorcycle •
cessories • Motorcycle Components • Mo-
cycle Apparel • The Tourer's Packing List
lanning a Tour • Co-Riders and Group
des • Motorcycle Camping • Touring Secu-
• Motorcycle Safety • Motorcycle Rallies
d Clubs • Organized Tours • Foreign
avel • Index
per, 8-1/4 x 10-1/2 in., 128 pp., 227 illus.
STER $24.95

Motorcycling Excellence:
Skills, Knowledge, and Strategies
for Riding Right
by The Motorcycle Safety Foundation

Here is a book for the motorcyclist who wants
to do it right—the most complete, authoritative
book ever published on safe riding techniques
and strategies. Statistics indicate that a substantial percentage of motorcycle accidents in-
volve riders with limited experience and
training. Prior to 1973 there were few organized programs to instruct beginners and experienced riders in safe motorcycle operation.
Since that time, over one million students have
completed courses developed by the MSF.
This book is the culmination of what they have
learned about teaching students of all ages and
experience. It is the perfect refresher for anyone who has taken an MSF course and will be
an eye-opener for those who have not yet discovered them.

In a clear, engaging style with detailed diagrams and extensive full-color photographs and
illustrations, the book covers rider attitude,
proper dress, performance, maintenance and
troubleshooting, as well as basic and advanced
street skills. Included are tips on how to stop
quickly when necessary; avoid traffic hazards;
apply evasive maneuvers; countersteer for better control; travel skillfully in a group; identify
and fix mechanical problems; ride more
smoothly at high and low speeds; maintain momentum in off-highway riding; and much, much
more. A remarkable source of riding wisdom,
this book is certain to become the definitive reference for the sport. It enables brand-new riders to learn safe riding habits from the start
while veterans can perfect their performance to
reduce accident risk.

The Motorcycle Safety Foundation courses
have been responsible for sparking in many
people a lifelong passion for motorcycling. As
they claim, "The More You Know, The Better It
Gets!" *MOTORCYCLING EXCELLENCE* provides the opportunity for every motorcyclist to
discover for him or herself the thrills of "riding
right" by getting the best from self and machine.

". . . an invaluable resource tool that will
help any rider become a better rider." –
Street Bike

Paper, 8-1/4 x 10-1/2 in., 176 pp., color illus.
MCX $24.95

Other Books From Whitehorse Press

• •

Blood, Sweat & Gears:
Ramblings on Motorcycling
and Medicine
by flash gordon, m.d.

There are two ways to teach. One way is to drill information into the listener's head. The other is to tickle it in. West Coast humorist and off-beat motorcycling personality flash gordon, m.d., (yes—that *is* his real name . . . no caps, please) author of a popular column in San Francisco's *CityBike* magazine, is a master of the "tickling" school of education. Reading this collection of his best essays would be a guilty pleasure if not for the sound information it contains.

flash's experience as an emergency room doctor and 33-year motorcycling veteran allows him a unique perspective—his suggestions are remarkably insightful, and could even prove to be lifesaving. Ever wonder what to check first when someone has an accident? How about treating road rash properly? Experiencing lower back pain, leg burns, hearing or sinus problems—even hemorrhoids? flash tells it like it is—giving sensible advice about what you can treat on your own and what you can't. Though you may have forgotten everything you learned about first aid and safety in school, you'll never forget it again after reading this book—flash spins cautionary tales that are as easy to remember as a song.

We're sure you'll find *BLOOD, SWEAT & GEARS* to be highly informative and entertaining. It's filled with the author's amusing—and sometimes sobering—anecdotes from many years of directing a free clinic in San Francisco. flash takes you from the high jinks of Haight Street to the high anxiety of the emergency room, and does it with intelligence and style. Addressing the most prevalent health issues facing those who spend a good deal of time in the saddle, flash delivers his advice with a strong dose of original humor. The possibility of saving the time and expense of a doctor's visit is certainly a sweet pill to swallow.

Paper, 5-1/2 x 8-1/2 in., 112 pp., 31 b/w illus.
FLASH $12.95

The Rider's Guidebook
by Bill Cooper

Here is a handy little book written by a man who has a lot to share and wanted to make life a little easier for other cycle enthusiasts. The book is filled with practical tips for making motorcycling more fun and enjoyable. Any one of Cooper's pearls of wisdom alone is worth the price of the book; together they provide a treasure chest of valuable information for riders at all levels of experience. You'll learn how to clean and protect your bike (aluminum and painted parts), how to stop brake squeal, how to stop annoying handlebar "buzz", care of face shields, bike security, making your seat more comfortable, riding in cold and hot weather. Even if you've been riding 30 years, you'll learn something from this book!

Paper, 5-1/2 x 8-1/2 in., 28 pp., 16 illus.
COOP $4.95

Quick Road Sign Translator,
Spanish to English
by Ed Culberson

If you've traveled to foreign countries before, you know that ordinary translation dictionaries are of little use with road signs because road sign phrases conform to local custom and not to formal language conventions. Take this handy road sign translator with you to Mexico or other Spanish-speaking countries. Clear plastic lamination keeps it looking good after long use; convenient size fits nicely in your shirt pocket for quick reference.

Paper, 2-3/4 x 5-1/4 in., 8 pp.
TRANS $2.95

elated Travel Guides

• •

ational Forest Scenic Byways
Beverly Magley

is book of America's most scenic drives was
t written just for motorcyclists, but for any
veler who wants to take to the road in search
America's abundant beauty. Beverly Magley
uses on the system of Scenic Byways estab-
ed by the USDA Forest Service to help trav-
rs see our National Forests. There are now
6 National Forests in 44 states, offering a
de range of outdoor recreational activity.
For each Scenic Byway, Magley provides a
neral description of the road, its location and
ite numbers, special attractions found
arby, information about the travel season, in-
mation about camping and other services
ailable, and contacts for further information.
empting selection of photos and maps adds
the convenience and allure of this nicely or-
nized, very useful book.

per, 6 x 9 in., 240 pp., approx. 175 illus.
BYWAY $11.95

ational Forest Scenic Byways II

is companion to *Scenic Byways* covers 48
ditional scenic byways in the National Forest
stem. From the multi-colored rock formations
Wyoming's Shoshone National Forest to the
diant reds, yellows and oranges of the
tumn oaks in Virginia's George Washington
tional Forest, *Scenic Byways II*, like its
edecessor, covers a variety of terrains
roughout the country. New to this edition is an
page section containing vivid, full-color photo-
aphs of the stunning scenery you'll encounter
some of these roads.

per, 6 x 9 in., 240 pp., many illus.
BY2 $11.95

ational Forest Scenic Byways Set

hy choose? Buy both books and save.
SET1 $22.00

ed & Breakfast in the Mid-Atlantic tates (4th Edition)
Bernice Chesler

avelling through America's diverse mid-Atlan-
region can be confusing without the proper
ide. Luckily, you can carry Bernice Chesler's
perb bed and breakfast guidebook at your
de and rest easy. Long recognized for setting
standard of excellence in the guidebook in-
ustry, Ms. Chesler's guide has been dubbed
e best B&B book on the market. Newly en-
rged and updated with over 425 urban, rural,

suburban and resort B&Bs, this volume covers
all the states from New York south to North
Carolina. Chesler also lists several reservation
services that offer thousands of selected accommodations of their own. It may seem hard
to believe, but this book *is* difficult to put down.
Each entry, in addition to providing all the necessary information needed to choose a lodging,
tells the unique story of the inn's owners and
occupants, making you want to read on and discover their whole history. If you're planning on
staying at B&Bs in any of the mid-Atlantic
states, this informative and fun guide will be an
excellent companion.

Paper, 5-1/2 x 8-1/2 in., 416 pp., maps & illus.
BBATL $17.95

Mountain Roads & Quiet Places
by Jerry DeLaughter

The Great Smoky Mountains Natural History Association publishes this fun and colorful adventure guide, which takes you step-by-step along
13 of the Smokies' breathtaking scenic highways and less traveled back roads. The introduction offers a short but fascinating history of
the area, while each chapter suggests interesting activities and hikes along the route and features informative sidebars about native plant
and animal life, complete with full color photographs and drawings. A large map of the area
is provided, and the text is keyed to color-
coded, numbered posts along the roads. If
you're looking for some of the windiest roads in
the country and have some time to "smell the
roses" along the way, this nicely produced book
will be your welcomed companion.

Paper, 9 x 8-1/2 in., 96 pp., color illus.
MRQP $9.95

National Park Vacations, The West
by Donald Pirie

This is a comprehensive and easy-to-use guide
to the spectacular Western National Parks:
Grand Canyon, Yosemite, Yellowstone, Glacier,
Arches, Bryce, Capitol Reef, Glen Canyon,
Zion, Rocky Mountain, Grand Teton, Sequoia
and Kings Canyon. Pirie has visited these
parks often with his family and shares personal
and practical tips on how best to enjoy them.
He covers in detail: getting there, where to
sleep and eat, how many days to spend, and
what to do. The informative text is highlighted
by good maps and the author's own beautiful
color photography.

Paper, 6 x 9 in., 182 pp., many illus.
NPVW $9.95

Incredible Journeys

• •

Two Wheels to Adventure
by Danny Liska

The late Danny Liska rode his BMW from Alaska to Argentina, recording one of the strangest motorcycle journeys ever made. Think of the most fantastic events that could happen to a man and they have probably happened to Liska: he's travelled through the jungle with smugglers, eaten lizard and monkey to stay alive, suffered from malaria, been attacked by vampire bats, and even doubled as a stunt man for Yul Brynner! Every page of this mammoth book is filled with surreal collages and unbelievable photographs. Our copies are autographed by the legend himself and are sure to become collector's items.

Hdbnd., 6-1/2 x 9 in., 759 pp., many illus.
LISKA $39.95

Hell's Angels
by Hunter Thompson

Here it is, Hunter Thompson's "strange and terible saga" of his hair-raising exploits among California's roughest motorcycle gangs. In the 1960s Thompson spent months riding, drinking, and pillaging with the Angels. The resulting account not only earned Thompson critical praise, but also a sound beating at the hands of the outlaw bikers.

While much has been written about the Hell's Angels, few writers can match Thompson's skewed wit and humor. His portrayal is both terrifying and hilarious. Enter the outlaw biker world, with America's premier gonzo journalist as your guide.

Paper, 4 x 7 in., 349 pp.   **HELLS $5.95**

Winging Through America
by Gary Shumway

Here is the tale to read if you've thought about getting on your bike and traveling cross-country. Author Gary Shumway presents an overview of the sights and sounds—uniquely American—that he encountered on his journey through America. During his marathon 24-day trip, Shumway touched all 48 of the continental states. You'll find appendices on recommended equipment and clothing, travel expenses, highway itineraries, overnight stops, tourist bureaus by state, and suggested attractions by city. If you're in the mood for some serious pavement flogging, *Winging through America* may reinforce your conviction.

Paper, 5-1/2 x 8-1/2 in., 172 pp., 46 b/w illus.
WINGA $10.95

Zen and the Art of Motorcycle Maintenance
by Robert M. Pirsig

One of the great books of our time, this story is not so much of Zen or even of motorcycles but of a man's attempt to find meaning in life. As Pirsig describes it, "The study of the art of motorcycle maintenance is really a miniature study of the art of rationality itself. Working on a motorcycle, working well, caring, is to become part of a process, to achieve an inner peace of mind. The motorcycle is primarily a mental phenomenon." This should already be on your bookshelf. If not, here's your chance.

Paper, 4-1/8 x 6-7/8 in., 380 pp. **ZEN $6.95**

Two Wheels to Panama
by William Carroll

In the mid-1950s, a frustrated Bill Carroll set out on a trip he would remember forever, riding his 1950 BSA B33 from Los Angeles to El Paso and then through Mexico and Central America to reach the Panama Canal. His 7,772-mile solo trip led him through often desolate and undeveloped terrain, where he encountered jungles, forest idols, deep rivers, burial grounds, mysterious and amusing characters and many other unexpected adventures. This fascinating and well-written book is filled with more than 175 incredible black and white photographs and maps of a wild and uncharted Central America that no longer exists. If you're considering a trek south of the border, this book will inspire you to do it . . . it's just as exciting today as it was then— and now there are roads!

Paper, 11 x 8-1/2 in., 144 pp., many b/w illus.
TWPAN $20.00

The Endless Ride
by Robert Auburn

You'll never forget Robert Auburn's odyssey— five years through 51 countries, covering 165,000 miles on the same Honda Magna 700 If you'd like to experience the sense of discovery he had riding in foreign countries, then the 312 National Geographic-quality photographs that appear in this dazzling book are the next best thing to being there. Also included is a priceless 19-language Parts and Service Phrasebook, compiled with the cooperation of 20 leading Honda distributors worldwide. ". . . more slide-show than travelogue, a great thumb-through for any erstwhile world traveler."—David Edwards, *Cycle World*

Paper, 6 x 8-3/4 in., 438 pp., color illus.
ENLR $29.95

credible Journeys

• •

vestment Biker: On the Road th Jim Rogers

Jim Rogers

1990, maverick investor Jim Rogers put over 000 miles on his BMW, traversing six conti- nts and earning a spot in the Guinness Book World Records. In this account of his jour- y, Rogers describes some of the world's st remote countries and offers surprising tips where an enterprising investor might want to his money. Described by *Time* magazine as great book," *Investment Biker* is fascinating ding for all motorcycle wanderers.

rdbound, 6-1/8 x 9-1/4 in., 416 pp., no illus.
IB $25.00

e Long Ride (Video)

James Rogers

urney with Jim Rogers as he becomes the st man to cross China by motorcycle. Starting Shanghai, Rogers travels the ancient Silk ute through China's remote villages and ex- c cities.

Through his travels, Rogers introduces you a culture that is steeped in tradition but also dually opening itself up to Western ideas d shedding the ways of the communist sys- m. You'll see the fledgling Shanghai stock ex- ange (with all of 12 company stocks being ded) and meet the new generation of Chi- se students, eager to experience the culture d ideas of the West. See martial arts masters rforming incredible feats of strength, and acu- ncturists curing all ills with needles and ated cups. You'll also see the gorgeous scen- y of a land all too few Westerners have ever ited.

deo, VHS, 52 min., color **LONGV $19.95**

e Party's Over (Video)

James Rogers

n Rogers' second great motorcycle adven- e takes him across the forbidding Siberian dscape as he attempts to become the first rson ever to cross the Soviet Union on a mo- cycle.

As this video shows, accomplishing this goal s no easy task, as the Soviet Union at the e had one of the worst road systems of any dustrialized nation. Often, Rogers and his mpanions find themselves navigating dirt ads that have become treacherously muddy, en hitching rides on freight trains to cross adless swamplands. An adventure that's sure inspire any long-distance traveler.

deo, VHS, 112 min., color **PARTV $19.95**

Jupiter's Travels

Since we first opened our doors in 1989, cus- tomers have been asking for a book called *Jupiter's Travels* by Ted Simon. When we looked into it, we found that the book had sold over 300,000 copies both here and abroad and had been translated into six languages, attest- ing to its immense popularity. Unfortunately, the US edition was no longer in print. With the help of the author we were finally able to bring in copies of the British paperback edition last year so that US enthusiasts could once again read the fabulous saga of Ted Simon's round-the- world journey by motorcycle.

We were totally unprepared for what hap- pened when we finally got the book. Orders came in by the droves and the press started calling, begging for review copies. We just couldn't keep the book in stock. Again, with the help of Ted, special couriers began to bring us case after case of the book, all of which sold out the minute they reached our office. One shipment arrived in the dead of night in the back of a stranger's station wagon!

Then the reviews started to appear! Mark Tuttle of *Rider* wrote "*Jupiter's Travels* is back on the American market after a long absence, and if you haven't read Ted Simon's vivid, lively metaphorical account of his four-year adven- ture across 54 countries on a Triumph Tiger in the early '70s, by all means take the plunge. Whether telling of his harrowing desert cross- ings while traveling the length of Africa, a prison stay in Brazil or dealing with floods in Australia, journalist Simon's knack for narrating his feelings and impressions makes for terrific imagery as the reader gets to know both him and the world." Alex Lloyd of *Street Bike* maga- zine was equally enthusiastic: "There are books about travel on a motorcycle, and then there's *Jupiter's Travels*. For me, there is no compari- son. There will never be another story so well described." It's been called "the world's most beloved motorcycle book," "wholly involving," and "a profound effect on [one's] perception of everyday life,"—superlatives reserved for books that truly speak to their readers.

If you haven't read *Jupiter's Travels,* treat yourself to this great masterpiece while our cop- ies still last! Ted Simon may have logged 78,302 miles on his trip, but the true journey of *Jupiter's Travels* is the one he takes into his soul. Riding across vast continents and meet- ing their peoples, Ted is seen as a spy, a glam- orous, astonishing stranger, and a deity—a true "Magellen on a motorcycle."

Paper, 4 x 7 in., 447 pp.   **JUPTR $19.95**

Motorcycle Touring for Adventurers

• •

How to Tour Europe by Motorcycle
by Beverly Boe and Phil Philcox

Written in 1983, this book is now somewhat dated in its listings and specific references, but much of its advice and wisdom are timeless and remain valuable to anyone thinking of motorcycling in Europe. This book offers countless tips and suggestions on many important topics: planning your trip, insurance, licenses, renting or buying a motorcycle in Europe, camping and hosteling, where to go, touring and the weather, what to take and how to take it, things to know about Europe, how to speak "European-ese." With this book you can tap into Philcox and Boe's years of experience motorcycling in Europe and make your own trip more productive and enjoyable.

Paper, 5-1/2 x 8-1/2 in., 135 pp., 80 illus.
                                    PHIL $9.95

The Best Roads of California
by Larry Blankenship

Read this amusing book before you even think of motorcycling in California. You'll learn the best this great state has to offer. Discover out-of-the-way back roads bursting with scenery, untouched by traffic and congestion. Gain new insight into old favorites like breathtaking Highway 1. For each route, this book covers the type of road, the road's best and worst parts, the scenery, accurate driving times and distances, road and weather conditions, degree of difficulty, interesting and off-beat people and attractions, historical background, and more!

Paper, 5-1/4 x 8-1/2 in., 161 pp., 10 illus.
                                    BLNK $13.95

The Roads of Colorado: Motorcycle Tour Guide
by Chris Maly

This guide offers the motorcycle touring enthusiast clear, practical information on the best roads to ride in the state of Colorado. The book contains 18 different rides suitable for sport, cruiser or touring bikes, complete with maps, photos, detailed information on road highlights, towns and restaurants. If you're planning a trip to this mountainous state, or just interested in learning more about the thrilling roads of Colorado, you'll want to consult this guide before you go. It's small enough to fit easily into your tank bag and the spiral binding lets you fold it to the correct page for easy viewing.

Paper, 6 x 9 in., 114 pp., maps &illus.
                                    RCO $14.99

Motorcycle Arizona! (Second Edition)
by Frank Del Monte

Save time, be prepared, and avoid hassles with this compact guidebook on Arizona and the southwest. The book has five sections, each covering one of the five essential touring subjects: how to tour, where to tour, how to get there, where to stay, and what to see.

The first section covers general traveling tips, such as how to pack, what to wear, and how to get emergency service. Sections 2 and 3 describe over 50 different motorcycling trips ranging in length from one day to two weeks. Clear maps and detailed route descriptions make it easy to stay on course. Section 4 provides complete listings of hotels and motels in all of the towns covered in the route descriptions. The final section describes some of Arizona's most interesting attractions, ranging from the Petrified Forest in Holbrook to the Living Ghost Town in Jerome.

Arizona offers some of the most breathtaking scenery in the country and this book ensures that you won't miss any of it.

Paper, 5-1/2 x 8-1/2 in., 144 pp., 19 illus.
                                    MCAZ $9.9

Trails of Colorado Guides

These guides offer the dual-sport motorcycle or ATV enthusiast clear, practical information on where to ride in Colorado's incredible system off-road vehicle trails. Each book contains 10 different dual-sport motorcycle and/or ATV trail suggestions, complete with easy-to-follow maps, telephone numbers of ranger districts, elevations, terrain type and difficulty, prime riding seasons, and scenic photographs of the mountain views you'll see along the way. Their spiral-bindings make it easy to keep the information you need at your fingertips. The motorcycle trail guides list primarily single-track trail while the ATV trail guides list trails that are appropriate for both bikes and other three- and four-wheeled vehicles. Carry one of these guides with you and prepare for an adventure.

ATV Trail Guide, Vol. 1   TCOA1 $14.9

ATV Trail Guide, Vol. 2   TCOA2 $14.9

Motorcycle Trail Guide, Vol. 1
                                TCOM1 $14.9
Motorcycle Trail Guide, Vol. 2
                                TCOM2 $14.9

Iotorcycling Videos

● ●

e Lives to Ride
ected by Alice Stone

s entertaining, critically-acclaimed documen-
y challenges a classic American icon: the
idy male biker with his back seat bimbo.
e very different, very strong women motorcy-
its share their passion for machinery, as-
alt, and the wind in their hair. These women
isider motorcycling a way of life, and their
aging stories illuminate issues of women's
ependence, self-reliance and thrill-seeking.
i'll meet an 82 year-old great-grandmother
o broke the gender barrier for female com-
itors in the 1930s, the entrepreneur who
nded Harley Women magazine, and many
er colorful and diverse personalities who are
anging the way America views motorcy-
its—and women. Interspersed with the film's
ebration of contemporary female bikers are
veral fascinating historical sequences that
truly awe-inspiring: a single black woman
es alone, and fearlessly, throughout the seg-
ated South in the 1930s, and two sisters
vel alone across America on unpaved and
nacing roads in 1916. They made it across
:cessfully, but were arrested for wearing
ats in public! "She Lives to Ride" has been
led "A winner from start to finish" (Variety),
sheer delight" (L.A. Times), and "An exhila-
ing celebration" (Boston Globe).

eo, VHS, 76 min., color   **SHEV $29.95**

n Any Sunday
Bruce Brown

Academy Award nominee for Best Documen-
y, this extraordinary film covers virtually
ery form of motorcycle competition, from Mo-
:ross to Desert Racing; the Widowmaker hill
nb to the Elsinore Grand Prix; the Bonneville
It Flats to the AMA Grand National Tour. The
ing footage is spectacular and features cham-
n riders Mert Lawwill and Malcolm Smith, as
ill as legendary actor Steve McQueen. Film-
iker Bruce Brown may be best remembered
his classic work, The Endless Summer, but
i Any Sunday gets every in-the-know motor-
clists' vote for Best Film Ever. Hard to find,
're thrilled to offer this newly re-mastered ver-
n from "the unofficial poet of the sports
rld." – N.Y. Times.

Jeo, VHS, 90 min., color   **ONANY $39.95**

Street Smarts (Video)
by Paul Winters and David West

Street Smarts is a practical course in two-
wheeled street survival. With tips and tactics
from experienced street riders and expert road
racers, you'll learn safety techniqes you can apply directly to your street riding. This is a valuable resource that will help riders at any level.
This video is nicely produced, with excellent action footage and helpful animation diagrams to
demonstrate every important point. Topics include rider clothing, street strategies, night riding, braking, countersteering, and much more.
Overall, the video shows you how to use your
head to keep out of trouble. Any one of the tips
you'll learn here could save your life.

Video, VHS, 55 min., color   **STRTV $29.95**

Street Smarts Volume 2 (Video)
by Paul Winters

More street riding techniques from some of the
world's best riders. Hear the pros talk first-hand
about how *they* deal with common riding hazards. Wes Cooley, Chuck Graves, David Emde,
and a host of other champion riders answer a
series of important safety questions, including:
"What do you do if you go into a turn too fast?";
and "Under what conditions should you use the
rear brake?" This video gives you the chance
to hear many different opinions about how to
approach these situations. Evaluate each answer and incorporate the best of them into your
own riding techniques.

Video, VHS, 45 min., color   **SSV2 $29.95**

Street Smarts Volume 3 (Video)
by Paul Winters

Any time a motorcyclist takes to the road, he or
she is at risk. Some situations, however, are
riskier than others. Street Smarts 3 focuses on
these situations, the "Danger Zones" in which
knowledge, anticipation, and reflexes are the
keys to survival. Crossing an intersection,
rounding a sharp mountain turn, lane splitting
on the freeway—these are a few of the high-
risk scenarios Street Smarts 3 addresses,
teaching you how to anticipate trouble and the
best techniques for avoiding it. You'll learn
where to place your vehicle in the lane, the
proper angle for rounding a sharp corner, and
the best ways to avoid road debris. Live action
footage and computer simulations help drive
the lessons home.

Video, VHS, 37 min., color   **SSV3 $29.95**

All Three Volumes   **SET3 $79.95**

Maps and Atlases

Fast Maps

When we first saw these maps, a cheer went up around the office. At last, a map maker realized that if maps are going to be used outside, they need to be protected from the weather. Fastmaps are the answer to every driver's prayers. They flip open and refold in a jiffy, are just the right size for a tank bag or side bag, and are laminated for protection against the elements. The plastic coating accepts grease pencil or non-permanent marker for write-on, wipe off trip routing. State maps show most roads in the entire state, indentifying national and state parks, forests and special features. The state's largest cities are blown up in detail on the reverse side. State map indexes include all cities and towns in the state. Get on track with colorful, convenient Fastmaps!

Paper, 4-1/2 x 11 inches, folded.

Arizona	FMAZ	$4.95
California North	FMNCA	$4.95
California South	FMSCA	$4.95
Cape Cod/The Islands	FMCOD	$5.95
Colorado	FMCO	$4.95
Florida/Disney World	FMFL	$4.95
Georgia	FMGA	$4.95
Illinois	FMIL	$5.95
Indiana	FMIN	$4.95
Iowa	FMIA	$4.95
Kentucky	FMKY	$4.95
Michigan	FMMI	$4.95
Minnesota	FMMN	$4.95
New Hampshire/Vermont	FMNHV	$4.95
New Jersey	FMNJ	$4.95
New Mexico	FMNM	$4.95
New York State	FMNY	$5.95
North Carolina	FMNC	$5.95
Oregon	FMOR	$4.95
Pacific Coast	FMPAC	$4.95
Pennsylvania	FMPA	$4.95
Puerto Rico and San Juan	FMPR	$5.95
South Carolina	FMSC	$4.95
Tennessee	FMTN	$5.95
Texas	FMTX	$5.95
United States	FMUSA	$5.95
Washington State	FMWA	$4.95
Wisconsin	FMWI	$4.95

DeLorme Atlases and Gazetteers

If you're interested in back roads, here are the books you've been trying to find. The DeLorme Atlas & Gazetteer Series are big, bold, colorful books that each chart an entire state in painstaking detail, with maps geared for backcountry exploration and adventure. These Atlases feature the most complete road coverage available and include a comprehensive index that lists even the smallest towns and villages.

Paper, 11 x 16 inches.

Alaska	GAZAK	$19.95
Arizona	GAZAZ	$16.95
Northern California	GAZCN	$16.95
Southern & Central CA	GAZCS	$16.95
Colorado	GAZCO	$16.95
Florida	GAZFL	$16.95
Idaho	GAZID	$16.95
Illinois	GAZIL	$16.95
Maine	GAZME	$16.95
Maryland/Delaware	GAZMD	$16.95
Michigan	GAZMI	$16.95
Minnesota	GAZMN	$16.95
Montana	GAZMT	$16.95
North Carolina	GAZNC	$16.95
New Hampshire	GAZNH	$16.95
New York State	GAZNY	$16.95
Ohio	GAZOH	$16.95
Oregon	GAZOR	$16.95
Pennsylvania	GAZPA	$16.95
Tennessee	GAZTN	$16.95
Texas	GAZTX	$24.95
Utah	GAZUT	$16.95
Virginia	GAZVA	$16.95
Vermont	GAZVT	$16.95
Washington	GAZWA	$16.95
Wisconsin	GAZWI	$16.95
Wyoming	GAZWY	$16.95

Kummerly and Frey Maps

We've found Kummerly + Frey road maps to be the very best available in terms of both accuracy and thoroughness. The legends are printed in English, French, German, and Italian for ease of understanding regardless of your native tongue. Each map folds up into a handy 5 x 9 inches and has a protective outer cover.

Alpine Roads, 1:500,000	KFALP	$9.95
Austria, 1:500,000	KFAUS	$9.95
Northern France, 1:600,000	KFFRN	$9.95
Northern Italy, 1:500,000	KFITN	$8.95
Rhone/Alps, 1:250,000	KFRA	$8.95
Southern France, 1:600,000	KFFRS	$9.95
Southern Germany, 1:500,000	KFGES	$9.95
Southern Italy, 1:500,000	KFITS	$8.95
Switzerland, 1:250,000	KFSWZ	$9.95

RDER FORM FOR BOOKS

. . . .

Whitehorse Press
424 North Main Street - P.O. Box 60
North Conway, NH 03860-0060, U.S.A.

Our e-mail address is:
75030.2554@compuserve.com

SOLD TO:
Customer Number: _____

UPS SHIPPING ADDRESS: *(If different):*
(UPS will not deliver to a P.O. box)

Name: _____

Name: _____

Street: _____

Street: _____

City: _____

City: _____

State: _____ Zip: _____

State: _____ Zip: _____

Daytime Phone: (_____) _____ (Speeds orders if we have a question.)

How Many	Item Code	Description	Size	Price Each Dollars	Cents	Total Price Dollars	Cents
		Prices subject to change without notice.		Subtotal			
				Shipping & Handling			
				Total Payment			

In USA & Canada Call Toll-Free 800-531-1133
To Order From Other Countries Call 603-356-6556
World-Wide Fax 603-356-6590
Or mail this form with your check or money order.

SHIPPING AND HANDLING:

U.S.: Add 10% of the total order,
but not less than $3.00. Expedited shipping is
available upon request, please call for rates.

Canada and Mexico:
Add 20% of the total order, but not less
than $4.00 U.S.

Other Countries:
We ship by air mail and charge actual cost. Estimate
$10.00 for the first book and $8.00 for each additional
book, or you may call for a quote.
Orders of $100 or more: FREE SHIPPING!
United States and Canada only.

PAYMENT: *(Payment required before shipment. Sorry, no C.O.D.s)*

( ) Check ( ) Money Order (U.S. dollars only, please)   Credit Card: ( ) Master Card ( ) VISA ( ) Amex

Expiration Date _____ / _____

__.__.__.__.__.__.__.__.__.__.__.__.__.__.__.
Credit Card Number *(please show spaces used in number)*

Name on Card: _____ Signature: _____

Thanks for your order!

Ridge Rider Dale Coyner strikes a pose in his favorite attire. (Photo by L.D.Graham)

The Author

Dale Coyner's journeys through the Appalachians began out of a curiosity for what was "around the next bend." He came to riding later than some, purchasing his first motorcycle, a Yamaha Radian, after he finished college. He credits the open, freewheeling nature of motorcycling with firing a sense of wonderment about his surroundings that led to rediscovering his native region. He shares his best finds with you in this, his first book.

For many of the tours in this volume, Dale relied on his trusty Honda Gold Wing. He's not sure if it was the size of the Wing, the pop-up camper he was pulling, or the bright red Aerostitch suit that garnered the most friendly smiles in his travels, but he got a lot of them. His current ride is a Honda ST-1100.

Dale's work in multimedia for an international consulting firm takes him on journeys of another type—the Internet. You can often find him zipping around the world in cyberspace, where he is experimenting with new forms of discovering and sharing information. He has constructed a World Wide Web site to catalog new discoveries about the Appalachians which you can find at http://www.his.com/~dale. In addition to the Web site, you may also contact him via Internet e-mail at dale@his.com.